AF077169

Re-situating Canadian
Early Childhood Education

Rethinking Childhood

Gaile S. Cannella
General Editor

Vol. 47

The Rethinking Childhood series is part of the Peter Lang Education list.
Every volume is peer reviewed and meets
the highest quality standards for content and production.

PETER LANG
New York • Washington, D.C./Baltimore • Bern
Frankfurt • Berlin • Brussels • Vienna • Oxford

Re-situating Canadian Early Childhood Education

EDITED BY
Veronica Pacini-Ketchabaw
& Larry Prochner

PETER LANG
New York • Washington, D.C./Baltimore • Bern
Frankfurt • Berlin • Brussels • Vienna • Oxford

Library of Congress Cataloging-in-Publication Data

Re-situating Canadian early childhood education /
[edited by] Veronica Pacini-Ketchabaw, Larry Prochner.
pages cm. — (Rethinking childhood; vol. 47)
Includes bibliographical references.
1. Early childhood education—Canada. I. Pacini-Ketchabaw, Veronica,
editor of compilation. II. Prochner, Larry, editor of compilation. III. Title.
LB1139.3.C2R47   372.210971—dc23   2012042561
ISBN 978-1-4331-1835-7 (hardcover)
ISBN 978-1-4331-1834-0 (paperback)
ISBN 978-1-4539-1039-9 (e-book)
ISSN 1086-7155

Bibliographic information published by **Die Deutsche Nationalbibliothek**.
Die Deutsche Nationalbibliothek lists this publication in the "Deutsche
Nationalbibliografie"; detailed bibliographic data is available
on the Internet at http://dnb.d-nb.de/.

© 2013 Peter Lang Publishing, Inc., New York
29 Broadway, 18th floor, New York, NY 10006
www.peterlang.com

All rights reserved.
Reprint or reproduction, even partially, in all forms such as microfilm,
xerography, microfiche, microcard, and offset strictly prohibited.

*To early childhood educators who
work daily to reconceptualize their practices*

Acknowledgements

Chapters 2, 3, 4, 5, 6, & 7 are revised versions of articles that appeared in 2010 in the *Alberta Journal of Educational Research*, Special Issue: "Blurring the Boundaries of Early Childhood Education's Theory/Practice Divide," volume 56, issue 3. We would like to thank the journal for permission to publish a revised version of the articles.

Contents

Foreword—Reconceptualist Her/Histories in Early Childhood Studies:
Challenges, Power Relations, and Critical Activism ix
Daphney L. Curry & Gaile S. Cannella

1 Resituating Early Childhood Education: Introduction 1
Larry Prochner & Veronica Pacini-Ketchabaw

2 The Integration of Cognitive and Sociocultural Theories of Literacy
Development for Instruction and Research: Why? How?. 15
Katherine Davidson

3 Valuing Subjective Complexities: Disrupting the Tyranny of Time 35
Sherry Rose & Pam Whitty

4 Addressing Divides and Binaries in Early Childhood Education:
Disability, Discourse and Theory, and Practice in a Bachelor of
Education Program. 53
Luigi Iannacci & Bente Graham

5 An Early Childhood Professional's Authority: How Can It Be Used
for Influencing and Instigating Action for Social Goods?. 73
Rachel Langford

6 When Queer Enters Early Childhood Teacher Training:
What's So Inappropriate about That?. 90
Zeenat Janmohamed

7 Immigrant Parents Taking Part in Their Children's Education:
A Practical Experiment 106
Judith K. Bernhard

8 Making Developmental Knowledge Stutter and Stumble:
   Continuing Pedagogical Explorations with Collective Biography. 125
   Kathleen Kummen, Veronica Pacini-Ketchabaw, & Deborah Thompson

9 Children's Representations of Cultural Scripts in Play:
   Facilitating Transition from Home to Preschool in an Intercultural
   Early Learning Program for Refugee Children. 146
   Anna Kirova

10 Resituating Practice through Teachers' Storying of Children's Interests 172
   Mary Caroline Rowan

11 Taking Children's Rights and Participation Seriously:
   Cross-national Perspectives and Possibilities 189
   Beth Blue Swadener, Lacey Peters, & Sonya Gaches

List of Contributors 211

Reconceptualist Her/Histories in Early Childhood Studies

Challenges, Power Relations, and Critical Activism

Daphney L. Curry & Gaile S. Cannella

For the past twenty or thirty years, groups of early childhood researchers and educators around the globe have stood for the reconceptualization of early childhood education, now often referred to as critical early childhood studies. Conceptually and ideologically, the rethought field emphasizes more socially just and diverse ways of knowing, being, and doing (Bloch, 1992; Cannella, 1997; Jipson, 1991; Mac Naughton, 2000; Silin, 1987). Reconceptualist early education is closely aligned with civil rights, equity, and diversity as reconceptualist scholars have challenged, and continue to challenge, dominant ideologies in the field that reinforce Euro-Western assumptions about human beings and life in general. The Enlightenment, modernist attempt to extinguish the premodern through the construction of a belief in science has created a self-named "Western" environment that has legitimated social control and regulation by those in power over "others" (Cannella, 1997; Cannella & Viruru, 2004; Dahlberg, Moss, & Pence, 1999; Shallwani, 2010). Shallwani (2010) explains that "the modern Enlightenment project has been characterized by belief in the power of sciences to discover objective universal truth, belief that the pursuit and attainment of this knowledge can lead to a better life, and belief in a liberal democratic state founded on rationality and knowledge" (p. 232).

Science as modernist practice, facilitated by technologies of power that continue to be used to literally conceptualize and control those who are younger, has been exposed by reconceptualist early childhood scholars as a universalizing and narrowing foundation for the field (Cannella & Viruru, 2004; Shallwani, 2010). The domination of developmental psychology over those labeled as "child" and the hierarchical relationship between psychology and education/pedagogy that privileges psychology are illustrations of foundational notions that serve to universalize and discredit ways of being and understanding that do not conform to the truths as constructed by that psychology.

As early as 1987 in the United States, early childhood scholars like Marianne Bloch, Janice Jipson, Shirley Kessler, Sally Lubeck, Beth Swadener, Johnathan Silin, and Lourdes Soto began the dialogue that questioned the knowledge bases that dominate the field. In 1991, the first annual Reconceptualizing Early Childhood Research, Theory and Practice (RECE) conference was held at the University of Wisconsin–Madison, in the United States. This event has since provided a means for early childhood reconceptualists to disseminate their work/research as regular meetings are held worldwide. In the 1990s, Joe Kincheloe and Janice Jipson introduced the Peter Lang book series Rethinking Childhood that serves as an avenue for reconceptualization to this day. Early childhood scholars from around the globe like Sue Grieshaber and Glenda Mac Naughton in Australia, Jeannette Rhedding-Jones in Norway, and Gunilla Dahlberg in Sweden practiced their own critical early childhood scholarship during the 1990s, at times directly associated with the reconceptualist label, and at other times contributing to the diversity of knowledges and perspectives in the reconceptualist tradition, but without direct association with the label.

Over the past twenty years, reconceptualist educators and scholars have placed at the forefront diverse, and traditionally marginalized, forms of knowledge as well as demonstrated practices for/with those who are younger that generate increased possibilities for social justice in education, care, and their lives in general. Multiple reconceptualist book series now exist with authorship from around the globe, as well as a readership from diverse fields and locations. Reconceptualist educator-scholars publish in a range of established journals across fields, as well as in the two major reconceptualist journals: *Contemporary Issues in Early Childhood* and *International Critical Childhood Policy Studies.*

The intent of reconceptualist scholars/scholarship is not to invent new truths, but to challenge the construction of truths that have placed particular groups of people, forms of knowledge, and ways of being in the margins. The purposes of reconceptualizations have been/are to embrace multiplicity, cultural studies, equity, and diversity, and to contribute to a world where social justice, environmental justice, and life possibilities are increased for all individuals regardless of their background, while critically acknowledging conditions that have created, and continue to create, marginalization and inequity (Cannella, 2002; Dahlberg et al., 1999; Grieshaber & Cannella, 2001; Kessler & Swadener, 1992).

The purpose of this foreword is to provide the reader with more specifics of reconceptualist herstory/history as a background for understanding the intersection of early childhood reconceptualist work in the range of communities, diverse locations, and countries around the globe. We ask the reader to begin by considering (and, it is hoped, understanding) the following: (1) As foundational scholarship from the past twenty or thirty years is presented in the first section, we use the term *herstory* rather than *history*, especially when discussing the work of early childhood scholars who are predominantly female. Upon reviewing a range of new manuscripts over the years for journals and new books as they have been submitted for publication, the more common practice noted is for the work of *males* (and sometimes a small number of others) *outside the field* to be used as the originating work. This practice is obviously problematic and represents the erasure of the field of early childhood education (children as overlooked) and women as the largest group of scholars in the field (whose scholarship is also often ignored, discounted, disregarded). (2) We then move to an overview, not a complete literature review, of the work related to understanding social power relations that has been, and is being, conducted by reconceptualist early childhood scholars or those whose work facilitates the reconceptualist tradition. This discussion foregrounds the call for critical activism, work that has begun but that can/should be expanded.

Rejecting Universalist Perspectives: Listening to Early Childhood Herstories and the Possibilities of Deconstruction

The specific work of various reconceptualist scholars within the field can be used to demonstrate the herstory of challenges to universalisms. There are multiple universalisms that have been/should be called into question. However, the most obvious of these constructed truths that have been universally imposed on early childhood education are the knowledge(s) from developmental psychology, thus the example overviewed here. Beginning in the 1980s, reconceptualist scholars (Bloch, 1987, 1992; Burman, 1994; Cannella, 1997; Lubeck, 1996; Silin, 1987) from around the globe began to speak out and question this dominance over the field. Child development research has been constructed as the foundation for a truth-oriented pedagogy grounded in Piagetian constructivism and designated as developmentally appropriate practice (DAP) (Bredekamp & Copple, 1997). Often even without engaging in modernist forms of scientific rational criticism that Piaget would likely have supported, this developmental knowledge has been/ is presented as truth directly applicable to classroom practice and rarely critiqued or questioned (Cannella, 1997; Silin, 1987; Soto & Swadener, 2002).

Jonathon Silin (1987) openly challenges the reliance of early childhood education on truth-oriented psychological perspectives. He discusses the influence of

Bacon, Descartes, Darwin, Piaget, G. Stanley Hall, and the child study movement on the privileging of a modernist scientific, early childhood education. Twenty-five years ago, Silin explained that although most early childhood educators have a sense of mission and commitment to the field, there remains a "certain forgetfulness about the history that has shaped the profession—early educators have borrowed heavily from some academic disciplines while totally ignoring others in order to rationalize existing practices" (p. 17). This forgetfulness results in knowledges and (most important) lives that are disregarded, discounted, and made invisible.

Marianne Bloch (1987) expands this critical perspective by examining the social, political, and cultural assumptions that have guided the field dating back to the colonial era in the United States. Her review brings attention to the scientific claims (e.g., early years as privileged determiner of one's life, regulation through notions of expert professionalism, necessity of graded classrooms, and views that privilege experimentalism) that have been used to legitimize early education in the United States since the nineteenth century. Bloch's herstorical research exposes a field that is guided by psychological theory and researchers (e.g., Hall, Thorndike), and deemed legitimate by invoking claim to positivist, scientific experimental research. The push to become scientific and professional dominated early nursery schools of the 1920s. Bloch (1987) writes that "after WWI, 'scientifically sound curriculum' became synonymous with 'legitimate' education" (p. 46), demonstrating how constructions of science were/are tied to modernism and the particular views of those in power.

Bloch's herstorical reexamination written in 1992 further critiques and expands understanding of the relationship between developmental psychology and early childhood research. She takes issue with the positivist research methodologies and traditions that dominate early childhood curriculum, theory, and practice. Bloch (1992) discusses how the assumptions of a legitimated scientific education (e.g., importance of teacher training, education's assumed role in the elimination of inequities like poverty), based on developmental psychology and Euro-Western ideologies, have marginalized other critical perspectives (e.g., feminist, postmodern, poststructual, postcolonial).

Erica Burman (1994), a feminist critical psychologist whose work has profoundly influenced early childhood reconceptualists, began by critiquing the dominance of developmental psychology as a field generally grounded in assumptions that human beings can be interpreted and judged. The work outlines the negative impact that the discipline has had on children and their families in modern society if they do not conform to Euro-Western mainstream ideologies. Central to Burman's discussions are illustrations of how developmental psychology serves to regulate marginalized populations (e.g., women, children, low socioeconomic status, minority ethnic populations) by singling them out as objects to study and measure based on normative descriptions deemed scientific and necessarily prescriptive. Burman (1994) explains how the field of developmental psychology literally creates theories and constructs that are then imposed on particular groups of people. An example is the emergence of theories of attachment that associate females with dependence and the requirement of human attachment, while privileging constructs like detachment (stereotypically associated with males) as the ultimate form of advanced human functioning. Further, these theories generate an acceptance of constructs like normality and abnormality. In a more recent edition, Burman (2008) continues to discuss how developmental psychology, and its dependence on measurement, reinforces the production of research objects and subjects, who are primarily mothers and children. Normative descriptions/prescriptions are imposed on groups of people to maintain gender, class, or racial order and result in discrimination. The construction of dominant views of mothering serves as an example illustrating how developmental psychology oppresses different ways of knowing, being, and doing in an attempt to construct, regulate, and legislate the adequacy of mothering, and is therefore used to control women.

Similarly, yet focusing on the specific content knowledge used to construct the field of early childhood education, Cannella's (1997) herstory explains that the knowledges and voices of children have been ignored and left out of the knowledge bases that dominate the field. The ways of being and living of those who are younger, as well as their families and communities, are referred to as the "voices of silent knowing" (p. 10). Similar to Bloch (1994), the ways in which developmental psychology has imposed foundational assumptions on the field of early childhood education are discussed. Universalist foundational assumptions include an acceptance of an adult/child dichotomy that privileges those who are older; progress as a necessity of the human condition both individually and as a species; and a one-size-fits-all linear, developmental, predetermined sequence model for human functioning. As an example, when a defined form of progress does not occur, the individual (most often one categorized as "child") is labeled deficient. Child development assumptions have led to social and cultural injustices, which in turn have limited life possibilities for those who are younger by creating (1) multiple forms of privilege and control, (2) covert methods for social regulation and domination, (3) an acceptance of hierarchical/patriarchal human relations, and (4) views of humanity as deficient. Finally, developmental psychology has "legitimized the surveillance, measurement, and social control of children and other marginalized groups in the name of growth and human change" (Cannella, 1997, p. 63).

In the United States during the 1990s, professionals from the National Association for the Education of Young Children (NAEYC) used child development "knowledge" to construct a discourse of classroom "best practices" labeled developmentally appropriate practice (DAP). This universalist discourse defines and imposes guidelines for "quality" on early childhood classrooms, programs, and even research (Cannella, 1997; Cannella & Soto, 2010). Although generated in the United States, DAP guidelines are disseminated around the globe as well as used to create requirements for accreditation and licensure in a range of locations. From DAP's inception, reconceptualists have directly challenged DAP as a universalist, deterministic imposition of developmental psychology. As an example, using three dimensions of early childhood curriculum (i.e., knowledge, development, and context), Jipson (1998) analyzed the personal journals, personal narratives, and philosophy statements of thirty early childhood educators discussing the implications of DAP and culturally appropriate practices for early childhood. Jipson's (1998) work clearly demonstrates the dominant Euro-American cultural bias of NAEYC's DAP model.

Over time and in a range of publications, Sally Lubeck's (1994, 1996, 1998) herstorical work has delineated the ways that developmental psychology has damaged/is damaging beliefs, practices, and research in early childhood education. In particular, her 1998 work outlines assumptions within DAP that dominate and narrow understandings and possibilities for children, their teachers, and caregivers as well as the field. Lubeck (1998) describes these assumptions as privileging: (1) belief in objective appraisal; (2) acceptance of the objective, detached, and unbiased observer; (3) truth-oriented generalization of research broadly applied to humans and social settings; and (4) the institutionalization of a universal hierarchy of knowledge.

In more recent work, Shallwani (2010) presents a textual analysis of the language in the NAEYC DAP document. The work illustrates how child development discourse "depicts families as deficient in caring for their children and the discipline/profession as the legitimate knowledge base regarding children and childhood" (p. 242). Like previous scholars, Shallwani discusses the impact that the Enlightenment modernist project has had on the belief in the powers of science to uncover a predetermined "normal" that ultimately discredits and disqualifies those constituted as abnormal. Using a Foucaultian lens, Shallwani's analysis reveals how the guise of quality imposed by DAP is a form of racism, and serves to oppress children and their families by monitoring and regulating their bodies and the settings and people in which, and with whom, they interact. Shallwani calls this a reproduction of imperialism in an attempt to divide, classify, and normalize children and adults into useful and docile human beings based on white and imperial dominant ideologies.

For decades, reconceptualist scholars (Bloch, 1987, 1992, 2000; Bloch, Kennedy, Lightfoot, & Weyenberg, 2006; Bloch & Popkewitz, 2000; Cannella, 1997; Cannella & Soto, 2010; Dahlberg et al., 1999; Kennedy & Bloch, 2010; Kessler, 1991; Kessler & Swadener, 1992; Lubeck, 1991, 2000; Silin, 1987; Soto & Swadener, 2002) have questioned the knowledge bases (e.g., child development;

developmental psychology; constructions of play, quality, cognition, gender, race) that frame the field of early childhood education. These challenges have led to new ways of thinking, as well as the acknowledgment of individuals, groups, ways of being and knowing, and social inequities that are usually hidden, placed in the margins, and even erased. Some have been concerned that critique and deconstruction lead only to negativity, inaction, even depression. However, those who are part of the reconceptualist tradition view critique as increasing possibilities and as a position from which action can be taken. These scholars around the globe are attempting to place at the center knowledges and ways of being that have been traditionally marginalized.

Multiple volumes could be written describing the range of reconceptualist work in different geopolitical locations that would deconstruct, while at the same time reconstruct new possibilities. The work of Canadian early childhood scholars in this volume provides excellent examples of this deconstructive action. Sherry Rose and Pam Whitty challenge the disciplinary power of "clock time" by working with child-care educators to focus on knowledges and relationships that are not governed by time. Veronica Pacini-Ketchabaw, Kathleen Kummen, and Deborah Thompson use collective biography to contest psychological universals as developmental memories are revealed as multiple and situated and as forms of knowledge that are constructed by the material world. Anna Kirova defies universalist notions of play by focusing on culturally initiated actions that result in hybrid spaces through which play, for children and adults, is a vehicle for the preservation of cultural knowledges, ways of being, and identities.

While this work is absolutely positive, certainly leads to unique possibilities, and should be understood as the future, dominant ideologies continue to construct theory, practice, and research in the field, and create power for those who accept them. This condition leads to the broader body of work by reconceptualists, research into social regulations and the construction of hierarchal power relations over and through those who are younger, as well as critical activism that is required to counter those power relations.

Continued Reconceptualist Work: Unmasking Social Power Relations and Constructing Critical Activism

Globally, and in specific cultures and locations, reconceptualists acknowledge that patriarchy, colonialism, and capitalism have resulted in social regulations as well as physical domination imposed by particular groups over others. Intersecting power relations produce and are produced by dominant discourse practices, resulting in inequitable power and oppressive relations. Those who are younger; their teachers and parents; and particular racial, gendered, and ethnic groups are placed in the margins.

As a broad example from outside early childhood education but as a circumstance in which the field is embedded, males continue to dominate females in a range of cultures and societies. This self-aggrandizing construction of "male superiority," or patriarchy, is most evident in the preferential treatment that privileges males across the construction of languages, discourse practices, accepted/expected human behaviors, and even national and international governmental and expectations for leadership (Cannella & Viruru, 2004). Thus, males are constructed as normal (and advanced) and females are constructed as abnormal (and inferior). Females are held responsible for reproduction and nurturance (as this ultimate power tied to reproduction is continually discredited), while males are to perform capitalist production as they explain, order, and regulate. Euro-Western Christian, white male ways of knowing and doing have dominated Western societies and maintained conceptualizations of the female as the eternal caretaker. Even in contemporary time periods in which females go to war (serving as the stereotypic male killing machine or servant to that machine), voices of nonviolence that would counter assassination and war are most often silenced, and the acceptance of female leadership is relatively rare (e.g., military, business, national governments dominated by males). This mind-set is carried over to education, and especially early childhood education and care, with most teachers being females who are controlled by the gatekeepers of the system. These gatekeepers and social regulators include principals, school boards, accountability systems that would regulate behavior, and even CEOs, all who label, discredit, control, and even fire teachers and caregivers from within contemporary agendas that would privatize traditionally public services for children. Critical action is obviously needed within this context in which complex and intersecting social relations produce power and are reinscribed by that power.

Power Relations

Early childhood reconceptualists demonstrate the ways that a preoccupation with capitalist patriarchy and colonialist social control and power is evident in discourses (ways of knowing and doing) that dominate early childhood beliefs, programs, curriculum, and research. The work of Michael Foucault (1977), a French philosopher and social theorist, is widely recognized and used by reconceptualist early childhood scholars. His critical, poststructural analyses of disciplinary and regulatory powers provide frameworks for understanding the current state of early childhood education. Foucault proposes that disciplinary power produces control over colonized populations through dominant discourses (Cannella & Viruru, 2004); thus, power dichotomies are created, for example normal versus abnormal, colonizer versus subaltern, adult versus child. An environment that accepts legislated regulatory power is also produced. Relations of power are created as "one group places restrictions on the human bodies of another group, controlling what oppressed bodies can do and what spaces they are allowed to inhabit and navigate" (Cannella, 2002, p. 207). By 1999, a large number of reconceptualist early childhood scholars were using poststructural analysis, feminist theories, and various forms of postcolonial critique as well as critical and queer theories to examine social relations and power as produced and producing. (See Cannella & Bailey, 1999, for example studies from the various perspectives.)

As we have discussed, reconceptualist scholars object to the imposition of universal truths on the minds and bodies of others, whether labeled child or adult (Bloch, 1992; Cannella, 1997). Further, universalist truths have been "used to legitimize intervening into the lives of 'others' (most often those labeled children) in order to 'save' those others from whatever we deemed to be a problem" (Cannella, 1997, p. 2). This legitimation of intervention results in all types of power relations and the privileging of particular groups (even individuals) over others.

For example, behind the mask of child-centered pedagogy, "children have been created as a group of people who must be observed and who are in opposition, at least in intellectual ability, agency, and behavior, to adults" (Viruru & Cannella, 2001, p. 102). Observation of children (or surveillance, as discussed by Foucault, 1977) is legitimated as necessary as adults must "protect" and "guide" those who are younger so that they will be "safe" and their development appropriately guided and controlled. Attempts to regulate the bodies and spaces of children in order to measure and control those who are younger are embedded within the child development discourse that has dominated, and continues to dominate, practice (Shallwani, 2010). In addition, Campbell and Smith (2001) share another insight on observation and how it even narrows opportunities and the directions for change for those who are younger:

> Because traditional observation values and privileges developmental forms of knowledge over other ways of knowing the child, the practice of observation acts as a disciplinary instrument of surveillance. The child's freedom to move toward adulthood is constrained by knowledge of what it is to be normal and desirable. (p. 92)

Another example of childhood surveillance and judgment by those who would maintain or construct power for themselves can be seen in the obsession with measuring the psychologically generated construct that has been labeled human intellect. Standardized testing and accountability measures used in schools perpetuate the acceptance of a predetermined normality or predetermined mental and intellectual truths by legitimizing testing discourses and notions of measurement as applied to human progress. "The discourse on testing diverts attention from how schools are failing poor children especially from minority populations, and from the inequities in school environments, resources, and opportunities provided to poor children" (Cannella & Viruru, 2004, p. 133). Testing is seen as the ultimate motivator for teacher and student success, as if to say that standardized tests provide some sort of pleasure to the test taker.

Again, reconceptualists have demonstrated that practices like surveillance, testing, and the assumption of the right to judge others are about regulation and control of everything and everyone—children, teachers, parents, even knowledges and behaviors that are accepted and rejected. Education is then tied to this testing and constructed as the savior of those who would be educated (Cannella, 2002). Therefore, "the dominant construction of what it means to be saved through education is to become an individual who intellectually conforms to notions of scientific progress and advancement" (p. 204), one who is observed as progressing developmentally and performing appropriately (as judged by adult observers and test constructors).

Reconceptualist scholars also confront power relations as constructed by acceptance of the notion of "expert" knowledge and the "expert" professional. Individuals and groups who differ from the experts are placed in the margins, their experiences and knowledges judged and labeled abnormal or even deficient. In modernist, technological societies, expert knowledge is disseminated through visual media, books, professional organizations, celebrities/athletes, corporations, and scholars—to name just a few. The self-identified West's obsession with measuring human progress and achievement has created a hierarchy of experts that dominates how we feed, educate, entertain, and discipline those who are younger. The notion of "expert" continues the acceptance of a "predetermined normality" or truth and the "right" to judge another person.

Acceptance of both a predetermined normality and the superiority and right of the expert to judge others is evidenced in the construct of the notion of play therapy. Play, for those who are younger, is accepted as universal and the notion of play knowledge is used to legitimate a play therapy expert, the therapist. In turn, the use of play therapy legitimizes surveillance and intervention because it is deemed as the child's natural medium of expression/communication. "Play as a universal construct, applicable to all, creates a corporate structure of normalization and, consequently, labels for those considered abnormal because they cannot or choose not to play" (Cannella & Viruru, 2004, p. 108). A range of reconceptualist scholarship demonstrates that intersecting power relations are constructed that produce and perpetuate particular knowledges. Expert professionals are then given the right to observe, judge, label, intervene, and use those knowledges as forms of control over those who are younger.

Mac Naughton (2000) illustrates how current early childhood pedagogy influences the gendering of children's identities, as well as gendered power relations within schools and care centers. Using a feminist lens, Mac Naughton outlines and challenges accepted myths (e.g., gender as biologically stable and unchanging, gender equity issues as solved by the field long ago, males as negatively affected in gender equity programs) related to gender equality in early childhood education. Gender roles/norms also carry over to teachers who are seen as the ultimate caregivers to their students (Hauser & Jipson, 1998). Hughes and Mac Naughton (2001) invite teachers to "actively seek, negotiate, and debate cultural and political meanings tied to gender" (p. 128). Theilheimer and Cahill (2001) use the metaphor of a "messy closet" to explain the "myths, beliefs, norms, and representations of sexuality and children that heavily influence the field of early childhood education" (p. 103). In Western society, identities have been created for gay, lesbian, and bisexual individuals using Euro-Christian male ideologies. Theilheimer and Cahill (2001) warn that schools represent the privileging of heteronormativity reflected in society overall, that children are receiving the narrow message that the appropriate expectation is to be heterosexual. Along a similar vein, Wickens (2010) explains that romantic notions of the innocent child have led to calls for censorship of certain books and media. She explains that childhood innocence is a myth. Censorship is an attempt to sanitize children's lives of any suggestions of sexuality, whether subtle or overt (Wickens, 2010). Child development models view the child as deficient and innocent, not yet complete, and therefore unable to progress without the watchful and protective eye of a more sexually competent adult.

Work in the reconceptualist tradition also addresses childhood public policy and the forms of legislation and discourse practices that construct that policy. A recent example is an analysis of the current shift from child protection (e.g., repressive and controlling action) to child welfare (e.g., supportive approach) conducted by Vandenbroeck, Roose, and De Bie (2010). Foucault's notion of pastoral power is used to illustrate that the welfare discourse, while seemingly equitable and caring, still creates a dichotomy of the expert (e.g., social worker) and the "other" in need of intervention or protection. "Remarkably, parents themselves are often excluded from the debates on what 'their' problem is supposed to be, reducing them to being spectators in their own life" (Vandenbroeck et al., 2010, p. 119). Thus, the people whom the welfare system is trying to help are often blamed for their own problems (e.g., poverty) (Swadener, 2000). Vandenbroeck et al. explain that the current welfare discourse calls for prevention as a way to intervene before problems occur. Thus, predetermined risk factors have been identified through positivist research methods to help identify these so-called risk factors. The notion that experts can fix the problems of their "high-risk" clients legitimizes the control of one group over another (e.g., superior/inferior, good parents/bad parents).

Cultural and intellectual globalization, the "new colonization, means that young children are increasingly exposed to western popular culture, complicating efforts by early childhood educators to provide children with access to local Indigenous histories and knowledge" (Ritchie & Rau, 2010, p. 366). Nsamenang

(2010) provides a discussion of social intellectual globalization. From dominant Euro-American perspectives, the mother is seen as the eternal caregiver of the child, a view that is invading other parts of the world. Western early childhood development programs are appearing throughout Africa in the name of saving the intellect of the children. Nsamenang labels these programs as part of a Eurocentric adjustment agenda that would promote Western child-care and development models. This type of reconceptualist analysis of social power relations has been conducted, and continues to be constructed, by a range of indigenous early childhood reconceptualist scholars and those who would employ postcolonial critique like Radhika Viruru (2001) in India, Jenny Ritchie and Cheryl Rau (2008) in New Zealand, and Lourdes Diaz Soto (2000) in the United States.

Early childhood reconceptualist scholars, and others who work in a reconceptualist tradition, have become increasingly aware of corporatization, the privileging of the notion of free markets, and the increased embeddedness of societal institutions within business model mentalities and power structures (Cannella & Kincheloe, 2002). Kincheloe (2002) defines a new childhood by uncovering the complex political and social power that corporations like McDonald's have over childhood. He also explains that "education takes place in a variety of social sites, including but not limited to schooling" (p. 84) by describing the incredible influence McDonald's has over Western society overall. Kincheloe explains how McDonald's and other corporations use marketing to employ a "pedagogy of pleasure" (p. 93), just like toy companies and other businesses that market to children.

Most recently, power is recognized as privileging Western ways of marketing and profiteering, especially within neoliberal globalization that interprets all aspects of life as generated by, and dependent on, capitalism (Lee, 2010; Perez & Cannella, 2010; Ritchie & Rau, 2010). Perez and Cannella (2010) offer a historical and contemporary review of the impact of neoliberalism on early childhood policy/legislation, curriculum, and practices. The authors provide in-depth analyses of current early childhood education/care policy, illustrating how notions of power and competition are evident in contemporary discourse practices (e.g., No Child Left Behind legislation) and in the privatization of public services. This combination of discourse with privatization is illustrated as disaster capitalism, as explained by Naomi Klein (2007), and is employed to create private charter schools out of public institutions following a catastrophic event (e.g., New Orleans public schools after Hurricane Katrina).

Lee (2010) examines neoliberal conceptualizations of freedom, equality, and choice in her analysis of the preschool voucher system in Taiwan and Hong Kong. She explains that an illusion of choice or freedom is created when parents use publically funded vouchers to select their child's preschool from a pool of government-controlled programs. The government then becomes the authority on what constitutes a "good" preschool program. Lee (2010) explains:

It is assumed that a market approach to education will not only empower the parents and students as "free choosers" but will also improve quality and equality of education and care for all children. Such assumptions of a market approach in the field of education reflect the core elements of a neoliberal political economic reasoning system that has been widely circulated at the global level to facilitate a universal intelligibility of educational vouchers. (p. 133)

Finally, the work of scholars like Sue Grieshaber (2010) in Australia illustrates the complexities of emerging neoliberal power relations that surround those who are younger. This recent work analyzes the public's reaction (in the media) to the publication of *Corporate Paedophilia: Sexualisation of Children in Australia*, demonstrating that performances of neoliberalism are embedded within both interpretations that go toward moral panic and readings that invoke discourses of tolerance/intolerance. Scholars in the early childhood reconceptualist tradition are increasingly recognizing these complex, contradictory, and paradoxical performances of neoliberalism as it invades the lives of everyone around the globe.

Critical Activism

Reconceptualist scholarship is itself a form of critical activism for social justice because the work stands for traditionally marginalized knowledges, positions, and peoples, and has placed those who would take a reconceptualist stance at risk (a point that is not always understood by scholars who use critical work for reasons of professional advancement, rather than social justice). However, in-depth analyses into the complexity of social power relations are also major components of critical activism because the scholarship facilitates the establishment of a context through which direct critical actions can be taken.

Recent reconceptualist scholarship in early childhood education seeks new humanistic and "decolonizing" methodologies (e.g., children as co-participants; child empowerment advocacy) that reject current positivist research traditions that continue the universal construct of childhood, as well as other universalisms (Soto & Swadener, 2005). Similarly, Cannella and Greishaber (2001) explain that reconceptualist perspectives have begun to uncover the voices of humankind that were once ignored and marginalized in early childhood education. They call for early childhood scholars to listen to the voices of younger human beings and embrace multiple and diverse constructions of early education and care.

The work of early childhood scholars in this volume illustrates the active acceptance of multiplicity and diversity, as well as the acceptance of those who are younger and traditionally marginalized peoples as partners in critical action. Mary Caroline Rowan's work is informed by Indigenous methodologies and knowledge as she uses cultural stories to construct an educational environment for young children that can aid in the resistance of normalization. Using the work of Friere,

Bourdieu, and Cummins in the construction of workshops for immigrant parents over a ten-year period, Judith K. Bernhard focuses on experiences that assist parents in understanding marginalized positions and actions that can be taken to support their children by using their own cultural capital. Western "rights-based" discourses are challenged by Beth Blue Swadener, Lacey Peters, and Sonya Gaches as they seek collective and culturally framed forms of praxis in diverse locations, while always focusing on sharing power with children, and giving the views of those who are younger due weight. This work takes concern for social power directly to those who have been harmed by those inequitable relations.

Early childhood reconceptualist critical activism, and related work in the reconceptualist tradition in fields like critical psychology, can be found in many forms. These activists are rethinking the purposes of research in ways that challenge our will to know the mind of the other, while focusing on systems and performances of oppression (Cannella & Lincoln, 2009; Cannella & Viruru, 2002; Mac Naughton, 2005; Soto, Cervantes-Soon, Villareal, & Campos, 2009). They are constructing alliances with children and families (Swadener, 2000) and teachers (Elliot, 2007), and helping to place Indigenous voices and ways of being at the center of educational institutions (Ritchie, 2001). They are uncovering new lines of flight embedded within the flows, rhythms, and intensities of early childhood curriculum as it is contestable, emergent, unsettling, and full of possibilities (Pacini-Ketchabaw, 2010) and generating new forms of knowledge that assist as we unthink what we think we know about childhood (Burman, 2010).

Again, scholars in this volume are taking direct critical action as they attempt to literally change our dominant practices. Teacher education is an area in which most early childhood scholars function, a field that tends to be both narrow and prescriptive, especially under conditions of neoliberal capitalism. In this volume, Luigi Iannacci and Bente Graham focus on the introduction of critical disability studies to teacher candidates, and Zeenat Janmohamed unveils the heteronormative nature of teacher education programs in early childhood education. This research could directly affect the content and practices of teacher preparation programs. As a profound example, and knowing that early childhood professionals often have difficulty with the concept of authority because of the power implications tied to the construct, Rachel Langford draws upon feminist and critical perspectives to illustrate how authority could/should be reconceptualized and claimed as the power to address the inequities within the neoliberal state.

Soto (2010) and the other authors of *Childhoods: A Handbook* urge us to open our minds and consider new possibilities by "pursuing newly evolving qualitative and experimental paradigms in order to emphasize decolonizing models as well as research capable of ameliorating oppressive dehumanizing situations, . . . pursuing . . . projects from the heart" (p. 377). Soto calls for early childhood professionals to evaluate their own perspectives through a process Freire calls "conscientization" where "we examine our perspectives, privileges, and our own world view, not as a naval gazing activity but as an intention to better understand" (Soto, 2010, p. 377). Soto asks us to consider whether we are trying to better our own condition or the condition of humankind. The reconceptualist early childhood tradition has generated research and forms of critical action that have reshaped the field academically. However, equity and social justice have not been attained for a large number of children, their families, or communities in our own countries or in distant locations. During this time of increased global capitalism, poverty, and inequity, radical reconceptualist work that addresses these power relations, locally and globally, specifically and systemically, has never been more important.

References

Bloch, M. N. (1987). Becoming scientific and professional: An historical perspective on the aims and effects of early education. In T. S. Popkewitz (Ed.), *The formation of school subjects* (pp. 25–62). Basingstoke, England: Falmer Press.
Bloch, M. N. (1992). Critical perspectives on the historical relationship between child development and early childhood education research. In S. Kessler & B. B. Swadener (Eds.), *Reconceptualizing the early childhood curriculum: Beginning the dialogue* (pp. 3–20). New York, NY: Teachers College Press.
Bloch, M. N. (2000). Governing teachers, parents, and children through child development knowledge. *Human Development, 43*(4/5), 257–265.
Bloch, M. N., Kennedy, D., Lightfoot, T., & Weyenberg, D. (Eds.). (2006). *The child in the world/the world in the child: Education and the configuration of a universal, modern, and globalized childhood.* New York, NY: Palgrave Macmillan.
Bloch, M. N., & Popkewitz, T. S. (2000). Constructing the parent, teacher, and child: Discourses of development. In L. D. Soto (Ed.), *The politics of early childhood education* (pp. 7–32). New York, NY: Peter Lang.
Bredekamp, S. (1987). *Developmentally appropriate practice in early childhood programs serving children from birth through age 8.* Washington, DC: National Association for the Education of Young Children.
Burman, E. (1994). *Deconstructing developmental psychology.* London, England: Routledge.
Burman, E. (2008). *Deconstructing developmental psychology* (2nd ed.). London, England: Brunner-Routledge.
Burman, E. (2010). Un/thinking children in development: A contribution from northern anti-developmental psychology. In G. S. Cannella & L. D. Soto (Eds.), *Childhoods: A handbook* (pp. 9–26). New York, NY: Peter Lang.
Campbell, S., & Smith, K. (2001). Equity observation and images of fairness in childhood. In S. Grieshaber & G. S. Cannella (Eds.), *Embracing identities in early childhood education: Diversity and possibilities* (pp. 89–102). New York, NY: Teachers College Press.
Cannella, G. S. (1997). *Deconstructing early childhood education: Social justice & revolution.* New York, NY: Peter Lang.
Cannella, G. S. (2002). Global perspectives, cultural studies, and the construction of the postmodern. In G. S. Cannella & J. Kincheloe (Eds.), *Kidworld: Childhood studies, globalization, and education* (pp. 4–26). New York, NY: Peter Lang.
Cannella, G. S., & Bailey, C. (1999). Postmodern research in early childhood education. In S. Reifel (Ed.), *Advances in early education and day care* (Vol. 10, pp. 3–39). Greenwich, CT: JAI Press.

Cannella, G. S., & Grieshaber, S. (2001). Identities and possibilities. In S. Grieshaber & G. S. Cannella (Eds.), *Embracing identities in early childhood education: Diversity and possibilities* (pp. 89–102). New York, NY: Teachers College Press.

Cannella, G. S., & Kincheloe, J. (Eds.). (2002). *Kidworld: Childhood studies, globalization, and education.* New York, NY: Peter Lang.

Cannella, G. S., & Lincoln, Y. (2009). Deploying qualitative methods for critical social purposes. In N. K. Denzin & M. D. Giardina (Eds.), *Qualitative inquiry and social justice* (pp. 53–72). Walnut Creek, CA: Left Coast Press.

Cannella, G. S., & Soto, L. D. (2010). *Childhoods: A handbook.* New York, NY: Peter Lang.

Cannella, G. S., & Viruru, R. (2002). (Euro-American constructions of) education of children (and adults) around the world: A postcolonial critique. In G. S. Cannella & J. Kincheloe (Eds.), *Kidworld: Childhood studies, globalization, and education* (pp. 265–287). New York, NY: Peter Lang.

Cannella, G. S., & Viruru, R. (2004). *Childhood and (post)colonization: Power, education, and contemporary practice.* New York, NY: Routledge.

Dahlberg, G., & Moss, P. (2005). *Ethics and politics in early childhood education.* London, England: RoutledgeFalmer.

Dahlberg, G., Moss, P., & Pence, A. (1999). *Beyond quality in early childhood education and care: Postmodern perspectives.* New York, NY: Routledge.

Elliot, E. (2007). *"We're not robots": The voices of infant/toddler caregivers.* Albany, NY: SUNY Press.

Foucault, M. (1977). *Discipline and punish: The birth of prison.* New York, NY: Pantheon.

Grieshaber, S. (2010). Sexualization of children in contemporary Australian media. In G. S. Cannella & L. D. Soto (Eds.), *Childhoods: A handbook* (pp. 173–188). New York, NY: Peter Lang.

Grieshaber, S., & Cannella, G. S. (2001). From identity to identities: Increasing possibilities in early childhood education. In S. Grieshaber & G. S. Cannella (Eds.), *Embracing identities in early childhood education: Diversity and possibilities* (pp. 3–22). New York, NY: Teachers College Press.

Hauser, M. E., & Jipson, J. A. (1998). *Intersections: Feminisms/early childhoods.* New York, NY: Peter Lang.

Hughes, P., & Mac Naughton, G. (2001). Fractured or manufactured: Gendered identities and culture in the early years. In S. Grieshaber & G. S. Cannella (Eds.), *Embracing identities in early childhood education: Diversity and possibilities* (pp. 114–132). New York, NY: Teachers College Press.

Jipson, J. J. (1991). Developmentally appropriate practice: Culture, curriculum, and connections. *Early Education and Development, 2,* 120–136.

Jipson, J. J. (1998). Developmentally appropriate practice: Culture, curriculum, connections. In M. E. Hauser & J. J. Jipson (Eds.), *Intersections: Feminisms / early childhoods* (pp. 221–239). New York, NY: Peter Lang.

Kennedy, D., & Bloch, M. (2010). Negotiating sameness and difference: American Jewish childhood. In G. S. Cannella & L. D. Soto (Eds.), *Childhoods: A handbook* (pp. 40–55). New York, NY: Peter Lang.

Kessler, S. (1991). Alternative perspectives on early childhood education. *Early Childhood Research Quarterly, 6,* 183–197.

Kessler, S., & Swadener, B. B. (Eds.). (1992). *Reconceptualizing the early childhood curriculum: Beginning the dialogue.* New York, NY: Teachers College Press.

Kincheloe, J. (2002). The complex politics of McDonald's and the new childhood: Colonizing kidworld. In G. S. Cannella & J. Kincheloe (Eds.), *Kidworld: Childhood studies, globalization, and education* (pp. 75–122). New York, NY: Peter Lang.

Klein, N. (2007). *The shock doctrine: The rise of disaster capitalism.* New York, NY: Metropolitan Books.

Lee, I. F. (2010). Global and local trends for governance and planning in early childhood education and care: Effects of preschool vouchers. In G. S. Cannella & L. D. Soto (Eds.), *Childhoods: A handbook* (pp. 131–144). New York, NY: Peter Lang.

Lubeck, S. (1991). Reconceptualizing early childhood education. *Early Education and Development, 2*(2), 168–174.

Lubeck, S. (1994). The politics of developmentally appropriate practice. In B. Mallory & R. New (Eds.), *Diversity and developmentally appropriate practices: Challenges for early childhood Education* (pp. 17–39). New York, NY: Teachers College Press.

Lubeck, S. (1996). Deconstructing "child development knowledge" and "teacher preparation." *Early Childhood Quarterly, 11,* 147–176.

Lubeck, S. (1998). Is developmentally appropriate practice for everyone? *Childhood Education, 74,* 283–292.

Lubeck, S. (2000). On reassessing the relevance of the child development knowledge base to education: A response. *Human Development, 43*(4/5), 273–278.

Mac Naughton, G. (2000). *Rethinking gender in early childhood education.* London, England: Paul Chapman.

Mac Naughton, G. (2005). *Doing Foucault in early childhood studies: Applying poststructural ideas.* New York, NY: Routledge.

Nsamenang, A. B. (2010). Childhoods within Africa's triple heritage. In G. S. Cannella & L. D. Soto (Eds.), *Childhoods: A handbook* (pp. 9–26). New York, NY: Peter Lang.

Pacini-Ketchabaw, V. (Ed.). (2010). *Flows, rhythms, and intensities of early childhood education curriculum.* New York, NY: Peter Lang.

Perez, M. S., & Cannella, G. S. (2010). Disaster capitalism as neoliberal instrument for the construction of early childhood education/care policy: Charter schools in post-Katrina New Orleans. In G. S. Cannella & L. D. Soto (Eds.), *Childhoods: A handbook* (pp. 145–156). New York, NY: Peter Lang.

Ritchie, J. (2001). Reflections on collectivism in early childhood teacher training in Aotearoa/New Zealand. In S. Grieshaber & G. S. Cannella (Eds.), *Embracing identities in early childhood education: Diversity and possibilities* (pp. 137–147). New York, NY: Teachers College Press.

Ritchie, J., & Rau, C. (2008). *Te Puawaitang—partnerships with Tamariki and Whanau in bicultural early childhood care and education.* Final report to the Teaching Learning Research Initiative. Wellington, New Zealand: TLRI/NZCER. Retrieved December 18, 2008, from http://www.tlri.org.nz/pdfs/9207_finalreport.pdf

Ritchie, J., & Rau, C. (2010). Kia mau kit e wairuatanga: Countercolonial narratives of early childhood education in Aotearoa. In G. S. Cannella & L. D. Soto (Eds.), *Childhoods: A handbook* (pp. 355–374). New York, NY: Peter Lang.

Shallwani, S. (2010). Racism and imperialism in the child development discourse: Deconstructing "developmentally appropriate practice." In G. S. Cannella & L. D. Soto (Eds.), *Childhoods: A handbook* (pp. 214–231). New York, NY: Peter Lang.

Silin, J. G. (1987). The early childhood educator's knowledge base: A reconsideration. In L. G. Katz (Ed.), *Current topics in early childhood education* (pp. 17–31). Norwood, NJ: Ablex.

Soto, L. D. (Ed.). (2000). *The politics of early childhood education.* New York, NY: Peter Lang.

Soto, L. D. (2010). Constructing critical futures: Projects from the heart. In G. S. Cannella & L. D. Soto (Eds.), *Childhoods: A handbook* (pp. 375–380). New York, NY: Peter Lang.

Soto, L. D., Cervantes-Soon, C., Villareal, E., & Campos, E. (2009). The Xicana sacred space: A communal circle of compromise for educational researchers. *Harvard Educational Review, 79*(4), 755–775.

Soto, L. D., & Swadener, B. B. (2002). Toward liberatory early childhood theory, research and praxis: Decolonizing a field. *Contemporary Issues in Early Childhood, 3*(1), 28–66.

Soto, L. D., & Swadener, B. B. (Eds.). (2005). *Power and voice in research with children.* New York, NY: Peter Lang.

Swadener, B. B. (2000). "At risk" or "at promise" from deficit constructions of the "other childhood" to possibilities for authentic alliances with children and families. In L. D. Soto (Ed.), *The politics of early childhood education* (pp. 117–134). New York, NY: Peter Lang.

Theilheimer, R., & Cahill, B. A. (2001). A messy closet in the early childhood classroom. In S. Grieshaber & G. S. Cannella (Eds.), *Embracing identities in early childhood education: Diversity and possibilities* (pp. 103–113). New York, NY: Teachers College Press.

Vandenbroeck, M., Roose, R., & De Bie, M. (2010). Governing families in the social investment state. In G. S. Cannella & L. D. Soto (Eds.), *Childhoods: A handbook* (pp. 119–130). New York, NY: Peter Lang.

Viruru, R. (2001). *Early childhood education: Postcolonial perspectives from India*. London, England: Sage.

Viruru, R., & Cannella, G. S. (2001). Postcolonial ethnography, young children, and voice. In S. Grieshaber & G. S. Cannella (Eds.), *Embracing identities in early childhood education: Diversity and possibilities* (pp. 89–102). New York, NY: Teachers College Press.

Wickens, C. (2010). The denial of sexuality and the power of censorship. In G. S. Cannella & L. D. Soto (Eds.), *Childhoods: A handbook* (pp. 281–290). New York, NY: Peter Lang.

Chapter One

Resituating Early Childhood Education

Introduction

Larry Prochner & Veronica Pacini-Ketchabaw

This book presents possibilities for resituating the theory and practice of Canadian early childhood education from a normative, developmental view to one grounded in postfoundational theory. While the conceptual framework guiding thinking in early childhood education (ECE) has shifted over the past twenty-five years, government policy guiding programs, services, and approaches to curriculum continues to draw largely upon a normative discourse. This chapter discusses educational change within the field in relation to the resilience of core ideas, presents key concepts in the normative and postfoundational discourses, and outlines the chapters that follow.

Change and Continuity in ECE

The term "reconceptualist" was used in the field of curriculum theory beginning in the 1970s to identify theorists who were dissatisfied with the how-to, technical-rational focus of what were called "traditional approaches." As described by Pinar (1975), reconceptualists "tend to study not 'change in behavior' or 'decision making in the classroom,' but matters of temporality, transcendence, consciousness, and politics" (p. xi). In the 1980s scholars in ECE who were critical of traditional curriculum approaches adopted a similar stance, marking the start of the reconceptualist movement in the ECE field.[1] The movement in

---
1   The history of this movement in the United States is described by Kessler and Swadener (1992) in their introduction to *Reconceptualizing the Early Childhood Curriculum: Beginning the Dialogue*, and more recently by Swadener and Cannella (2007) in the Canadian Child Care Federation's magazine, *INTERACTION*. See also Cannella (2010); Cannella, Swadener, and Che (2007); and Jipson and Bailey (2000). Pacini-Ketchabaw and Pence (2005) have provided an analysis of Canadian developments.

ECE coincided with and was influenced by several events. One was the publication of the first edition of the National Association for the Education of Young Children's (NAEYC) *Developmentally Appropriate Practice* (DAP), edited by Bredekamp in 1986, planned as a "tool for early childhood professionals" (Bredekamp, 1986, p. 56) to disseminate DAP ideas and DAP-based programs. Although Bredekamp (1991, p. 199) cast DAP as a means for "*redeveloping* early childhood education" [emphasis added], it is more correctly interpreted as an effort to place practice on an alternate basis in relation to new child development knowledge. This is consistent with Weber's (1984) characterization of ECE in a pre-DAP era, in which the field continually "redeveloped" theory and practice to reflect behavioural psychology, cognitive psychology, psychoanalytic psychology, neuropsychology, and so on. Another event coinciding with the 1980s reconceptualist movement was the introduction to the United States of the alternative approach to childhood education represented by the Reggio Emilia schools (New & Kantor, 2009). It appeared as a counterpoint to the academic kindergarten curriculum (cf. Walsh, 1989), which was itself a motivation for both the DAP framework and programs and the reconceptualist movement.

Reconceptualists argued that developmental psychology was flawed as a theoretical foundation for ECE programs and practice (cf. Cannella, 1997), with potential to contribute to serious inequities (Lubeck, 1985). Over time, the focus of reconceptualists expanded beyond critiques of developmentalism (e.g., Lenz Taguchi, 2009; Olsson, 2009). The scope of the work was similar to that of the reconceptualist movement in generalist curriculum theory described by Pinar (1999) in his retrospective analysis:

> What identifies 25 years of curriculum theorizing is not the term reconceptualist, per se, but rather collective although diverse approaches to resisting technologies of education that try to separate content, pedagogy, and learning into discrete, measureable, and observable units of behaviour and product. (p. 506)

It is now twenty-five years from the initial reconceptualist work in ECE in the 1980s, and perspectives in this field include similarly diverse responses to curriculum problems, united by a concern for "equal and emancipatory early childhood education" (Swadener & Cannella, 2007, p. 26). Reconceptualists in ECE called for research and policy that included the voices of parents, children, and teachers as an alternative foundation to child development knowledge, expecting that this would lead to more responsive and respectful practices grounded in the values, interests, and desires of local culture and community (cf. Ayers, 1989; Duncan, Bowden, & Smith, 2006; Pence, 1998). Others looked to the "lost" potential of older ideas, for example, the ideas of Dewey (Bentley, 2011; Wood, 2007), or sought to redefine what were seen as problems in a normative discourse as strengths instead (Souto-Manning, 2006).

This has been a slow process. As observed by Freeman and Hatch in their 1989 article "Emergent Literacy: Reconceptualizing Kindergarten Practice": "A disparity exists between existing knowledge of how children develop literacy and initial instruction in kindergarten. . . . Why does this disparity exist? How can kindergarten practice be reconceptualised to reflect an emergent literacy perspective?" (p. 23). We are not there yet. Davidson addresses an argument for sociocultural perspectives to be joined with the cognitive view on literacy development in this volume. With reference to postcolonial theory in ECE, Viruru (2005) concluded that "postcolonial thought has had only minimal if any impact on the field of early childhood as an academic discipline and even less on the daily practices of early childhood educators" (p. 7). We know from studies of educational history that change in curriculum and pedagogy can be piecemeal, even "haphazard" (Goodson, 2002, p. 13), and this has been true in the field of ECE. We observe that reconceptualist theory largely remains outside "contemporary theory" and thus "reconceptualist," indicated, for example, by its positioning in a 2007 encyclopedia of ECE in which the editors noted, "In addition to entries on contemporary theories of teaching and learning, alternative and post-modern perspectives on the field are represented by entries on the reconceptualist movement, feminist theory, and children's sexuality" (New & Cochran, 2007, p. xxi). Our key word search for the terms "reconceptualist" and "reconceptualize" in the online database of articles from NAEYC's professional journal *Young Children* (1985–2011) resulted in no matches (with the same result for "postcolonial theory").

The persistence of core ideas in early childhood education has restricted a wider influence of reconceptualist theory and practice. By core idea we mean those ideas about learning and teaching that have endured across time, and to the extent they have been exported or borrowed, exist across space (Cleghorn & Prochner, 2010). An example is a belief in the importance of children's self-activity through play and with materials for successful development. This was a core idea in the early kindergarten movement (Weber, 1969), expressed in its pedagogy and curriculum, and enacted in programs in which children used specialized materials under the direction of a teacher.[2] Its resilience is shown in the experience of kindergarten teacher and teacher educator Grace Fulmer. From 1901 to 1903 Fulmer taught the youngest children at Dewey's Laboratory School at the University of Chicago, a school famous in the history of progressive education for its freer approach to the use of materials and emphasis on cooperative learning. Fulmer's predecessor at the Lab School was Georgia Scates, whose account of

---

2   See Rogers (2005) for an analysis of the idea of "self-activity" in Hegelian thinking as it was interpreted by members of by the St. Louis philosophical movement in the nineteenth century, which included kindergartener Susan Blow. "Through play young children create an alternative reality in which they . . . are faced with otherness, and thus a form of self-estrangement. When the play has ended, they are . . . enriched by their experience" (p. 231. In the 1920s Russian psychologists employed the concept of "creative self-activity" in activity theory using an entirely different philosophical base (Arce, 2006; Umrikhin, 1997).

the kindergarten co-authored with Dewey included a plea for its "emancipation" from the formalized use of Froebel's blocks and other materials (Scates, 1900).³ Fulmer was Froebelian Elizabeth Harrison's niece (Annual Convention, 1898), and had received her training under Harrison at the Chicago Kindergarten College in traditional methods. Fulmer expressed her commitment to Froebel in her book on kindergarten methods published eighteen years after her work at the Dewey School.⁴

> The materials peculiar to the kindergarten were selected because of their value in the organization and control of human experience—because of their universal significance—and not because they happened to be the few things in which the founder of the kindergarten became interested, or because of their appeal to a few individuals. (Fulmer, 1918, p. 7)

Fulmer acknowledged her intellectual "debt" to Dewey in the preface, later drawing on his ideas to emphasize the need for teachers to control children's use of materials: "Direction or guidance," says Dr. Dewey, "is not external imposition; but it is freeing the life process for its own most adequate fulfillment" (Fulmer, 1918, p. 69).⁵ Here, Fulmer and Dewey agree that appropriate constraints lead to "emancipation," which in Froebelian theory referred to a move to a spiritual state.

The point is not that change is difficult—this will not be surprising to readers—but rather, that a shift from traditional thinking (Froebelian kindergarten theory, in this case) was constrained by adherence to core ideas. We observe that constancy has been considered a positive professional attribute in the field. With reference to the "rebirth of great ideas," textbook author George Morrison (2011) comments, "I hope you will always be as amazed as I am about the way early childhood professionals recycle enduring ideas and practices and use them in their teaching" (p. 58). Here we see recycling valued over critical reflection and reconceptualization.

A second example of a core idea as a constraint on change is a belief in early education's potential to ameliorate social and educational problems in the future, a trigger for the rediscovery of early childhood in the 1960s and the programs that ensued, as well as the renewed attention to childhood education in current times as a remedy for children determined to be at risk (Bloch, 2005). Then and now there has been a preoccupation with determining the best way to achieve this goal, conceived as the best approach. Writing in the early 1970s, Weikart (1972) commented, "The field of compensatory preschool education is littered

---

3   The kindergarten was referred to as the "sub-primary" department. The article is attributed to Scates, but includes sections published by Dewey in *The School and Society* in 1899.

4   *The Use of the Kindergarten Gifts* was used as a textbook in Fulmer's private teacher training school in Los Angeles until the late 1930s.

5   Quoted from Dewey's *The Child and the Curriculum* (1902, p. 22).

with debris from the battles of the last decade between the ideas of traditional child-developmental educators and the more modern approaches espoused by educational researchers" (p. 22). The battle continues in the twenty-first century, with many of the same approaches vying for attention.

Currently, there is intense political attention worldwide on the potential for early education as an early years investment, based on the idea of social melioration. Examples include reports from Australia (Robinson, Silburn, & Arney, 2011) and from Ireland (Start Strong, 2010), where the National Association of Head Teachers (2011) warned government to "invest in early years' education or risk wasting the potential of the children of Northern Ireland." In Scotland, early years investment was discussed at a meeting of child health and welfare experts and a government finance committee as part of an inquiry into preventative spending (Scottish Parliament Committee, 2010). Examples in Canada include reports from Prince Edward Island (Flanagan, 2010) and the Early Years studies (McCain & Mustard, 1999, 2002; Mustard & McCain, 2007). The Ontario government's website explaining the value of full-day kindergarten begins with the sentence "Early learning is an investment in the future" (Ontario Ministry of Education, 2011). Investments are made with an expectation of future benefit, and this is part of the dictionary definition of investment: "to employ (money) in the purchase of anything from which interest or profit is expected" (Onions, 1973, p. 1108). In the case of early childhood programs, the "return on investment" includes brain growth as well as "higher future economic output" through "a more highly skilled workforce, . . . greater social inclusion and equity of access to economic opportunities" (Organisation for Economic Co-operation and Development [OECD], 2006, p. 133). Investment is clearly a show of commitment to children's and society's well-being. However, as Bloch (2005) explains, while

> emphasis on the costs and benefits . . . is a language that catches the ideas of legislators and calls attention to the importance of early childhood education and child care programs for all children and their families, this same language often "frames" and constructs children and their families as different, dangerous, and abnormal. (p. 426)

There is thus a need to shift discussions of theory and practice to a new place, to resituate location of analysis away from traditional core ideas, to change the conversation in its entirety.

Resituating ECE in Relation to Postfoundational Theory

Although change has been slow and uneven, we cannot deny the important contributions that the reconceptualist early childhood literature has made to the field, from policy development to training to daily practice. Reconceptualist scholars have transformed the ways in which we view, think about, and research early childhood. The breadth and depth of the reconceptualist movement is difficult to reflect on in just a few pages. Therefore, we do not attempt to define the reconceptualist movement in Canada or to provide a history of its genealogy. Plotting its history and creating a definition of reconceptualist ideas in early childhood is not a linear and simple task. At the same moment that definitions are demarcated, exclusions are created. Furthermore, a historical account needs to take into consideration time and place as uneven and dynamic, something that would require much more space than we have here. Our hope is that the brief review that follows gives the reader a glimpse into the contributions of scholars who have brought disruptions to the constancy of ECE theory and practice.

The reconceptualist movement, drawing on a range of postfoundational theories,[6] brought the loss of certainty, control, and predictability; openness to the presence of many voices and views; and the need to engage with silenced "other" views and explore a world of profound diversity and complexity. Through the reconceptualist movement, process, engagement, dialogue, and co-construction took precedence over routines, prescribed best practices, exclusivity, and predetermined outcomes.

Reconceptualist ECE scholars, as we mentioned above, challenge the existence of a singular *truth* and, consequently, of universality (Cannella, 1997; Dahlberg et al., 1999). Reality, according to reconceptualist thinkers, does not exist independently of the knower and the process of knowing. It is essential to acknowledge the importance of context and politics when making decisions. There is an acknowledgment that ECE is a political enterprise that always requires ethical and situated decisions (Dahlberg & Moss, 2005). At the core level, what these ideas have done is to problematize the *true* child constructed in ECE, questioning our reliance on a specific ideal image of the child (Burman, 2008). An intersectional race, class, gender, sexuality, nationalism, and age-situated analysis of the child has been promoted (Grieshaber & Cannella, 2001). This fluid and strength-based approach disestablishes the developmental psychology perspective of the unified, rational, vulnerable child. Also, it allows for multiplicity and diversity in how we understand children. It shifts the focus from shaping the "normal" child (a child that fits the norms of developmental psychology) to paying attention to how we can understand children from a multiplicity of perspectives and the effects that our understandings of childhood have on the lives of children and families.

The reconceptualist movement has also been influenced by poststructural theories that see language as a discursive system of socially construed signs, a meaning-filled practice, rather than modernity's view of language as an instrument for delivering *reality* (Grieshaber & Cannella, 2001; Hultqvist & Dahlberg,

---

6 Theories such as feminist, critical, poststructuralism, postcolonialism, anti-racist, and posthumanism, amongst others.

2001). Recognizing the discursive nature of language, unquestioned terms embedded in the field's core ideas such as "developmental practice," "daily routines," and "normal" are viewed as social constructs into which we infer or build meanings (Cannella, 1997; Dahlberg et al., 2007; Moss & Petrie, 2002).

Reconceptualist thinkers also question the binary/dualistic thinking that permeates early childhood education (Dahlberg et al., 1999; Lenz Taguchi, 2009; Mac Naughton, 2005). Distinctions between rational and irrational, ordered and unordered, included and excluded, appropriate and inappropriate, objective and subjective have been framed as natural and are mostly invisible in the field. However, reconceptualist scholars remind us, these distinctions are contingent upon dualistic conceptions of power and, as such, they are problematic. Instead, some scholars have written about the need to engage in a practice of "both/and" rather than "either/or" (Dahlberg et al., 2007; Lenz Taguchi, 2009; Olsson, 2009).

By acknowledging the political nature of ECE, the role of ECE institutions and professional disciplines has also been questioned by scholars within the reconceptualist movement (Moss & Petrie, 2002; Olsson, 2009). Moss and Petrie (2002), for example, argue that ECEC institutions need to be considered sites of disciplinary power, surveillance, and regulation. A key element in the existence of institutions is their legitimization of discourses. Many reconceptualist scholars have embraced this assumption to rethink ECE practices and, over time, have engaged in conceptualizing everyday early childhood practices differently using tools such as rhizoanalysis, deconstruction, ethics of resistance, and assemblage of desire, among others (see Lenz Taguchi, 2009; Mac Naughton, 2005; Olsson, 2009).

Postcolonial studies provide useful critical lenses for understanding the histories and continuing influences of colonialism, imperialism, and neocapitalist ideologies. Decolonization is also a political act taken up by postcolonial studies that have influenced the work of early childhood scholars like Soto and Swadener (2002) and Cannella and Viruru (2004). These scholars argue against colonial, oppressive, and exclusionary ECE practices. They have been influential in questioning the taken-for-granted globalization of developmental theories that reflect the colonial pattern of the minority world, "helping" the majority world to understand children (see also Nsamenang, 1993, 2007; Pence & Hix-Small, 2007; Viruru, 2001).

The work of Indigenous scholars has also been influential in rethinking the exclusionary and oppressive nature of normative, colonial discourses on Indigenous communities around the world. Linda Tuhiwai Smith's important contribution, *Decolonizing Methodologies: Research and Indigenous Peoples* (1999), has been used to think about the invisibility and silence of Indigenous knowledges, and these ideas have found expression in certain early childhood education and training programs (Ball & Pence, 2006; Pakai, 2007; Pence, Kuehne, Greenwood,

& Opekokew, 1993; Ritchie, 2007). We note that the academic sharing of diverse Indigenous perspectives regarding early childhood care and development is at a very early stage of development in Canada (e.g., see Rodriguez de France, Pence, & Greenwood, 2007).

The Chapters Ahead

Is there evidence of change in Canadian ECE? Do reconceptualist discussions remain outside the Canadian ECE mainstream? Perhaps there is not much change in the mainstream, but there are important movements that cannot be ignored, movements that are making a difference and are bringing disruptions and interruptions to the practice of ECE as usual. This book is a testament to the challenges that are constantly present in the Canadian mainstream landscape.

The contributions that Canadian scholars have made to this book represent the diversity of perspectives and approaches that the reconceptualist movement embraces. The chapters in this volume reassured us that Canadian scholars have much to contribute to current discussions in reconceptualist ECE, but also and especially to Canadian mainstream ECE as early childhood education emerges as a key priority for various provincial jurisdictions. In our view, an expanded early childhood education system cannot be pursued without critically engaged conversations about our common understandings of childhood and learning. The chapters in this volume engage in this conversation.

Katherine Davidson, in "The Integration of Cognitive and Sociocultural Theories of Literacy Development for Instruction and Research: Why? How?" argues for an "and/both" practice. Cognitive and sociocultural theories of literacy development are historically considered incommensurable in practice and in research. Cognitivists view literacy development as a succession of qualitatively varied skills, whereas socioculturalists view literacy as socially and culturally embedded. Traditional educational discourses tend to reflect cognitivist perspectives, which risk creating and maintaining social inequities in our increasingly diverse society. The underpinnings and differences of these two theories are discussed. Davidson argues that integration of the theories is possible and desirable in educational practice and research in order to equalize the learning opportunities for all students.

Sherry Rose and Pam Whitty, in "Valuing Subjective Complexities: Disrupting the Tyranny of Time," provide a critical examination of experimentations and interpretations provoked through communally produced texts. They uncover the ways in which educators both slide into and disrupt cultural orientations toward individualism, deficit, and the tyranny of clock time. For the past five years, they have been working with child-care educators while researching, piloting, and developing curriculum materials and workshops for infants, toddlers, and other children. As they move in and out of university and child-care spaces where "people are not equally located" (Eyre, 2007, p. 99), their work is rife with contradictions and ethical tensions. Out of this complex and contradictory landscape, they hear and ask a recursive question: "Where do we find the time to do this?" Questions such as this one incite experiments and interpretations that enliven and invigorate their pedagogical co-authorings in order to reimagine themselves and their worlds.

In "Addressing Divides and Binaries in Early Childhood Education: Disability, Discourse and Theory, and Practice in a Bachelor of Education Program," Luigi Iannacci and Bente Graham explore teacher candidates' understandings of young children with special needs or a learning disability prior to, during, and after a special education–focused course and a tutoring practicum that they were required to complete as part of their bachelor of education degree. Discourses that informed the students' understandings are examined in order to critically assess theory/practice gaps in a teacher education context as they relate to disability, and to develop future special education curricula that destabilize dominant and problematic discourses about disability.

Rachel Langford, in "An Early Childhood Professional's Authority: How Can It Be Used for Influencing and Instigating Action for Social Goods?," engages with the concept of authority as an uncomfortable subject for early childhood educators. The chapter outlines tensions in recognizing and asserting an early childhood professional's authority and the implications of these tensions for educators themselves and the changes they envisage in their work with young children and, more broadly, in Canada's early childhood system. Drawing on a range of feminist educational philosophers, critical pedagogy, and early childhood theorists, critiques of both traditional and professional authority as well as the rejection of an early educator's authority are examined. A description is offered of an early childhood professional's authority that emerges out of a retheorizing of authority as the means for influencing and instigating action for social goods.

In "When Queer Enters Early Childhood Teacher Training: What's So Inappropriate about That?" Zeenat Janmohamed challenges the heteronormative nature of early childhood teacher training, arguing for a more complex understanding of diversity that includes queer parents and their young children. Through a queer reading and feminist analysis, the chapter uncovers dominant assumptions of universality underlying the heteronormative discourse of developmentally appropriate practice that pervades postsecondary early childhood programs and its implications for practice.

In "Immigrant Parents Taking Part in Their Children's Education: A Practical Experiment," Judith K. Bernhard outlines the development of a series of theoretically based interventions for newcomer (immigrant) parents undertaken over a ten-year period through an iterative method of designing and analyzing a series of ethnographic studies. The work was based on the critical theory of Freire and the post-Marxist and radical theories of Bourdieu and Cummins. Specifically, the interventions were designed to help immigrant groups of parents (of Latino origin) to understand their position of marginality and to provide them with a basis for acting in support of their children's education in the new host country. The findings of the interventions reported show how the research program evolved along with the dialectic refinement of practice and theory.

Kathleen Kummen, Veronica Pacini-Ketchabaw, and Deborah Thompson, in "Making Developmental Knowledge Stutter and Stumble: Continuing Pedagogical Explorations with Collective Biography," draw on data gathered through collective biography in a child development graduate course in a child- and youth-care program, and propose the notion of a developmental worker as mutually constituted in and emerging through an intra-action with the discursive and the material. They base their arguments on the premise that in addition to deconstructing how developmental knowledge as discourse works, it is important to unmask how matter (bodies, materials, physical world) comes to have significance in developmental knowledge, highlighting the complex materiality of the social. The chapter uses the metaphor of making developmental knowledge stutter and stumble as the authors revisit their work in an attempt to make visible how we might not only engage in pedagogical practices that cause us to stutter in the discursive but also to stumble into the material understanding of developmental theory. They borrow from the work of feminist theorists Karen Barad, Rosi Braidotti, and Susan Heckman.

Anna Kirova, in "Children's Representations of Cultural Scripts in Play: Facilitating Transition from Home to Preschool in an Intercultural Early Learning Program for Refugee Children," focuses on the role of play as a cultural activity in refugee children's transition from home to preschool. She reports on a study that challenged the "culture-free" view of play as a means for development of a "universal" child. The study provided an alternative view of play as cultural leading activity in the development of a culturally situated child based on the work of Vygotsky and Leont'ev. These authors provided the theoretical frame for a community-initiated project that aimed to provide learning opportunities in both children's home languages and English. The ultimate goal was for linguistic and cultural continuity as well as the children's smooth transition from home to school cultures. The pilot study demonstrated that the intercultural approach to education could open possibilities for new directions in early childhood practice, in which a hybrid space is open for the children and adults who share it to bring their knowledges and ways of being in the world. In this space, play is a vehicle for preserving cultural group identities while creating a common culture.

Mary Caroline Rowan, in "Resituating Practice through Teachers' Storying of Children's Interests," troubles the impacts of colonialism and the imposition of Euro-Western systems. The chapter is informed by Indigenous methodologies to examine how stories provide a mechanism for transformation. The stories she presents are situated in the Tasiurvik Child Care Centre in Inukjuakin Nunavik, Arctic northern Quebec. The chapter shows how validating Inuttitut language usage, revealing Inuit knowledges, making visible relationships, and prompting educators to reflect on the cultural nature of the educational endeavour can open up the possibility of resisting institutionalized normalization.

Drawing from international research, Beth Blue Swadener, Lacey Peters, and Sonya Gaches examine early childhood scholarship, policy, and practice that is framed in children's rights and foregrounds children's participation. In their chapter, "Taking Children's Rights and Participation Seriously: Cross-national Perspectives and Possibilities," the authors do not view rights discourse as primarily a Western, neoliberal, or individualistic framework, but as a means of resituating early childhood research, policy, and practice; seeking collective and culturally framed praxes; sharing power with children; and giving children's views due weight.

References

Annual Convention of the N.E.A. Department of Kindergarten Education. (1896). *Kindergarten Magazine, 11*(1), 9–21.

Arce, A. (2006). The importance of play in pre-school education: Naturalisation versus a Marxist analysis. In P. Sawchuk, N. Duarte, & M. Elhammoumi (Eds.), *Critical perspectives on activity: Explorations across education, work, and everyday life* (pp. 75–88). Cambridge, England: Cambridge University Press. Retrieved from http://lib.myilibrary.com.login.ezproxy.library.ualberta.ca?ID=95575

Ayers, W. (1989). *The good preschool teacher: Six teachers reflect on their lives*. New York, NY: Teachers College Press.

Ball, J., & Pence, A. (2006). *Supporting Indigenous children's development: Community university partnerships*. Vancouver: University of British Columbia Press.

Bentley, D.F. (2011). "I smile with my mind": Reconceptualizing artistic practice in early childhood. *Journal of Research in Childhood Education, 25*(2), 160–176.

Bloch, M. (2005). Making progress? Conceptualizing and reconceptualizing approaches to ECE and child care in the twenty-first century. In J.L. Roopnarine & J.E. Johnson (Eds.), *Approaches to early childhood education* (4th ed., pp. 423–435). Upper Saddle River, NJ: Prentice Hall.

Bredekamp, S. (Ed.). (1986). *Developmentally appropriate practice*. Washington, DC: National Association for the Education of Young Children.

Bredekamp, S. (1991). Redeveloping early childhood education: A response to Kessler. *Early Childhood Research Quarterly, 6*(2), 199–209.

Burman, E. (2008). *Deconstructing developmental psychology* (2nd ed.). London, England: Routledge.

Cannella, G. S. (1997). *Deconstructing early childhood education: Social justice and revolution*. New York, NY: Peter Lang.

Cannella, G.S. (2010). Early childhood curriculum. In C. Kridel (Ed.), *Encyclopedia of curriculum studies* (Vol. 10, pp. 306–308). Thousand Oaks, CA: Sage.

Cannella, G. S., Swadener, B.B., & Che. Y. (2007). Reconceptualists. In R.S. New & M. Cochran (Eds.), *Early childhood education: An international encyclopedia* (pp. 693–696). Westport, CT: Praeger.

Cannella, G. S., & Viruru, R. (2004). *Childhood and postcolonization: Power, education, and contemporary practice.* London, England: RoutledgeFalmer.

Cleghorn, A., & Prochner, L. (2010). *Shades of globalization in three early childhood settings: Views from India, South Africa and Canada.* Rotterdam, the Netherlands: Sense.

Dahlberg, G., & Moss, P. (2005). *Ethics and politics in early childhood education.* New York, NY: RoutledgeFalmer.

Dahlberg, G., Moss, P., & Pence, A. (1999). *Beyond quality in early childhood education and care: Postmodern perspectives.* London, England: Falmer Press.

Dahlberg, G., Moss, P., & Pence, A. (2007). *Beyond quality in early childhood education and care: Languages of evaluation* (2nd ed.). New York, NY: Routledge.

Duncan, J., Bowden, C., & Smith, A.B. (2006). A gossip or a good yack? Reconceptualizing parent support in New Zealand early childhood centre–based programmes. *International Journal of Early Years Education, 14*(1), 1–13.

Eisele, C. (1984). The Dewey School: A record of success and a reality of failure. *Journal of the Midwest History of Education Society, 12,* 29–39.

Eyre, L. (2007). Whose ethics? Whose interests? The Tri-Council Policy and feminist research. *Journal of Curriculum Theorizing, 23*(2), 91-102.

Flanagan, K. (2010). *The early years report. Early learning in PEI: An investment in the island's future.* Prepared for the Department of Education and Early Childhood Development, Department of Community Services, Seniors, and Labour, Department of Health and Wellness, Executive Council Office, Government of Prince Edward Island. Charlottetown, PE.

Freeman, E.B., & Hatch, J.A. (1989). Emergent literacy: Reconceptualizing kindergarten practice. *Childhood Education, 66*(1), 21–24.

Fulmer, G. (1918). *The use of kindergarten gifts.* Boston, MA: Houghton Mifflin.

Goodson, I. (1998). *School subjects and curriculum change: Studies in curriculum history* (3rd ed.). Bristol, PA: Falmer Press.

Grieshaber, S., & Cannella, G. S. (2001). *Embracing identities in early childhood education: Diversity and possibilities.* New York, NY: Teachers College Press.

Hultqvist, K., & Dahlberg, G. (Eds.). (2001). *Governing the child in the new millennium.* New York, NY: RoutledgeFalmer.

Kessler, S.A., & Swadener, B. B. (Eds.). (1992). *Reconceptualizing the early childhood curriculum: Beginning the dialogue.* New York, NY: Teachers College Press.

Lenz Taguchi, H. (2009). *Going beyond the theory/practice divide in early childhood education: Introducing an intra-active pedagogy.* New York, NY: Routledge.

Lubeck, S. (1985). *Sandbox society: Early education in black and white America.* Philadelphia, PA: Falmer Press.

Mac Naughton, G. (2005). *Doing Foucault in early childhood studies: Applying poststructural ideas.* London, England: Routledge.

Morrison, G. (2011). *Fundamentals of early childhood education.* Upper Saddle River, NJ: Pearson Education.

Moss, P., & Petrie, P. (2002). *From children's services to children's spaces: Public policy, children and childhood.* London, England: RoutledgeFalmer.

McCain, M., & Mustard, J.F. (1999). *Early years study: Final report.* Toronto, ON: Canadian Institute for Advanced Research.

McCain, M., & Mustard, J.F. (2007). *Early years study 2: Putting science into action.* Toronto, ON: Council for Early Childhood Development.

Mustard, J.F., & McCain, M. (2002). *The early years study three years later: From early childhood development to human development—enabling communities.* Toronto, ON: Canadian Institute for Advanced Research.

National Association of Head Teachers (NAHT). (2011, March 11). School leaders' manifesto calls for early years' investment in Northern Ireland. *NAHT Northern Ireland News.* Retrieved from http://www.naht.org.uk/welcome/about-you/your-location/northern-ireland/northernireland1/naht-northern-ireland-news/manifesto-for-northern-ireland/

New, R. (2000, December). *Reggio Emilia: Catalyst for change and conversation*. Champaign, IL: ERIC Clearinghouse on Elementary and Early Childhood Education. (ERIC Document Reproduction Service No. ED447971)

New, R., & Cochran, M. (2007). Preface. In R.S. New & M. Cochran (Eds.), *Early childhood education: An international encyclopedia* (pp. xviii–xxii). Westport, CT: Praeger.

New, R., & Kantor, R. (2009). Reggio Emilia's approach to early care and education: Creating contexts for discussions. In J.L. Roopnarine & J.E. Johnson (Eds.), *Approaches to early childhood education* (5th ed., pp. 287–311). Upper Saddle River, NJ: Merrill/Pearson.

Nsamenang, B. (1993). *Human development in cultural context*. Newbury Park, CA: Sage.

Nsamenang, B. (2007). (Mis)understanding ECD in Africa: The force of local and global motives. In M. Garcia, A. Pence, & J. Evans (Eds.), *Africa's future—Africa's challenge: Early childhood care and development in sub-Saharan Africa*. Washington, DC: World Bank.

Olsson, L. (2009). *Movement and experimentation in young children's learning: Deleuze and Guattari in early childhood education*. New York, NY: Routledge.

Onions, C.T. (Ed.). (1973). *The shorter Oxford English dictionary on historical principles* (Vol. 1). Oxford, England: Oxford University Press.

Ontario Ministry of Education. (2011). Full day kindergarten: What we have heard. Retrieved from http://www.edu.gov.on.ca/kindergarten/what.html

Organisation for Economic Co-operation and Development (OECD). (2006). *OECD economic surveys: Canada 2006*. Paris, France: Author.

Pacini-Ketchabaw, V., & Pence, A. (2005). The reconceptualizing movement in Canadian early childhood education, care and development. In V. Pacini-Ketchabaw & A. Pence (Eds.), *Canadian early childhood education: Broadening and deepening discussions of quality* (pp.5-20). Ottawa, ON: Canadian Child Care Federation.

Pakai, E. (2007).Initial teacher education in Aotearoa/New Zealand. *Canadian Journal of Native Education, 30*(1), 158–175.

Pence, A., & Hix-Small, H. (2007).Global children in the shadow of the global child. *International Journal of Educational Policy, Research, and Practice, 8*(1), 83–100.

Pence, A., Kuehne, V., Greenwood, M., & Opekokew, M.R. (1993). Generative curriculum: A model of university and First Nations cooperative post-secondary education. *International Journal of Educational Development,13*(4), 339–349.

Pence, A.R. (1998).Reconceptualizing ECCD in the majority world: One minority world perspective. *International Journal of Early Childhood, 30*(2), 19–30.

Pinar, W. (1975). Preface. In W. Pinar (Ed.), *Curriculum theorizing: The reconceptualists*. Berkeley, CA: McCutchan.

Pinar, W. (1999). Introduction: A farewell and a celebration. In W. Pinar (Ed.), *Contemporary curriculum discourses: Twenty years of JCT* (pp. xi–xx). New York, NY: Peter Lang.

Ritchie, J. (Ed.). (2007). Seeking pathways beyond colonization [Special issue]. *Childrenz Issues, 11*(1).

Robinson, G., Silburn, S.R., & Arney, F. (2011). *The value of investment in the early years: Balancing costs of childhood services*. Topical paper commissioned for the public consultations on the Northern Territory Early Childhood Plan. Darwin, Australia: Northern Territory Government.

Rodriguez de France, C., Pence, A., & Greenwood, M. (Eds.). (2007). Indigenous approaches to early childhood care and education [Special issue]. *Canadian Journal of Native Education, 30*(1).

Rogers, D.G. (2005). *America's first women philosophers: Transplanting Hegel, 1860–1925*. London, England: Continuum.

Scates, G. (1900). The sub-primary (kindergarten) department. *The Elementary School Record, 1*(5), 129–142.

Scottish Government. (2008). *The early years framework*. Edinburgh, Scotland: Author.

Scottish Parliament Committee. (2010, November 2). Finance Committee 1. BBC Democracy Live. Retrieved from http://news.bbc.co.uk/democracylive/hi/scotland/newsid_9145000/9145294.stm

Soto, L.D., & Swadener, B.B. (2002). Toward liberatory early childhood theory, research and praxis: Decolonizing a field. *Contemporary Issues in Early Childhood, 3*(1), 38–66.

Souto-Manning, M. (2006). Families learn together: Reconceptualizing linguistic diversity as a resource. *Early Childhood Education Journal, 33*(6), 443–446.

Start Strong. (2010). *Planning now, for the future: Children's early care and education in Ireland*. Dublin, Ireland: Author. Retrieved from http://www.startstrong.ie/files/Children_2020_Planning_Now_for_the_Future.pdf

Swadener, B.B., & Cannella, G. S. (2007, Winter). Reconceptualizing early childhood education in North America. *Interaction*, 25–26. Retrieved from http://www.cyc.uvic.ca/uccr/documents/07.Swadener_Cannella_Reconceptualizing_Interaction.pdf

Umrikhin, V. (1997). Russian and world psychology: A common origin of divergent paths. In E.L. Grigorenko, P. Ruzgis, & R.J. Sternberg (Eds.), *Psychology of Russia: Past, present, future* (pp. 17–38). Commack, NY: Nova Science.

Viruru, R. (2001). *Decolonizing early childhood education: An Indian perspective*. New Delhi, India: Sage.

Viruru, R. (2005). The impact of postcolonial theory on early childhood education. *Journal of Education* [South Africa], *35,* 7–30.

Walsh, D. (1989). Changes in kindergarten: Why here? Why now? *Early Childhood Research Quarterly,4*(3), 377–391.

Weber, E. (1969). *The kindergarten: Its encounter with educational thought in America*. New York, NY: Teachers College Press.

Weber, E. (1984). *Ideas influencing early childhood education: A theoretical analysis*. New York, NY: Teachers College Press.

Weikart, D. (1972). Relationship of curriculum, teaching, and learning in preschool education. In J.C. Stanley (Ed.), *Preschool programs for the disadvantaged: Five experimental approaches to early childhood education* (pp. 22–66). Baltimore, MD: Johns Hopkins University Press.

Wood, E. (2007). Reconceptualizing child-centred education: Contemporary directions in policy, theory and practice in early childhood. *Forum: For Promoting 3–19 Comprehensive Education, 49*(1), 119–134.

Chapter Two

The Integration of Cognitive and Sociocultural Theories of Literacy Development for Instruction and Research

Why? How?

Katherine Davidson

Literacy is inarguably vital for the social and economic welfare of individuals and society (Canadian Language and Literacy Research Network [CLLRNet], 2009b; Purcell-Gates & Tierney, 2009; Snow, Burns, & Griffin, 1998). This reality is particularly relevant today in a progressively more globalized world, where political, economic, and social exchanges challenge individuals and nations to be ever more competitive. In response, governments and agencies have increasingly promoted policies and practices to advance students' literacy skills. For example, we have witnessed the No Child Left Behind Act (2002) and the Reading First initiative in the United States, which were based on the National Reading Panel's report *Teaching Children to Read* (2000), the Ontario Ministry of Education's (2003) *Early Reading Strategy: The Report of the Expert Panel on Early Reading in Ontario*, and more recently, the *National Strategy for Early Literacy* (CLLRNet, 2009b) to address an apparent literacy crisis in North America. Underpinning these reports and initiatives is a predominantly cognitive, scientifically based view of literacy development that Cummins et al. (2005) claimed disregards "affect, identity, respect, and human relationships" (p. 39). Lacking in these recent initiatives is an explicit attempt to address the needs of an increasingly pluralistic population. Such a narrow, cognitive perspective of literacy development risks perpetuating inequalities that stem from social and cultural diversity, which characterizes this population. In Ontario, for example, diversity is defined as

> the presence of a wide range of human qualities and attributes within a group, organization, or society. The dimensions of diversity include, but are not limited to, ancestry, culture, ethnicity, gender, gender identity, language, physical and

intellectual ability, race, religion, sex, sexual orientation, and socio-economic status. (Ontario Ministry of Education, 2009, p. 4)

The 2006 census revealed that residents of Ontario reported more than 200 languages as their first language; the Aboriginal population grew five times faster than did the non-Aboriginal population; 2.7 million Ontarians represented visible minorities; and the visible minority (excluding the Aboriginal population) increased more than four times the rate of the population in total (Ontario Ministry of Education, 2009, p. 4). In Canada as a whole, more than 200 ethnicities were reported in 2006 and 1.1 million new residents arrived between 2001 and 2006 (Ontario Ministry of Education, 2009). Visible minorities made up 75% of the newcomers and in 2006 these minorities amounted to more than 5 million Canadians (Statistics Canada, 2006). Equity and inclusivity in education for students with diverse backgrounds therefore need to be priorities.

A sociocultural view of literacy proposes that the influences of familial and cultural communities on students' literacy development must be considered in order to provide such equality in educational access and opportunity for all students (Gee, 2001; Purcell-Gates & Tierney, 2009), and particularly for students with diverse backgrounds (Au, 2000). This chapter addresses the question, How should cognitive and sociocultural perspectives of literacy development be integrated to meet present education needs?

Some researchers have contended that cognitive and sociocultural perspectives are diametrically opposed. For example, Holzman (1995) reported that a "traditional" view of development that consists of stages and an unfolding of internal capabilities is considered to be "hierarchical, elitist, and ideological" and therefore inappropriate (p. 200). Instead, development should be seen as a transformation of individuals as they participate in activity; it should not be assumed that individuals simply acquire predetermined skills by responding to their environments (Holzman, 1995). Wilkinson, Freebody, and Elkins (2000) also rejected the concept of reading as only a curricular subject composed of specific stages and skills. They promoted the broader view that literacy development is affected by sociocultural influences that emanate from outside as well as inside of school. Luke (2005) succinctly stated that "literacy is a malleable repertoire of practices, not an unchanging or universal set of skills" (p. xi). While cognitivists may propose that literacy development follows a fluid trajectory of skill acquisition, sociocultural theorists contend that literacy practices are multiple and varied, as well as socially and culturally dependent.

However, Gee (2001) and Purcell-Gates, Jacobsen, and Degener (2004) rejected the notion that the sociocultural and cognitive views are autonomous and incommensurable. Rather, they proposed that the cognitive occurs within a sociocultural context and that both are necessary for educational success. In this chapter, I examine the core premises of cognitive and sociocultural theories of literacy development and attempt to demonstrate that neither theory alone is adequate, but that an integration of the two theories into a unitary framework for literacy instruction and research has the potential to equalize access to quality education for all students.

The definition of literacy varies considerably throughout the literature, encompassing viewing, listening, speaking, reading, writing, and representing (Language and Literacy Researchers of Canada, 2009). The New Literacy Studies, for example, refer to multimodal literacies and multiliteracies, which include diverse languages and modes of texts and technologies; these practices refer to "an approach to literacy and language learning that looks at how literacy is used in everyday life—from literacy events like guided reading at school, to reading a newspaper in a café" (Pahl & Rowsell, 2005, p. 156). Debates about the meanings of literacy are frequent (Street, 1999), and the meanings vary depending on the particular theory to which one ascribes. In this chapter, literacy refers to reading and writing the printed form of language: to construct meaning from written text and to encode written text in writing (CLLRNet, 2009a).

Cognitive Theory of Literacy Development

Underlying the cognitive perspective of print literacy development is the dogma that the acquisition of reading and writing skills follows specific developmental milestones generalized to apply to everyone; in other words, there is a "universalized theory of development" (John-Steiner & Mahn, 1996, p. 197). According to Purcell-Gates et al. (2004), it is believed that cognitive researchers are interested in normative behaviour (e.g., the learning-to-read process), and their emphases are on operations that take place in the head. Cognitivists believe that literacy is transmitted; it is largely taught and learned. For alphabetic languages, print is a code that represents phoneme/grapheme correspondence; therefore, learning to read and write begins with learning the code. In addition, cognitive theorists believe that stages of reading or writing development are necessary to guide teaching; the stages illuminate the competency that is optimal for specific purposes, and they identify and explain the inadequacies exhibited by certain groups (Chall, 1983; Ehri, 2005). Street (1984) referred to the cognitive perspective as "autonomous" (p. 2) because it implies that literacy consists of technical skills that are learned independently from social or cultural influences, and that literacy learning is neutral and apolitical. Although the stage theory of reading development was foreshadowed by Quantz as early as 1897 (Venezky, 1984), Chall is credited with strengthening its momentum and it is therefore presented here as an example of a cognitive theory of literacy development. In the review that follows, I also discuss a more current cognitive model of reading development that was developed by the Southwest Educational Development Laboratory (now SEDL), published by Sebastian Wren (2001), and adopted by CLLRNet (2009a). In addition, phonological processing, which has been identified as a core component of reading acquisition, exemplifies yet another cognitive perspective of literacy development. Last, an example of proposed stages of writing development is presented.

Chall (1983) explained that all individuals, including those with special needs, progress through stages of reading acquisition in characteristic ways, within certain age limits, and following the same sequence. Chall proposed the following six stages of reading: (1) Stage 0: Pre-reading (birth to age 6); (2) Stage 1: Initial Reading or Decoding (ages 6–7); (3) Stage 2: Confirmation, Fluency, Ungluing from Print (ages 7–8); (4) Stage 3: Reading for Learning the New (ages 8–14); (5) Stage 4: Multiple Viewpoints (ages 14–18); and (6) Stage 5: Construction and Deconstruction (age 18 and above). Progression through the stages is characterized by the recognition and decoding of words, by relating the spoken word to the printed word, by learning the rules about relating letters to sounds, by learning the meanings of uncommon words (abstract words, ideas, concepts), and by acquiring world knowledge that is necessary for comprehending what is read. Chall's stages may be used to identify what an individual has learned and what is yet to be taught; she also recommended norm-referenced tests to diagnose a reading problem.

More recently, Wren (2001) proposed a framework of reading development, depicted in the Appendix. The figure portrays comprehension of the written word as the ultimate objective of reading. This comprehension is dependent upon two foundational competencies: language comprehension and decoding. Furthermore, each competency is based upon underlying abilities. More explicitly, language comprehension, which is the ability to glean meaning from spoken language, requires background knowledge combined with linguistic knowledge (the ability to compose and comprehend proper sentences), which is composed of understanding the sounds of knowledge (phonology), grammar (syntax), and vocabulary or word meaning (semantics) (CLLRNet, 2009a). The second competency, decoding, refers to the ability to recognize and process written information (Wren, 2001). Decoding further relies on knowledge of printed words (lexical knowledge) and comprehension of the rules for spelling and writing (cipher knowledge). The base for lexical and cipher knowledge is composed of concepts about print (knowing the form and purpose of written text), phoneme awareness (hearing and manipulating the sounds in language), and knowledge of letters and their sounds (CLLRNet, 2009a). Wren proposed that language comprehension and decoding skills are requisite for successful reading comprehension, and the "A" structure of the framework implies that the two develop concurrently as the underlying abilities grow. However, Wren (2001) also stressed that the framework does not suggest a particular order of instruction; rather, he stated that the "cognitive elements . . . tend to develop congruently," that they "serve to reinforce each other," and that the development is "unpredictable" and "varies from child to child" (p. 43). Educators need to be aware of each child's literacy development. The SEDL website (http //www.sedl.org/) provides tools and resources and CLLRNet (2009a) has published a guide to assist teachers in implementing this framework of reading development.

With respect to phonology and literacy, Gillon (2004) reported that a "vast body of research employing differing methodologies and conducted in a variety of alphabetic languages has convincingly demonstrated that a powerful relationship exists between phonological awareness and literacy development" (p. 1). This finding has been substantiated by a number of cognitive theorists and researchers (Ehri et al., 2001; Goswami, 2003; Shaywitz, 2005; Snow, Burns, & Griffin, 1998). As a predictor of early reading success, phonological awareness acquisition also consists of a hierarchy of sub-skills that progress from word level to syllable, to onset and rime, and to phoneme level. At the word level, individuals are able to discriminate between words in a sentence. Progressing from word discrimination is the ability to understand that words can be divided into smaller parts such as syllables, onset and rime, and phonemes. Some theorists contend that all the sub-skills should be taught in order for reading to develop (Gillon, 2004), while others claim that phoneme awareness is the most significant factor for reading success (McGuinness, 1997; Shaywitz, 2005). Clearly, distinct cognitive skills make up these reading acquisition theories.

With respect to writing development, Bear, Invernizzi, Templeton, and Johnston (1996), as cited by Purcell-Gates et al. (2004), proposed that writing skills progress according to the following stages: (1) emergent (ages 1–7): drawing, scribbling, pretend writing, printing letter-like to actual letters, no sound-symbol correspondence; (2) beginning (ages 5–9): initial writing is laborious but it improves to the point of accomplishing half a page of written work, the content of which is often a summary or retelling; (3) transitional (ages 6–12): more fluency, planning, organization, and details characterize this stage; and (4) intermediate and specialized writing (ages 10–100): fluent writing with expression and voice; varied styles and genre are seen. Accompanying these writing stages are levels of spelling skills: (1) preliterate (emergent): draw a picture or scribble and later write unrelated letters; (2) early letter name (early beginning): write predominant sounds in words and then initial and final consonants; (3) middle and late letter name (later beginning): use of initial and final consonants with a vowel in most syllables, progressing to short vowel patterns, consonant blends and digraphs, some long vowel words; (4) within-word pattern (transitional): spell short vowel words, most one-syllable long-vowel words, *r*-controlled words, and use of some Latin suffixes; and (5) syllable juncture and derivational constancy (intermediate): learn how syllables fit together, double consonants, drop the *e* to add an ending, know suffixes and prefixes. While theorists of writing once depicted writers as autonomous individuals who mainly contended with and documented their thoughts (Nystrand, 2006), interest in evaluating and researching writing prompted the identification of specific skills to target and measure. Furthermore, the influence of cognitivist views is also manifested by researchers who are concerned with cognitive factors that underpin the development of these writing stages and skills. For example, Bourke and Adams (2010) confirmed that working memory, vocabulary knowledge, nonverbal cognitive ability, and reading skill influence individuals' development in writing. Further, they supported instruction that fosters an understanding of phonology and its relationship to communication and literacy as a foundation for effective writing as it is for reading. Molfese et al. (2011) determined that writing achievement was related to letter/word identification skills, while Hooper, Roberts, Nelson, Zeisel, and Fannin (2010) discovered that core language abilities and prereading skills predicted students' levels of writing in grades 3 to 5. In addition, Fitzgerald and Shannahan (2000) proposed that reading development and writing development share several common cognitive processes (e.g., understanding functions of reading and writing, concepts about print, phonological awareness, graphemes, word making, morphology, vocabulary, syntax) that should be assessed and taught for optimal growth in literacy.

The preceding cognitive views of literacy development demonstrate the common features that are valued and continue to be emphasized by influential institutions and current policies. If theories in practice reflect the lenses through which individuals see the world (Tracey & Morrow, 2006), the cognitive lens implies that individuals who stray from the prescribed stages are deficient in their literacy skills. From a critical literacy theoretical position (Tracey & Morrow, 2006), one must question whether adherence to this view disadvantages students who stem from non-mainstream backgrounds, whose first language is not English or not even phonetic, and whose out-of-school literacy practices differ from the skills represented by these stages of development. If this is the case, school literacy practices risk discriminating against students from diverse backgrounds, potentially incorrectly identifying them as unable or disabled learners, and impeding their success in literacy learning. An alternate school of thought posits that the cognitive perspective of literacy is indeed too limited in its understanding of how individuals learn to read and write; rather, the roles that social and cultural environments play in literacy development must also be considered. This brings us to consider the value of sociocultural theory.

Sociocultural Theory of Literacy Development

The theory that learning and development are socially and culturally situated versus a "unidimensional construct" (Purcell-Gates, 2007, p. 3) is credited largely to the Russian psychologist Lev Vygotsky. In the 1920s and 1930s, Vygotsky proposed that all human activities take place in cultural contexts, are mediated by language and other symbols, and can be best understood in the context of their historical development (John-Steiner & Mahn, 1996). According to Vygotsky, development is the transformation of socially shared activities into internalized processes (John-Steiner & Mahn, 1996). Development begins with interactions among people, and it results in socialization as well as in higher mental functions. The family, community, and society into which a child is born create the higher mental processes in the child (McNamee, 1995). A main Vygotskian tenet is that "more knowledgeable members of a group engage in social mediation to bring others into the cultural practices" (Pérez, 1998, p. 4).

From the sociocultural perspective, therefore, children's literacy development is understood by exploring the cultural, social, and historical contexts within which the children have grown. One is obliged to consider how the thinking of a particular group of individuals has directed the children's thinking, how the children understand who they are in relation to others, and how they interpret their world (McNamee, 1995; Pérez, 1998). Pérez (1998) also credited Jerome Bruner with the insight that individuals bring their cultural experiences with the world and text, and their knowledge and skills with letters, words, and text, to their interpretation of written language. As explained by Tracey and Morrow (2006), "knowledge is constructed based on social interactions and experience" (p. 103). Huerta (2011) referred to it as a "humanizing pedagogy" (p. 39) in which teachers are aware of and acknowledge the sociohistorical and political contexts of their own lives and the lives of their students, while Cummins et al. (2005) labeled it a "pedagogy of respect" (p. 42).

Sociocultural theorists therefore make up the "social practice camp [that] sees literacy as primarily social and cultural" (Purcell-Gates et al., 2004, p. 26); learning to read cannot be separated from the setting in which it occurs (Tracey & Morrow, 2006). As cited by Purcell-Gates et al. (2004), Brian Street referred to this model of literacy as "ideological" (p. 64), pointing out that literacy relates to power structures in society. The dominant culture has traditionally imposed its language and concept of adequate skill on minority groups who may not share the dominant experiences and values, thereby maintaining the existing power dynamics. The cognitivists' premise that literacy consists of decontextualized, discrete linguistic skills (sounds of letters, knowledge of words, etc.) is rejected, as is the concept that reading and writing skills are transmitted from one individual to another (Pérez, 1998). Pérez (1998) clarified that from the sociocultural standpoint, being literate means being able to read and write in a culturally appropriate way, that the skills are not only in the individual's head, but that literacy is also an interactive process that is modified according to the sociocultural environment. In addition, "skills, strategies, and understandings are appropriated, not transmitted" (Maloch, 2004, p. 2). Purcell-Gates et al. (2004) corroborated that "literacy practice" replaces "literacy skill" (p. 26) and that literacy development occurs inside and outside of schools and across the life span.

Consider the example given by Purcell-Gates et al. (2004), wherein paying a bill is a literacy event that comprises a number of literacy practices. Paying a bill entails interpersonal interactions, which are social because to do so usually involves reading what someone has written on the bill, writing a cheque or addressing an envelope to pay the bill, and possibly speaking to a teller. There is social discourse of some form between individuals. The domain of life in which the event occurs could be personal or work related: in a bank, office, or store. The practice is governed by social conventions, law, and/or personal morals and responsibility. For example, it might be criminal not to pay; one might be penalized by others in power; one's accessibility to the service might be cancelled; and one might feel guilt or others might be inconvenienced if the bill is not paid. The event conceivably reflects an action that one has historically performed or that has been influenced by past occurrences. However, the practices within this act could change if technology such as telephone-banking or computer use were to be employed. Despite the obvious application of reading and writing skills, the social and cultural implications of paying a bill are multiple. The values, beliefs, and practices that one's community possesses with respect to a particular literacy event such as this one affect how one engages in the event.

The concept of situated literacy practices brought to mind my own childhood church literacy experiences, which differed from the school literacy I encountered. In contrast to completing phonics worksheets and reading basal readers, I learned to read German hymns in Gothic print through repeated exposure and song—literally, choral reading. The sociocultural context of the German church provided an interactive learning experience in which the skills, strategies, and understandings needed to read German and Gothic print were indeed appropriated rather than explicitly taught. An appreciation for and a valuation of hymnbooks as literary works and of the German language were fostered. The church experience may be considered one "cultural model" (Gee, 2001, p. 720) that reflected the perspective that reading and singing in German and learning to do so by way of active interaction were normal activities. This is yet another example of a socially situated literacy experience; however, it was detached from and foreign to the culture of the school that I attended.

Gee's (2001) example of a child's home-based literacy experience also exemplified how the family is a cultural model with respect to instilling certain perspectives regarding literacy. In Gee's anecdote, a pre-reader was engaged in an activity book in which he used a "magic pen" to rub an area of a picture to uncover a missing piece of the picture. Under the picture was the question, "In what are Donald and Daisy riding?" The child's father asked the child to "read" the question. The child's response was, "What are Donald and Daisy riding in?" The missing piece was indeed a car; therefore the child's response was appropriate for the picture. However, it was inaccurate with respect to the actual text. The father, cognizant of the child's inability to yet decode print and the child's wavering self-image as a reader, accepted the child's response. This interaction communicated to the child that reading was valued and that he was capable of reading. In this case, the home and school perspectives of literacy may be considered to be compatible regarding the significance of reading and the use of meaning, but possibly incompatible regarding the lack of accurate decoding.

The preceding scenarios demonstrate how literacy practices vary and occur outside of school and across ages. Street (1984) concurred that literacy is always embedded in some social form, and it is always learned in relation to uses within specific social conditions. We have recognized that home environments play a large role in the literacy learning of children (Snow et al., 1998). However, the sociocultural standpoint presses educators to understand, respect, and utilize the literacy knowledge that students bring to the classroom from outside of school, and to recognize the sociocultural conditions within the classroom that affect students' literacy learning as well.

A Comparison of Cognitive and Sociocultural Views of Literacy Development

The contrasting perspectives of the cognitive and sociocultural theories are clearly evident. Cognitive theorists promote a developmental approach to literacy learning with distinct skills and milestones; cultural differences in learning are largely disregarded. As a result, the cultural practices of the dominant group in society are considered to be the norm and the culturally diverse are often judged to be deficient (Gutiérrez & Rogoff, 2003). School literacy tends to reflect the values of the dominant and powerful socioeconomic group.

Sociocultural theorists, conversely, strive to make literacy equitable for all social groups by recognizing various forms of literacy (Purcell-Gates et al., 2004). The sociocultural approach attempts to accept, understand, and employ the practices of culturally diverse groups to foster literacy learning. The sociocultural belief is that cognitive reasoning works in conjunction with beliefs, values, and habits of mind that form an individual's identity and that need to be considered when interventions are designed for maximum learning (Lee, Spencer, & Harpalani, 2003). Cognitivists treat literacy as if it is autonomous, a technical skill that is context free, neutral, and decontextualized. However, socioculturalists contend that all literacy is ideological, context dependent, and value ridden (Street, 1984).

Despite these apparent diverse views regarding literacy development, the differences between cognitive and sociocultural theories are not necessarily irreconcilable. Each one alone is conceivably too narrow; therefore, the potential for the two theories to complement each other should be considered.

Why Integrate Cognitive and Sociocultural Theories?

While the theories on their own may be insufficient for guiding literacy instruction and research, each theory plays a valuable role in providing accessible and equitable literacy instruction for all students. Cognitive theories provide guidelines and benchmarks for assessment and instruction in literacy skills. These guidelines assist teachers to plan and judge the success of their tutelage, and they may serve as goals and measures of achievement for students. However, when the language and culture of the school and students clash, these guidelines may very well be invalid for teachers and damaging to students. The sociocultural perspective acknowledges, respects, and incorporates students' languages and cultures; yet alone it lacks guidelines and academic objectives for teaching and learning. In addition, theorists with seemingly opposing views actually concede that each perspective has virtues.

Cognitive theories have dominated for a number of reasons. These theories guide instructional activities in classrooms (Tracey & Morrow, 2006), and literacy experts have concluded that direct skills teaching is necessary for successful literacy acquisition (CLLRNet, 2009a; National Reading Panel, 2000; Snow et al., 1998; Wren, 2001). Chall (1983) suggested that the stage theory of literacy development "might help to prevent some of the persistent controversies that occur in the field of reading research and practice" (p. 30). The stages provide a framework by which to gauge individuals' development and assess instructional methods. Chall, who was also concerned about the poorer reading performances of children from bilingual, minority, and low-socioeconomic-level families, contended that the stage theory helps to identify their difficulties in order to guide teaching for the students' improvement. Moreover, Street (1984) also included abilities such as directionality (reading and writing from left to right and top to bottom), letter-sound correspondence, word recognition, spelling, and handwriting among the recommended functional literacy skills necessary for "ordinary everyday tasks" (p. 229). In addition, Pérez (1998) recognized that "literate students will understand that a written language is a code, and that there are particular rules for decoding and encoding and making meaning, . . . that there are conventions to help the reader make the written text sound as much like oral speech as possible when read aloud (e.g., periods, commas, quotation marks, boldface) (pp. 60, 61). Purcell-Gates (2007) also admitted that "an obvious link between learning to read in school and using literacy in one's life is that of skill acquisition," which requires some form of "focused instruction" (p. 203). Last, Purcell-Gates and Tierney (2009) agreed that children must be systematically taught the skills of reading and writing. Guidance from cognitive perspectives is undeniably needed for promoting print literacy.

However, the issue of equity in literacy instruction has long been ignored in the traditional educational process (Au, 2000), and in reality is jeopardized by the latest scientifically based education reforms in the United States (Cummins et al., 2005). These reforms incorrectly assumed that students' home language is irrelevant and even an impediment to literacy development; English language learners' cultural knowledge and linguistic abilities have minimal relevance; instruction should focus on developing English literacy; students learn only what teachers teach; and culturally and linguistically diverse parents cannot contribute to their children's literacy development (Cummins et al., 2005). The roles of ethnicity, social class, and language in the gap in literacy achievement between students from diverse backgrounds and mainstream backgrounds have been "underrated" (Au, 2000, p. 837). Au's point is key to this discussion. The cultural factors of diverse backgrounds have persistently been related to underachievement. Traditional instructional approaches have underserved students who have already been disadvantaged with respect to social and economic capital. These approaches typically represent the values and customs of the dominant in society, concurrently disadvantaging some groups (Finnegan, 1999). For mainstream children whose culture and language are reflected and extended in the classroom, academic performance is facilitated; however, if the sociocultural experiences of all children are not considered, the academic performance of children whose home culture and/or language differ from that of the classroom is compromised (Huerta, 2011). Furthermore, students who do not speak standard American English might perceive that their own way of speaking is inferior; they may feel alienated from teachers, and as a result they surmise that they do not belong in school (McCafferty, 2002). The students' identities are socially situated; therefore, in a school setting, if their self-perceptions are of being unaccepted then their confidence and motivation to participate will be jeopardized. In addition, pressure for students to abandon a first language may also create ambivalence toward English and lessen their chances for success (Pérez, 1998). One might argue that traditionally schools have been agents in fostering and maintaining the status quo regarding power and privilege by privileging the beneficiaries of the already dominant culture and language.

Fortunately, from a sociocultural view, educators have begun to reflect critically on the values, expectations, and social pressures that are expressed in traditional school settings. There is increased concern about the universal process of teaching reading and writing. Rogers (2000) challenged educators to critique present literacy practices in order to create new teaching and learning situations that support equality, social change, and justice. Sociocultural theory suggests that educators seek to understand the cultural and social contexts in which children have grown and developed (Pérez, 1998). Concern for diverse languages and backgrounds is brought to the fore when teaching practice embraces this theory. As expressed by Cummins et al. (2005), in order to teach the whole child, we cannot demand that students leave their languages and cultures at the school door. In fact, an optimal condition for effective learning occurs when students' prior understanding and background knowledge are engaged, even from the cognitive perspective (Ontario Ministry of Education, 2005). Since preexisting knowledge is "encoded" in students' home languages (Cummins et al., 2005, p. 38), educators are called upon to encourage students to maintain the language that they share with friends and family (McCafferty, 2002) and to use strengths in their home language as a basis for learning to read and write in English (Cummins et al., 2005; Huerta, 2011; Pérez, 1998). Pérez referred to "additive bilingualism" (p. 12), which can result in positive cognitive gains, a greater chance of retaining students in school, and in fostering parent-child communication. Cultural and linguistic diversity should also be considered a social resource that has potential to benefit cooperation and competition in the global marketplace. Cummins et al. (2005) proposed that (1) students' cultural knowledge and language abilities in their home language are valuable resources for engaging students; and (2) English language learners are more engaged when their identities are affirmed and they are enabled to activate their identities in learning.

Even Chall (1983) recognized the significance of sociocultural factors. She stated that "individuals progress through stages by interacting with their environment—the home, school, larger community, and culture" (p. 11) and "individual people progress through the reading stages at different rates. . . . The rate of advancement depends upon an interaction between individual (biological, motivational, cognitive, and so on) and environmental (home, community) factors" (p. 82). Snow et al. (1998) also recognized that cultural differences, including language, may create a "mismatch between the schools and the families" (p. 29), and that this incongruence may unfairly and inappropriately present obstacles to children's ability to learn to read in school.

In reality, therefore, cognitivist and socioculturalist views of literacy development are not diametrically opposed; each has its merits and each recognizes the value of the other. How then can a theoretical framework for literacy instruction and research integrate the cognitive and the sociocultural perspectives?

How to Integrate Cognitive and Sociocultural Theories of Literacy

A paucity of actual research on combining cognitive and sociocultural theories of literacy instruction and research precludes the reporting of much empirical evidence on its effectiveness; however, potential means to employ an integrated approach for instruction and research are discussed below.

For example, since cultural diversity may be manifested in students' home or first languages, which may differ from the dominant language of their schools, a combined cognitive-sociocultural approach would employ students' languages as resources to engage the students and to draw on their prior knowledge, as mentioned above. After all, "students' first languages are a critical foundation, not only for language learning, but for all learning" (Ontario Ministry of Education, 2005, p. 14). Therefore, students (i.e., English language learners) might initially be encouraged to utilize their first language to complete classroom tasks. Such a task may consist of a cross-curricular project that incorporates persuasive writing and research in geography, culminating in the creation of a travel brochure. In order to combine the cognitive objectives and sociocultural approach, a student from Tanzania, whose first and strongest language is Swahili, might be given the option to compose a convincing ad for Tanzania in Swahili. With the assistance of an adult or peer translator, an English version would subsequently be collaboratively created as well. This project provides an opportunity for the student to demonstrate his or her potential because it permits written expression in the student's first language, it enlists the student's prior knowledge, and as a result it may engage the student more than a traditional assignment might. Concomitantly, the project meets curricular expectations in language and geography while at the same time strengthening the student's English language skills.

A vignette reported by Pahl and Rowsell (2005) also demonstrated how a home language of Chinese may be integrated into an English language classroom teaching reading and writing. In this scenario, a child created illustrations and composed accompanying Chinese text with her mother at home. At school, the teacher helped her to translate the Chinese into English, and to combine the pictures and texts into a dual language book for herself and other Chinese students.

Compton-Lilly (2006) demonstrated how to incorporate a child's out-of-school literacy experiences with Pokémon stories to bolster his identity as a reader and writer by employing the stories for reading and the familiar topic for writing until he gradually felt confident with school literacy activities. In addition, Maloch (2004) demonstrated how the sociocultural school setting affected the dynamics of students' group work. The researcher considered the students' personal, family, and educational backgrounds as the students were observed during shared literacy experiences. In addition, Lee et al. (2003) commented that "interventions and educational research that are based on norms for psychosocial-cognitive development that do not reflect young people's histories and their unique cultural riches often miss opportunities to influence generative change or to understand what researchers purport to study" (p. 6). The concept of cultural modeling was promoted by Lee et al.; norms for talk and instruction in school were taken from the family and community practices of the students. For example, skills in critiquing literature might start with the analysis of rap lyrics, which are extracted from the students' culture, and gradually the acquired skills would be applied to more traditional academic texts.

Cummins et al. (2005) described the use of "dual language identity texts" (p. 40), which involves collaboration, independent problem solving, and home languages and English as well as the knowledge gained from the students' diverse experiences and backgrounds. This process demonstrates respect for students' first languages and experiences external to school; it allows for a "transfer of knowledge and skills across languages" (p. 42) while fostering students' positive identity in the school setting.

Huerta (2011) similarly found that the most effective teachers of Latino students possessed and implemented a degree of sociocultural knowledge. Among the teaching practices that Huerta's employed were the regular use of students' home languages and experiences; acknowledgement and respect of the Latino culture; and the use of multicultural literature and resources, participatory group structures, and networking opportunities.

Several additional complementary strategies for supporting English language learners may be found in the Ontario Ministry of Education's (2005) publication *Many Roots, Many Voices*. Underpinning the successful literacy strategies for students of diverse backgrounds is the understanding that the one-size-fits-all paradigm is an unacceptable philosophy; efforts to respect and include diversity are demanded.

In addition, since cognitivists tend to conduct empirical research and socioculturalists employ qualitative methods, integration of the two would suggest that researchers would also use both. Alton-Lee (2006) demonstrated such integration. Alton-Lee's concern for helping teachers understand how to manage the classroom and create activities for optimal student outcomes led her to study the teacher's role as well as the classroom culture's impact on student learning. Her methodology included pre- and post-unit testing of knowledge (the cognitive component) as well as comprehensive observations of students' actions and interviews. During the instruction sessions, she followed quarter minute by quarter minute the learning of three to six students. The data included observations of students' engagement, audio recordings of their public talk, video recordings, and tapings of private speech. The analyses of the data reportedly traced the relationships between the select students' experience in the classroom and changes in their attitudes and their knowledge (measured by tests). Post-testing and interviews were conducted a year later as well. Alton-Lee concluded that it is imperative to attend to culture (in this case, within the classroom) and cognition when studying the effectiveness of instruction. She referred to similar findings of Graham Nuthall that challenged the notion that ability is a fixed characteristic that explains learning. More important is engagement by students with classroom activities. These considerations of the classroom culture have implications for teaching diverse students—an understanding of processes of the mind and of the ways that culture shapes classroom experiences is critical.

Another integrated research approach was practiced by Reveles, Cordova, and Kelly (2004), who studied students' acquisition of science knowledge and literacy skills related to science by videotaping and audio taping classroom activities, taking field notes, conducting interviews of students, and collecting student work. The tapes and field notes provided data that could be analyzed regarding teacher–student and student–student interactions that related to the students' learning of science and use of science language. The classroom dynamics, therefore the social and cultural features of the classroom, could be examined. The degree of science language used and the student work also provided evidence of cognitive skill growth.

With respect to literacy, Purcell-Gates et al. (2004) reported their integrated research methods with adult literacy learners. They found that the use of authentic texts that corresponded with the adults' daily use increased the students' literacy skills and frequency of reading. In addition, the literacy experiences of the children in the homes of these adult students increased, and children experienced subsequent emergent literacy and early reading success.

The integration of sociocultural concepts into school practices was also studied by Raham (2004) in her investigation of literacy instruction in Canadian Aboriginal settings. Raham discovered that the most effective schools for Aboriginal students routinely provided instruction in Aboriginal languages and they incorporated the students' cultural practices into the programs. The effective educators also drew on and partnered with the students' community members to enhance student engagement and success. An example of how these practices may be manifested is demonstrated by the work of McKeough et al. (2008). These researchers studied the effectiveness of storytelling on the literacy development of Aboriginal children. From a cognitive perspective, oral language expression and understanding are considered to be precursors to successful written language skills (e.g., Wren, 2001), and culturally, oral story transmission is a longstanding Aboriginal custom (McKeough et al., 2008). Furthermore, McKeough et al. incorporated cultural aspects by consulting a First Nations advisory group regarding culturally relevant content themes, teaching materials, and lesson plans for Aboriginal children. The students were instructed in story structures, themes, and vocabulary by way of pictures, graphic mnemonics (story frames, icons, picture cards, picture books), oral discussion, and text that were relevant to their experiences. Both independently and collaboratively they created oral and written stories that supported their drawings and icons. The students advanced considerably in their oral storytelling skills. Successful integration of cognitive and sociocultural issues was exemplified in the methods employed in this study.

Evidence from these scenarios and studies demonstrates that it is possible and desirable to combine cognitive and sociocultural theories. Whether conducting a literacy intervention study or attempting a particular teaching strategy to improve word recognition, a sociocultural conscious researcher or teacher would also attend to factors within the classroom milieu and to students' out-of-school experiences that might affect the results. An integrated approach appears to be much more inclusive and respectful of all students, and it would seemingly result in a more equitable provision of literacy instruction. The suggested amalgamation of perspectives also readily complies with the recommendations of the Language and Literacy Researchers of Canada (2009) that policy and practices should "seek: (a) a convergence of evidence from a variety of research methodologies; (b) an open-mindedness to different research approaches and perspectives; (c) ways of integrating diverse (and sometimes conflicting) perspectives and domains" (p. 2).

Conclusion

Students from diverse social and cultural backgrounds experience inequality in education and lost achievement opportunities (Au, 2000; Cummins et al., 2005; Duffy, 2004). A cycle of continued underachievement has been perpetuated by a narrow view of literacy development, instruction, and research. It could be said that the education system has been instrumental in reproducing cultural and social repression, fostering hegemony of the English language and of the values and expectations of the dominant society, while marginalizing individuals with varied languages and sociocultural experiences. A potential challenge to the status quo has been forwarded in this chapter. Two theories of literacy development have been explored: the cognitive and the sociocultural. Both perspectives have been forwarded by accomplished and respected theorists, and at times they appear to be diametrically opposed. The cognitive view emphasizes skill acquisition along a universal developmental continuum and instruction that promotes growth through the stages or phases of literacy learning. The sociocultural standpoint is that literacy learning is socially situated and that it is appropriated from more knowledgeable others within one's social and cultural environment. The cognitive view attributes differences in learning achievement to ability and instructional variations, while the sociocultural theory attributes diversity in literacy learning to experiential variances. I have made the argument that these two theories can and should be integrated into a unitary theoretical framework for literacy instruction and research. In fact, the hypothesis of Purcell-Gates et al. (2004) that cognitive development occurs nested within a sociocultural sphere of experience precludes separation of the two concepts. In addition, the reported studies demonstrate that conscientious researchers and practitioners cannot disregard the value of both perspectives. North America's increasingly diverse population demands that responsible educators acknowledge, respect, and draw upon students' cultural and social experiences with respect to literacy learning, and that they adopt pedagogical perspectives that foster social and educational equity as well as academic achievement. To further develop these concepts, more research is needed to explore how to accomplish optimal literacy instruction and research through a wider, effective, and humanistic cognitive-sociocultural lens.

REFERENCES

Alton-Lee, A. (2006). How teaching influences learning: Implications for educational researchers, teachers, teacher educators and policy makers. *Teacher and Teacher Education, 22,* 612–626.

Au, K. H. (2000). A multicultural perspective on policies for improving literacy achievement: Equity and excellence. In M. L. Kamil, P. B. Mosenthal, P. D. Pearson, & R. Barr (Eds.), *Handbook of reading research* (pp. 835–851). Mahwah, NJ: Erlbaum.

Bourke, L., & Adams, A. (2010). Cognitive constraints and the early learning goals in writing. *Journal of Research in Reading, 33*(1), 94–110.

Canadian Language and Literacy Research Network (CLLRNet). (2009a). *Foundations for literacy: An evidence-based toolkit for the effective reading and writing teacher.* London, ON: University of Western Ontario.

Canadian Language and Literacy Research Network (CLLRNet). (2009b). *National strategy for early literacy.* Retrieved from http://nselwiki.cllrnet.ca/index.php/National_Strategy_for_Early_Literacy

Chall, J. S. (1983). *Stages of reading development.* New York, NY: McGraw-Hill.

Compton-Lilly, C. (2006). Identity, childhood culture, and literacy learning: A case study. *Journal of Early Childhood Literacy, 6*(1), 57–76.

Cummins, J., Bismilla, V., Chow, P., Cohen, S., Giampapa, F., Leoni, L., et al. (2005). Affirming identity in multilingual classrooms. *Educational Leadership, 63*(1), 38–43.

Duffy, A. (2004). *Class struggles: Public Education and the new Canadian.* Retrieved from http://atkinsonfoundation.ca.

Ehri, L. C. (2005). Development of sight word reading: Phases and findings. In M. J. Snowling & C. Hulme (Eds.), *The science of reading: A handbook* (pp. 135–154). Malden, MA: Blackwell.

Ehri, L. C., Nunes, S. R., Willows, D. M., Schuster, B. V., Yaghoub-Zadeh, Z., & Shanahan, T. (2001). Phonemic awareness instruction helps children to read: Evidence from the National Reading Panel's meta-analysis. *Reading Research Quarterly, 36*(3), 250–287.

Finnegan, R. (1999). Sociological and anthropological issues in literacy. In D. A. Wagner, R. L. Venezky, & B. V. Street (Eds.), *Literacy: An international handbook* (pp. 89–94). Boulder, CO: Westview Press.

Fitzgerald, J., & Shannahan, T. (2000). Reading and writing relations and their development. *Educational Psychologist, 35*(1), 39–50.

Gee, J. P. (2001). Reading as situated language: A sociocognitive perspective. *Journal of Adolescent and Adult Literacy, 44*(8), 714–725.

Gillon, G. T. (2004). *Phonological awareness.* New York, NY: Guilford Press.

Goswami, U. (2003). Early phonological development and the acquisition of literacy. In S. B. Neuman & D. K. Dickinson (Eds.), *Handbook of early literacy research* (pp. 111–125). New York, NY: Guilford Press.

Gutiérrez, K. D., & Rogoff, B. (2003). Cultural ways of learning: Individual traits or repertoires of practice. *Educational Researcher, 32*(5), 19–25.

Holzman, L. (1995). Creating developmental learning environments: A Vygotskian practice. *School Psychology International, 16,* 199–212.

Hooper, S. R., Roberts, J. E., Nelson, L., Zeisel, S., & Fannin, D. K. (2010). Preschool predictors of narrative writing skills in elementary school children. *School Psychology Quarterly, 25*(1), 1–12.

Huerta, T. M. (2011). Humanizing pedagogy: Beliefs and practices on the teaching of Latino children. *Bilingual Research Journal, 34,* 38–57.

John-Steiner, V., & Mahn, H. (1996). Sociocultural approaches to learning and development: A Vygotskian framework. *Educational Psychologist, 31*(3/4), 191–206.

Language and Literacy Researchers of Canada. (2009). *Rethinking literacy education in Canada.* Retrieved from http://rethinkingliteracyeducationca.blogspot.com/

Lee, C. D., Spencer, M. B., & Harpalani, V. (2003). "Every shut eye ain't sleep": Studying how people live culturally. *Educational Researcher, 32*(5), 6–13.

Luke, A. (2005).*Foreword.* In K. Pahl & J. Rowsell (Eds.), *Literacy and education: Understanding the new literacy studies in the classroom* (pp. x–xiv). Thousand Oaks, CA: Sage.

Maloch, B. (2004). On the road to literature discussion groups: Teacher scaffolding during preparatory experiences. *Reading Research and Instruction, 44*(2), 1–19.

McCafferty, S. G. (2002). Adolescent second language literacy: Language-culture, literature, and identity. *Reading Research and Instruction, 41*(3), 279–288.

McGuinness, D. (1997). *Why our children can't read.* Toronto, ON: Free Press.

McKeough, A., Bird, S., Tourigny, E., Romaine, A., Graham, S., Ottmann, J., et al. (2008). Storytelling as a foundation for literacy development for Aboriginal children: Culturally and developmentally appropriate practices. *Canadian Psychology, 49*(2), 149–154.

McNamee, G. D. (1995). A Vygotskian perspective on literacy development. *School Psychology International, 16,* 185–198.

Molfese, V. J., Beswick, J. L., Jacobi-Vessels, J. L., Armstrong, N. E., Culver, B. L., White, J. M., et al. (2011). Evidence of alphabetic knowledge in writing: Connections to letter and word identification skills in preschool and kindergarten. *Reading and Writing, 24,* 133–150.

National Reading Panel. (2000). *Teaching children to read: An evidence-based assessment of the scientific research literature on reading and its implications for reading instruction.* Retrieved from http://www.nationalreadingpanel.org/

No Child Left Behind Act of 2001, Pub. L. No. 107-110, 115 Stat. 1425. (2002). Retrieved from http://www.ed.gov/policy/eisec/leg/esea02/index.html

Nystrand, M. (2006). The social and historical context for writing research. In C. A. MacArthur, S. Graham, & J. Fitzgerald (Eds.), *Handbook of writing research* (pp. 11–27). New York, NY: Guilford Press.

Ontario Ministry of Education. (2003). *Early reading strategy: The report of the expert panel on early reading in Ontario.* Toronto, ON: Queen's Printer for Ontario.

Ontario Ministry of Education. (2005). *Many roots, many voices.* Toronto, ON: Queen's Printer for Ontario. (Available at http://www.edu.gov.on.ca)

Ontario Ministry of Education. (2009). *Ontario's equity and inclusive education strategy.* Ottawa, ON: Author. Retrieved from http://www.edu.gov.on.ca

Pahl, K., & Rowsell, J. (2005). *Literacy and education: Understanding the New Literacy Studies in the classroom.* Thousand Oaks, CA: Sage.

Pérez, B. (1998). Literacy, diversity, and programmatic responses. In B. Pérez (Ed.), *Sociocultural contexts of language and literacy* (pp. 3–20). Mahwah, NJ: Erlbaum.

Purcell-Gates, V. (2007). Comprehending complexity. In V. Purcell-Gates (Ed.), *Cultural practices of literacy* (pp. 197–216). Mahwah, NJ: Erlbaum.

Purcell-Gates, V., Jacobson, E., & Degener, S. (2004). *Print literacy development: Uniting cognitive and social practice theories.* Cambridge, MA: Harvard University Press.

Purcell-Gates, V., & Tierney, R. (2009). *Public policy brief: Increasing literacy levels of Canadian students.* Vancouver: University of British Columbia. Retrieved from http://cpls.educ.ubc.ca/content/pdfs/LiteracyPolicyBrief.pdf

Raham, H. (2004). Literacy instruction in Aboriginal settings. *Society for Advancement of Excellence in Education.* Research Brief. Retrieved from www.saee.ca/pdfs/AboriginalBrief.pdf.

Reveles, J. M., Cordova, R., & Kelly, G. J. (2004). Science literacy and academic identity formulation. *Journal of Research in Science Teaching, 41*(10), 1111–1144.
Rogers, T. (2000). What will be the social implications and interactions of schooling in the next millennium? *Reading Research Quarterly, 35*(3), 420–421.
Shaywitz, S. (2005). *Overcoming dyslexia.* New York, NY: Vintage Books.
Snow, C. E., Burns, M. S., & Griffin, P. (1998). *Preventing reading difficulties in young children.* Washington, DC: National Academy Press.
Statistics Canada. (2006). *Canada's ethnocultural mosaic, 2006 census.* Ottawa, ON: Author. Retrieved from http://www.statcan.gc.ca
Street, B. V. (1984). *Literacy in theory and practice.* New York, NY: Cambridge University Press.
Street, B. V. (1999). The meanings of literacy. In D. A. Wagner, R. L. Venezky, & B. V. Street (Eds.), *Literacy: An international handbook* (pp. 34–42). Boulder, CO: Westview Press.
Tracey, D. H., & Morrow, L. M. (2006). *Lenses on reading.* New York, NY: Guilford Press.
Venezky, R. L. (1984). The history of reading research. In P. D. Pearson (Ed.), *Handbook of reading research* (pp. 3–38). Mahwah, NJ: Erlbaum.
Wilkinson, I. A. G., Freebody, P., & Elkins, J. (2000). Reading research in Australia and Aotearoa / New Zealand. In M. L. Kamil, P. 3. Mosenthal, P. D. Pearson, & R. Barr (Eds.), *Handbook of reading research* (Vol. 3, pp. 3–16). Mahwah, NJ: Erlbaum.
Wren, S., 2001. *The cognitive foundations of learning to read: A framework.* Austin, TX: SEDL. Retrieved from http://www.sedl.org/

Appendix:
The Cognitive Foundations of Learning to Read: A Framework
(Wren, 2001)

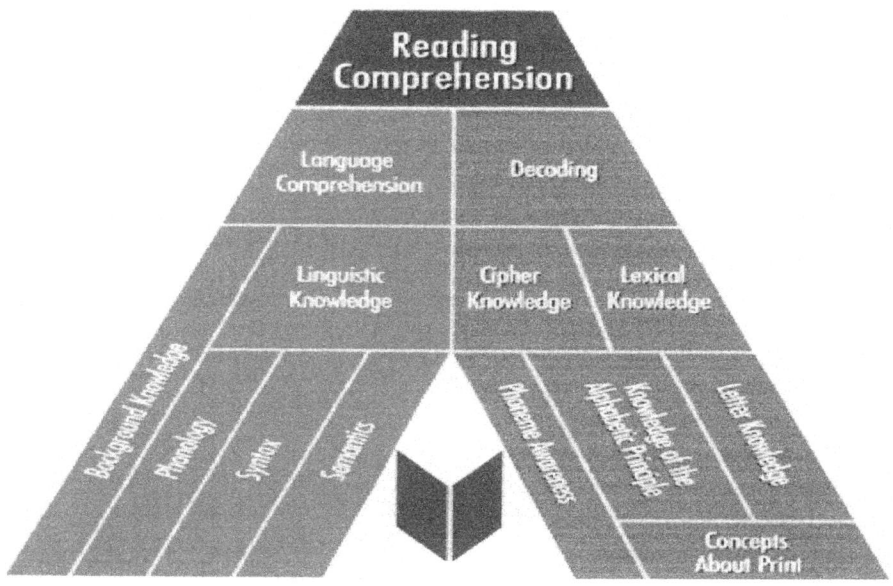

Valuing Subjective Complexities

Disrupting the Tyranny of Time

Sherry Rose & Pam Whitty

> We live in a world that is increasingly time governed, driven by new technologies and demands for increasing productivity. We are saturated with information. We demand and expect instant answers and quick fixes. We do not make time for other things, not least reflection, dialogue, critical thinking, working the tensions between theory and practice. Perhaps one answer to "What can we do?" is to say that we will struggle against the tyranny of time governance; we will risk crises by choosing to work with complexity, finding ways to think critically and searching for new questions; by doing so we will open up the possibility of new understandings and practices. (Dahlberg et al., 2007, p. 17)

For the past six years, the Early Childhood Centre at the University of New Brunswick (UNB-ECC) has had a contracted responsibility to research, pilot, and implement curriculum materials for young children, and has provided a program of professional learning for child-care educators.[1] From the start, these efforts have been informed by reconceptualist literature (Dahlberg & Moss, 2005; Greishaber & Cannella, 2001; Hughes & Mac Naughton, 2000; Mac Naughton, 2001, 2005; Pacini-Ketchabaw & Schecter, 2002; Penn, 2005) and reconceptualized practice (Rinaldi, 2006), with overlapping scholarship on children's rights (Burr, 2004; Friendly, 2006), equity research (Delpit, 1995; Derman-Sparks & the Anti-Bias Task Force, 1989/2001; Mac Naughton, 2001; Ramsey, 2004), and a valuing of children's daily lives (Dahlberg, Moss, & Pence, 1999; Penn, 2005; Rinaldi, 2006). The New Brunswick Curriculum Framework for Early Learning and Care—English (Early Childhood Centre, University of New Brunswick,

---

1 Funded through the New Brunswick Department of Social Development and the New Brunswick Early Learning and Childcare Trust Fund (http://www.gnb.ca/ 0017/Promos/0003/curriculum-e.asp*).

2008) and five curriculum support documents have been published to date (Ashton, Hunt, Nason, & Whitty, 2010; Ashton, Hunt, & White, 2008; Ashton, Stewart, Hunt, Nason, & Scheffel, 2009; Elliot, Ashton, Hunt, & Nason, 2010; Rose & Whitty, 2010a). These publications are produced through an ongoing process of reflection, dialogue, critical thinking, and meaning making inside workshop spaces, team meetings, daylong institutes, site visits, external consultations, and the co-authoring of multiple drafts of the documents.

The *New Brunswick Curriculum Framework for Early Learning and Child Care* (NBCF) introduced broad-based learning goals, values, and narrative documentation. These learning goals, influenced by the New Zealand (Carr, 2001; Ministry of Education, New Zealand, 1996) and Tasmanian (Department of Education, Tasmania, 2004) curricula, include well-being, play and playfulness, communication and literacies, and diversity and social responsibility. Values such as a zest for living and learning, creativity and play, and living democratically overlap with aspects of the goals and stress the distinctiveness of childhood as a time in its own right rather than merely as a preparation for school life. Narrative documentation potentially creates critical spaces for cultivating a "postmodern sensibility" (Popkewitz, 1998, as cited in Dahlberg et al., 1999, p. 27) and "to be more sensitive to the importance of focusing on questions . . .[being] fully aware that we are all inscribed in modernist discourses" (Dahlberg et al., 1999, p. 28).

Although we continually "work the tensions between theory and practice" in our work, we acknowledge that "educational practice, whether it be authoritarian or democratic, is always directive" (Freire & Freire, 2004, p. 66). A permeable, negotiable curriculum is difficult to achieve in a printed format. In spite of our efforts to textualize and affirm curriculum making as an ongoing and changing encounter among humans, companion species environments, materials, and technologies (Haraway, 1991, 2008), we are continually reminded how difficult it is to disrupt curriculum as directive in the context of officially mandated processes and products. Our continuous process of reflection, dialogue, critical thinking, and meaning making within workshop spaces and site visits is rife with contradictions and productive ethical tensions as we move in and out of university and day-care spaces where "people are not equally located" (Eyre, 2007, p. 99). How possible is it to disrupt authoritarian directives when creating and implementing an official curriculum in a culture ruled by hierarchical systems of knowledge production? How might continual conversations and a return to the documented artifacts challenge and re-author official documents?

Writing and implementing a values-based NBCF (Early Childhood Centre, 2008) involved the creation of many relational spaces that activated many lines: lines that are rigid, lines that are supple, and lines of flight (Deleuze & Guattari, 1987; Olsson, 2009). Recognizing that we are all caught in a constant interweaving of these lines, we ask, How do we cultivate favourable conditions for lines of flight to be created and activated in curricular practices (Olsson, 2009) in our ongoing work with child-care centres?

In an earlier article (Rose & Whitty, 2010b), we troubled the question, Where do we find the time? This question was reiterated throughout the curriculum implementation process in many contexts and in various forms: Where do I/we find the time? How do I/we find the time to follow one child's interests? How can I/we document narratives and be with children at the same time? How do I/we fit this all in? In this previous work, we foreground the tensions of time in three texts: curriculum documents, field notes from a semistructured focus group, and field notes from educators' responses to video documentation. Our critical examination of experimentations and interpretations, provoked through three communally produced texts, uncovered how educators both slide into and unsettle cultural orientations toward individualism, deficit, and clocked time. Being with these texts, (re)reading, (re)interpreting them in relational spaces uncovers (e)merging (dis)connections that expose rigid and supple lines and activate possible lines of flight. Opening a new way to think about time exposes our rigid authoring of time and its impact upon others and ourselves while inviting new choices and authorings of time, which incite different relational implications.

In this chapter, we continue our troubling of disciplinary time, a construction of time that calls for the correct use of time and the correct use of the body (Foucault, 1979, as cited by Tobin, 1997). Our intention is "to keep the problem of time alive so that educators [and ourselves] may follow the lines of flight that [another] inquiry might take" (Rose & Whitty, 2010b, p. 271).

We begin to explore "the conditions necessary for lines of flight and leakages to appear" in order to create movements in learning and subjectivities (Olsson, 2009, p. 75). In our work we strive to keep relational spaces open. We re-search for conditions where early childhood centres as places of encounters cultivate project identities (Delgado, 2006, p. 2, as cited in Moss, 2009), in which children and adults collectively construct knowledge and values (Dahlberg et al., 1999; Moss, 2009; Olsson, 2009), authoring alternatives to oppressive mainstream ideas (Delgado, 2006, p. 207, as cited in Moss, 2009).

We continue to ask, How do we invest in processes that productively support curriculum work as an engaging, contingent, unpredictable, intense, collective, and dialogic process? What practices might value educators as initiators of the in-between spaces of theory and practice that enliven local affirmation and experimentation (Olsson, 2009)? How might we further investigate how to listen for and value people's subjective use of time?

Drawing on our previous work (Rose & Whitty, 2010b), we continue to think about the intersection of time and relationships. We consciously cultivated a space to work with/in the context of longstanding relationships with educators, directors, and curriculum advisors. These longstanding relationships became "a precious resource, capable of making synergistic potential flow among educators, children and families" (Malaguzzi, 1995, p. 55). Our desire was to deepen our curricular understandings through these relationships by deepening our collective relationships with listening, documentation, materials, human and companion species, places, and time. Before examining our experiences of time through these documentation workshops and site visits, and the new utterances they put into circulation among our group (Foucault, 1997), we bring in the writings of others to illuminate the social construction of time.

Constructing Clock-Bound Worlds

> Mechanical timekeeping devices have been with us for more than two thousand years. Their history began with geared clockwork instruments in ancient times and they would reach a turning point when cumbersome weight-driven clocks of fourteenth century Europe began to strike twenty-four more or less equal hours a day. Improvements in clock-making would eventually make it possible to tell the time to the minutes and to the second. (McCready, 2001, p. 158)

Infringements of clock time on people's lives and freedoms are longstanding. In the late thirteenth century, particular European monasteries began calling monks to prayer at prescribed times (McCready, 2001). Hoffman (2009) notes that early in the fourteenth century, the telling of time shifted from natural signs or events to measurement by the clock. By the seventeenth century, clock-measured time "had enormous consequences for the regularization of all human activity" (p. 133). The continuing standardization of time and its links with human efficiency spread into the twentieth century and is epitomized by Frederick Taylor's industrial ethos (Levine, 2006). The new man and woman were to be objectified, quantified, and redefined in clockwork and mechanistic language. "Above all, their life and their time would be made to conform to the regime of the clock, the prerequisites of the schedule, and the dictates of efficiency" (Rifkin, 1987, p. 111). By the twenty-first century, in many parts of the world, the clock in its multiple analogue and digital forms calls people to work, to work efficiently, to work faster, and to work more productively. It calls us to standardize work with time, with our bodies, and with other's "bodies"—sometimes propelling us at speeds that feel beyond our control.

Others have problematized the governance of time, and its perpetuation of normalized subjectivities (Foucault, 1997; Marshall, 2007). Jonathan Swift's (1726) Lilliputians considered Gulliver's watch to be his god, an object of worship, to be attended to (Gleick, 1999). In the late nineteenth century, Warner (1884, as cited in Gleick, 1999) cautioned, "The chopping of time into rigid periods is an invasion of freedom, and makes no allowances for differences in temperament and feeling" (p. 44). This invasive standardization of people, work, and time is prevalent in the school system where a "modern industrial conception of time is strongly present . . .where timetabling symbolizes the finite, ordered and scarce nature of 'school time'" (Ball et al., 1984, p. 41, as cited in Wien, 1996, p. 398).

Challenging this construction of time in early learning and care sites, Wien and Kirby-Smith (1998) articulate the connection between "an integrated curriculum, unhurried time, and sustained complex activity" (p. 8) as it appears historically in early childhood. Calling forward the pedagogical thinking of Montessori (1912/1965), Isaacs (1930/1968), Bredekamp (1987), Katz and Chard (1989), Elkind (1990), Bredekamp and Rosegrant (1992), and Jones and Nimmo (1994), Wien and Kirby-Smith (1998) note that despite this historical line of thought, there exists a lived contradiction between educators' pedagogical values and the linear, lockstepped scheduling that undermines these values. Wien (1996) theorizes that the schedule and its component parts become taken-for-granted scripts for organizing time. Passed on from one year to the next, ritualistic routines such as calendar time, snack time, outdoor time, and field trips remain embodied and unchallenged (Wien, 1996) because "no one has the time to think consciously about how time undermines what educators value" (Wien & Kirby-Smith, 1998, p. 9). When Kirby-Smith invited two educators "to remove the clocks and watches from their classroom," the two discovered that removing the timepiece as the decisionmaker allowed them to break open the old scripts and imagine new possibilities (Wien & Kirby-Smith, 1998, p. 11).

In New Brunswick, Linda Gould, the director of Chatham Day Care, invited educators to remove clocks and watches for a two-week period (Rose & Whitty, 2010b). This provocation caused the educators to step back from a way of acting or reacting, to detach from their embodiment of clock time as a problem of thought: to question its meaning, conditions, and goals. By establishing clock time as an object, they reflected on it as a problem to open up new possibilities (Foucault,1997). With clock time, the efficient movement of children and educators became the overriding priority: the more activities, the better it seemed to be for the children, and more also contributed to a perceived successful measure of educators' performance. "We were teaching the kids to stay on schedule, to be ready for school, to rush through everything "(personal communication, Linda Gould, August 25, 2009). And as one child-care educator sadly lamented, "There was no time to spend time" (J. McGraw, personal communication, August 25, 2009). The educators discovered that they were "programmed and programming. The children were learning how to rush though life. They were learning how to 'live their dash! You know—you are born, you dash, and then you die'" (S. Karasek, personal communication, August 25, 2009).

Shifting their attention from the clock to the children meant that the educators were letting the children know they mattered. Educators reported that they slowed down, wrote positive documentation notes, noticed where the learning occurred, and listened to what occupied the children. They reported that they let the children know they mattered. They sat with the children, relaxed, listened, and recorded their observations: actions that changed their mind-set. This image of a listening educator runs counter to modernist notions of good use of time and in particular how silence is valued in teaching practices. "When silence is valued, it ceases to be wasted time. It no longer drags on the clock" (Levine, 2006, p. 42). When educators welcomed children as contributors to both curriculum and community responsibilities, they valued children serving meals, setting tables, stacking chairs, washing tables, sweeping floors, and determining their own bathroom and hunger needs. "Respecting children's participation in community responsibilities takes time and requires the respect of the time it takes to learn communal responsibilities," noted one of the educators (A. Savoy, personal communication, August 25, 2009).

Listening Encounters

Being with Documentation . . .

> We are talking about an approach based on listening rather than speaking, where doubt and amazement are welcome factors along with scientific inquiry and the deductive method of the detective. It is an approach in which the importance of the unexpected and the possible are recognized, an approach where educators know how to waste time, or better yet, know how to give time back to the children all of the time that they need. It is an approach which protects originality and subjectivity without creating isolation of the individual and offers to children the possibility of confronting special situations and problems as members of small peer groups. . . .Our task is to ask ourselves good questions. (Rinaldi, 1995, pp. 103–104)

Our previous work (Rose & Whitty, 2010b) addressed how time slowed down for educators who collectively interpreted educator Donna Baisley's video of cooking with two-year-olds. As these educators shared their interpretations and responses, they described a shift in time. As one educator stated, "When I first saw Donna put all those prepared ingredients out on the table and saw those 2-year-olds just jump in—dumping and mixing—I thought, to myself, this is going to result in chaos. But soon I found myself relaxing and thinking how wonderful it felt. It felt like we could take all the time in the world to finish this activity" (workshop participant, personal communication, February 2008). Video documentation honors "[subjective], relational concepts—dialogue, conversation, negotiation, encounter, confrontation, and conflict" (Dahlberg et al., 1999, p. 58)—that are difficult to depict in the printed formats of learning stories (Carr, 2001) and official curriculum documents. As educators interpreted Donna's cooking video, many of them were flooded with memories from their own childhood, recalling cooking with moms and grandmothers, failed recipes, how they approached cooking with their own children, and lessons learned through experience and relationships. Inside these workshops, time became "a time of reflectiveness, of pauses, memory, and interior listening" (Edwards & Rinaldi, 2009, p. 14).

Inspired by Donna's video and with a vision that other educators might like to experiment with video documentation, we provided five flip cameras to early learning and child-care educators at an earlier workshop. Charley took one of those cameras. Jill, Charley's director, attended a two-day institute at a Canadian national conference in Saint John, New Brunswick, where participants repeatedly viewed video documentation. Jill excitedly told us about a wonderful video clip that Charley had shared with parents: "I didn't know what else to do with the video, but now I do. Can I bring it to our next workshop?" (personal communication, Jill Shaw, June 2, 2011).

Excitedly, we planned a large chunk of time for repeated viewing of this video, a text that would be new to all of us in the room except Charley. To linger on Charley's work, we invited the workshop participants to view Charley's video documentation three times. The first viewing was framed with the goal of viewing it and sharing responses in small group discussions. Then we invited educators to share how their "thinking together" informed their second viewing. The third time we viewed the video, we were thinking about the questions that children might be exploring through their play. We discussed these questions and the possible materials, observations, and other questions that we might take back to the children to deepen their engagement and representation of their invented game. Finally, we invited the documenter, Charley, to comment on her interpretations and experience with the children's invented game.

The video shows a group of four-year-olds who, having discovered a basket of scarves new to their environment, initiate a range of playful scarf games. Soon the range of playfulness evolves into a group game of sling-shooting one another across the room in which tension, distance, body position, timing, and turntaking are all explored and negotiated with great joy and laughter. Charley clearly gives time back to children; she respectfully and silently documents their game. These children are not docile bodies ruled by the time of the clock.

Our repetitive viewing, interspersed with a flow of small group and whole group reflections, enables a more layered telling in which educators could "find and relate to the unpredictable, incorrigible, uncontrollable, unmanageable disobedient aspects that are also part of the pedagogical relationship" (Ellsworth, 1997, p. 7). Our viewing, interwoven with critical face-to-face dialogue, allowed us to take "seriously enough the conditions of teaching as well as the perspectives" of others (Craig & Ross, 2008, p. 301). The educators were courageous in uncovering their own assumptions and constructions of children. For example, one curriculum advisor honestly explained, "I found myself getting frustrated with the girl who was bossing everybody around. I think that is because I hate to be told what do." This brave revelation, perhaps a construction others held privately, provoked a rich debate represented by the following range of questions and comments:

> "What girl? I didn't even notice the girl. I was taken by the boy who watched from the side lines before joining in."
> "I didn't see her as bossy at all, but as a strong leader."
> "Yes, but does she always take the leadership role?"
> "What kind of leader is she?"
> "What other ways do children lead each other?"
> "How can we help children share leadership?"
> "Did you notice when she couldn't explain how others should position their body, she demonstrated?"
> "Did you notice that she was making sure everyone got a turn?" (Workshop participants, personal communication, June 7, 2011)

By bringing her practice in video form to a public forum, Charley co-constructs an encounter that shifts us from an individual gaze to an in/be/tween gaze. We witness how children encounter one another and new materials. Through our collective viewing, we encounter one another's interpretations and constructions influencing and redirecting curricular interpretations as our "individual contributions are taken up by the group creating a collective culture" (Olsson, 2009, p. 100).

Reflecting on Charley's video publicly, we can find "inspiration to break out of old assumptions and unproductive thought patterns that block our capacity to see the beauty of what is before us in everyday events of teaching and learning" (Moonja Oh, as cited in Edwards & Rinaldi, 2009, p. 5). Our constructions of the "bossy girl" can come to be questioned—large made more complex. We realize the diverse range of interpretations and possible flights though our collective dialogue. Curricular flights explode into possibilities to be discovered: What other ways can we propel our bodies? What other things might be propelled? What about slingshots, catapults? Are there other ways to propel? What if we invited the children to represent their game graphically? How might their game change if it were played outside? What if we provided them with large rubber exercise bands? Olsson (2009) asks what conditions are necessary to recognize and cultivate lines of flight through narrative documentation. Drawing on our experiences, described here, possible conditions may include: time dedicated to relationships that value communal interpretation; courageous confrontation of our own constructions and vulnerabilities; a desire to re-search our documentations through new questions, and a shared faith in new imaginings—time and a collective space where educators can "articulate, examine, confirm and/or transform their narrative knowledge" (Orr & Olson, 2007, p. 829).

Being with Materials...
What does it mean for an educator to plan "the environment as a third teacher" (Edwards, Gandini, & Forman, 1995; Fraser, 2000)? How might this be implemented within workshop spaces? Planning the environment as a third teacher is a challenging task of translating values into concrete factors such a choice of materials and use of time, spaces, equipment, and social interactions. Realizing our curriculum values in workshop spaces, we aim to bring the indoors out and outdoors in, and create beautifully inviting spaces that include a range of seasonal objects paired with books and representations. We plan for individual, small group, and whole group collaborations, all of which have choice embedded within them. We invite participation and visibility through representation using a wide range of open-ended materials. We welcome flexibility by encouraging movement through a range of spaces, relationships, and uses of material and time, and by seeking joy in the extraordinary or unanticipated discovery.

Given these conditions, our efforts continue to be governed by our internal press of time. This means we worry that participants (children) have lost interest and are uncomfortable with silence, hesitation, or challenge, and we move on too quickly. Rarely do we return to artifacts; listen to the artifacts; listen to the experiences of creation; listen to the silences, hesitations, or challenges. Rarely do we interpret our "being-with" in ways that might complicate and energize our curricular creations. With this contradictory complexity in mind we invite workshop participants to revisit adult- and children-produced artifacts and experiences as a call for slowing down, revisiting, listening for new lines of flight.

Inside one particular workshop assemblage of different activities involving claymaking/water-sand play/watercolour/poetry, a small group of educators chose to be with water in the outdoor space. In this space, educators negotiated materials; experimented with siphons, tubing, and funnels; problem solved water flowing in desired directions; and figured out how to saturate a moat so that it would hold water. There was a discussion about the importance of water conservation as the participants explored what water could do. A solution was to recycle the siphoned water by watering the flower garden. Clipboards with blank paper were available for participants to use to document observations, discoveries, and theories. Upon the completion of this outdoor playtime, the educators wrote a thank you note in the sand for the children who would discover their elaborately constructed sandcastle the next day. In spite of all this and much undocumented richness and complexity in participants' learning, language, and play, Charley was provoked into a troubling flight. She asked, "Can I really stay outside the whole time?" At this point the workshop participants erupted with many effectively charged and passionate suggestions: "Think about how much you learned outside; think about the range of activities; you even wrote out there." Educators located in home centres were most adamant that one could spend the whole day outside—learning.

Charley troubled their experience with her own reality: "But I am a preschool teacher. If I was with the children all day or even if it was an afterschool program it would be different. I would feel more comfortable being outside for longer periods." Charley's counterpoint connects with Tobin's (1997) argument that daily classroom routines "imitate and anticipate the adult cycle of pleasureless office work broken up by packaged pleasures in the form of . . . coffee and lunch breaks and vacations" (p.18). This regimentation of clocked pleasures produces

> Postcolonial citizens, alienated from our bodies and desires—[who] consume rather than produce passion. Our social and economic life is structured on this dynamic of laboring in alienating jobs to produce wealth that is then used to purchase value-added, manufactured, imported, highly processed, (refined, acquired) forms of pleasure. The reproduction of the system depends on the production of children alienated from desire, habituated to the cycle of work and consumption. (Tobin, 1997, p. 18)

Charley's distinction between preschool teaching and afterschool or full-day teaching raises the power of the primacy of institutional time over lived time (Polakow, 1992). Her question illustrates the point that "cultural beliefs are like the air we breathe, so taken for granted that they are rarely discussed or even articulated but provoke volatile reaction when these rules are violated" (Levine, 2006, p. 123). By speaking what is so rarely uttered, Charley's question raises other questions: How does a preschool category continue to exist across the province—when the NBCF-E, officially in use in all early learning and care sites, is intended to reconcile the care and education divide? The mythically prepared school-ready child governs time, organization of resources, and desires, while contributing to the financial viability of centres.

Being with Human and Companion Species . . .

A morning visit to a home-based child care facility, Bridget's Playhouse of Learning in Sunny Corner, New Brunswick, on the bank of the Northwest Miramichi River, brings forward a different experiencing of time—one that stands in contrast to institutionalized schooled time where the ease of stilling bodies, fragmenting time, and monitoring actions is ever present. Bridget's Playhouse enacts time with young children as they live, learn, and play in the seasonal cadence of northern New Brunswick. It is a construction of time where their bodies move through familiar spaces, natural and constructed, spaces that are in constant flux (Lenz Taguchi, 2010)—spaces where these children can act within and upon the world in factual and imaginary ways. Relationships over time, with/in nature's time and in/between family time and Bridget's time shape and are shaped by the lives of a collective of children within a particular locality.

The arrow on the sign means "We are out back." A group of children make their way from the river to the front of the house. They are wearing their rubber boots and yelling hellos. It feels like visiting friends. They have just been down to check the rock by the river, the one that tells them whether it is high tide or low. It turns out that it is high tide when we are visiting, and we are on our way up to the farm across the road to visit the people, the animals, and the buildings that have clearly become a part of their everyday lives. The conversations up the drive and to the road were rhizomatic in nature, taking many flights. "Do the three beaded girls on that brooch have a name? No! Why not? Let's name them." Mostly the conversation is about the dandelions that the children were picking to wear and to share, ongoing and excited invitations to come and see the recently acquired pigs and chickens, and the newly born calves. One child in particular was preoccupied with mosquitoes. It is Spring!

As we approach the road, the children pair up and Bridget takes the hand of one of the children. The children have crossed this road many times, care has been taken, and the farm, across the way, is an accessible and familiar place. At the farm, there are men on the roof taking down the old shingles, preparing to put up the new. The farmer opens the gate for all of us. The children run to the barn and some of them notice the piglets have become a bit bigger—they try luring them over to where they are with a bit of vegetable. They take turns standing in the best viewing spot—the conversation is about how much less shy the pigs seem and which one is which—the ears up or down being the distinguishing physical marker that helps with the naming. The chickens are still small enough to need a warming light and the calves behind the fence look over at us, keeping their distance. Most of the children run ahead to another outbuilding where two of them find the winter sliding mats and play that motion out on the grass, while two others balance on the loosened floorboards that behave in the manner of a low-lying teeter-totter.

The walk takes us to Stella's verandah. Stella died two months ago. The house stands empty. A few of the children play on the verandah where Stella used to share snacks and conversation with them while a few more run to the nearby entwined growth of three trees to play. Another child runs to the mailbox. It is Thursday and she is retrieving the sale fliers that arrive on that day.

We go back across the road and take another way back to Bridget's house so that the children can share their favourite tree and favourite rock. They do this but are more engaged with the brook that runs along the side of the drive—it is full of water from last night's rainfall. They embark, all but one, on a trek into the brook with their imaginations, rubber boots, and sticks. There is a deeply felt sense that they know their world, they notice differences within it, and they love to explore it. Once we reach the house, wet socks and boots are shed and we all go inside, the children spreading out to different spaces.

We come together for lunch at the dining room table. The children know Bridget's husband, Bernard, and her daughter Emily, who has just returned home from university; they know her dog, Isabelle, and her piano.

Revisiting this piece of text with Bridget, in the spirit of Lenz Taguchi's (2010) notion of counter-actualisation, our conversation was not about the *New Brunswick Curriculum Framework*. Instead it focused upon "flows, rhythms and intensities" of the day and the way that curriculum moves with, rather than controls, children (Pacini-Ketchabaw, 2010, p. xi). As Bridget responded verbally to the text, she talked about how the rhythm and activities of each day were planned with the children; how they made choices about going to the farm; which parts of the farm they wanted to visit; whether they wanted to take the shortcut through the woods to the neighbours; go to the river and engage with frogs, butterflies, or daisies or whatever natural phenomena caught their attention; or go to see the dog-grooming neighbour right next door. At Bridget's Playhouse, there is a strong sense that these children know about and belong to their world (Fraser, 2000); exercise freedom in their use of time (Hoffman, 2009); and both human and companion species (Haraway, 1991, 2008) are part of the flow and intensities of their everyday and seasonal living, learning, and caring. Bridget also spoke about safety—how everything is dangerous, how she hopes children can live without fear, so she has them using blenders, being aware of tidal flows, and crossing roads. In speaking of one particular child, Bridget recounted the following:

> I held her hand. Sometimes she gets preoccupied and doesn't pay attention to her surroundings. I don't want her to feel she can't walk on her own or with anyone else; so I sometimes let her be in charge of the dog. It is very important that the dog does not go on the road. She is very alert to where the dog is and makes the dog stay on the walkway. I make that job an important one that everyone wants to do. She also has many days she walks on her own. It all comes down to getting to know each and every child and how their day is going, while still giving them the utmost respect. (Personal communication, Bridget O'Shea, June 24, 2011)

Recognizing the hurried life of working parents, Bridget knows the importance of taking time. Learning with/in relationships is carried out "in a generally unhurried pace that creates a sense of security, self-esteem and the opportunity to work problems through" (Gandini, 1995, p. 147). In terms of the life cycle, Bridget reflects, "I wait for the opportunity to bring things up and talk to the parents about how much information they would like me to give and what they may like to give." Following Stella's death, she reflects, "Stella was a big part of the children's everyday visits. I felt the children should share their feelings, have questions answered and let them know I was sad too" (personal communication, Bridget O'Shea, June 24, 2011).

Bridget also commented that the visit had the effect of compressing and speeding up time, as the children wanted to share everything on the visit, and did not follow the usual daily rhythm of spending longer intervals of time engaged in fewer encounters. To gain a different sense of being with the children and Bridget on-site might require extended visits over time.

Learning Together, Subjective Time, and Insider Insights

At this particular moment in time our efforts are troubled by the recent shift of the Department of Early Learning and Child Care into the Department of Education in New Brunswick. For us, this means a need to be even more vigilant concerning the very real governance of schoolification and institutionalization on these ways of being with young children, their families, and educators. Many circulating questions involve time, are difficult to address, and rise to the surface again and again: Will the kids be ready for school? How will we know? How do I do everything in three hours? How do we get parents more involved? The language of these questions is embedded with modernist, neoliberal discourses—discourses that sediment subjectivities, relationships, values, time, and learning affecting our individual and collective participation and/or disengagement. If, as Hoffman (2009) writes and as we have narrated in this chapter, "human time...is in important ways subjective...[but] it is also, just as importantly, relational and intersubjective" (p. 119). The choices we make through our explorations of these problems need to include a scrutiny of time toward the creation of movements in learning and subjectivities (Moss, 2009; Olsson, 2009).

We are trying to create workshops for educators that value and work from insider perspectives (McDonald, Mohr, Dichter, & McDonald, 2007). Educators are invited to bring in documented artifacts for the group to research, opening up new questions and interpretations. Important in these workshop spaces was a time for educators to be with a wide range of open-ended materials and books, either alone or with one another. Some educators chose to work with a range of materials in a range of ways, while others remained with their chosen material for the duration of the workshop. Some worked silently, while others laughed, chatted, shared experiences, and evaluated one another's efforts. Meaning making, developing local possibilities out of local questions and challenges, means that evaluation is more "about constructing and deepening our understand of the early childhood institution than about conforming to predetermined standards" (Dahlberg & Moss, 2005, p. 88). "Professional development activities for educators that are designed and conducted without the benefit of inside perspectives...involve a kind of de-skilling in as much as they discount or dismiss the subtleties of dealing with real complexity" (McDonald et al., 2007, pp. 1–2). Scripted professional development constitutes a rigid line, becomes costly, often silences educators' knowledge, and often distances educators from their own authority. What if professional development valued insider insights while engaging with the creation of meaning with others? What if school readiness was a value of the school rather than a mismeasure of children and their family? What if parents' involvement was a value of the centre or school and not a mismeasure of the parents (Moss, 2009)?

Supple lines and lines of flight (Deleuze & Guattari, 1987; Olsson, 2009) occur when we open up relational participatory spaces; cultivate a pedagogy of listening (Rinaldi, 2006); live with our questions; resist recognition and representation (Olsson, 2009); value people's subjective use of time; be with materials, places, human and companion species; and collectively construct project identities by communally researching multimodal artifacts created by educators and children. Each of these ways of being open up critical curricular spaces that potentially disrupt taken-for-granted notions of children, childhood, and curricula privileged and produced by dominant neoliberal and modernist discourses (Cannella, 1997; Dahlberg et al., 1999; Edmiston, 2008; Mac Naughton, 2005).

Disruptive Possibilities

How possible is it to disrupt authoritarian directives when creating and implementing an official curriculum in a culture ruled by hierarchical systems of knowledge production? As Pinar, Reynolds, Slattery, and Taubman (1995) noted, "Curriculum is an extraordinarily complicated conversation. Curriculum as an institutionalized text is a formalized and abstract version of conversation, a term we usually use to refer to those open-ended, highly personal, interest driven events in which persons encounter each other"(p. 848). How do we generate and sustain complicated conversations in at the University of New Brunswick "that employ others' conversations to enrich our own?" (Pinar et al., p. 848). We recognize the need to publicly disrupt our embodied desires and expectations for instant answers and quick fixes. We are learning to make time for other things, not least reflection, dialogue, critical thinking, working the tensions between theories and practices. We are choosing to work with complexity, finding ways to think critically and searching for new questions in the hopes that we will enliven local affirmation and experimentation (Dahlberg et al., 2007; Olsson, 2009).

As we continue to explore how to listen for and value people's subjective use of time, we have opened up our workshop spaces to the (re)reading of documentation that educators introduce us to at the workshop. We realize that learning to be with materials, documentation, and with each other means we are taking "the time to think consciously about how time undermines what educators' value"

(Wien & Kirby-Smith, p. 9). We note that taking the time to observe participants' entry and flow through self-selected activities varies greatly. For example, one person stays with a book for an hour, another person moves through clay and watercolours, and another person roams the environment, scanning materials and looking for inspiration. Often educators are so engaged with their representations that they claim more time to persist in their creations. By consciously describing these subjective entries, rhythms, and flows to the group, we hope to connect theses differences to their experiences with children. In this way, we make public the subjective use of time.

Our collective relationships with listening to documentations, materials, human and companion species, places, and time suggests that we need to think about/value individual powerful-ness inside the collective. We noticed how quickly educators jumped in to answer Charley's question. These well-intended responses left little space for Charley to live with and through her question. It is a challenge in such a public space to keep questions open. It was also a challenge for us to refrain from offering an authoritative curricular answer when Charley approached each of us privately after the workshop. Could we have slowed down the collective desire to answer Charley's question by inviting individuals to produce their own interpretation of her questions; to articulate that interpretation in small groups; and to reflect on how others' interpretations connect to and change their thinking, just as we did with the video documentation? Would such a process have deepened and broadened the landscape of possibilities and constraints for all of us to create space in which Charley could then re-author her own practice?

Other questions we would like to investigate in the future also arise out of the on-site visit to Bridget's Playhouse. In this home centre, there seems to be more opportunities for relationships between human and companion species, and interactions with natural signs and events: relationships that are not governed by the clock. What lessons might be learned from these home centres that could open up the governance of clock time in larger, more institutionalized centres?

REFERENCES

Ashton, E., Hunt, A., & White, L. (2008). *Well-being: Professional support document.* Fredericton: University of New Brunswick Early Childhood Centre.

Ashton, E., Hunt, A., Nason, P., & Whitty, P. (2010). *Diversity and social responsibility: Professional support document.* Fredericton: University of New Brunswick Early Childhood Centre.

Ashton, E., Stewart, K., Hunt, A., Nason, P., & Scheffel, T.L. (2009). *Play and playfulness: Professional support document.* Fredericton: University of New Brunswick Early Childhood Centre.

Bredekamp, S. (Ed.). (1987). *Developmentally appropriate practice in early childhood programs serving children from birth through age 8.* Washington, DC: National Association for the Education of Young Children.

Bredekamp, S., & Rosegrant, T. (Eds.). (1992). *Reaching potentials: Appropriate curriculum and assessment for young children*. Washington, DC: National Association for the Education of Young Children.
Burr, R. (2004). Children's rights: International policy and lived practice. In M.J. Kehily (Ed.), *An introduction to childhood studies* (pp.145–159). Milton Keynes, England: Open University Press.
Cannella, G. S. (1997). *Deconstructing early childhood education: Social justice and revolution*. New York, NY: Peter Lang.
Carr, M. (2001). *Assessment in early childhood settings: Learning stories*. London, England: Paul Chapman.
Craig, C.J., & Ross, V. (2008). Cultivating the image of teachers as curriculum makers. In M.F. Connelly, M. Fang He, & J. Phillion (Eds.), *The Sage handbook of curriculum and instruction* (pp. 282–305). Los Angeles, CA: Sage.
Dahlberg, G., & Moss, P. (2005). *Ethics and politics in early childhood education*. New York, NY: RoutledgeFalmer.
Dahlberg, G., Moss, P., & Pence, A. (2007). *Beyond quality in early childhood education and care: Postmodern perspectives*. London, England: Falmer Press.
Deleuze, G., & Guattari, F. (1987). *A thousand plateaus: Capitalism and schizophrenia*. Minneapolis: University of Minnesota Press.
Delpit, L. (1995). *Other people's children: Cultural conflicts in the classroom*. New York, NY: New Press.
Department of Education, Tasmania. (2004). *Framework 1 and 2 overview, essential learnings framework. Key resource to support the essential learnings curriculum*. Hobart, Tasmania: Author. Retrieved from http://www.ltag.education.tas.gov.au/references.htm#ELresources
Derman-Sparks, L., & the Anti-Bias Task Force.(1989/2001). *Anti-bias curriculum: Tools for empowering young children*. Washington, DC: National Association for the Education of Young Children.
Early Childhood Centre Research Team, University of New Brunswick. (2008). *New Brunswick curriculum framework for early learning and child care—English*. Fredericton: Department of Social Development, University of New Brunswick.
Edmiston, B. (2008). *Forming ethical identities in early childhood play*. New York, NY: Routledge.
Edwards, C., Gandini, L., & Forman, G. (1993). *The hundred languages of children: The Reggio Emilia approach to early childhood education*. Norwood, NJ: Ablex.
Edwards, C., & Rinaldi, C. (Eds.). (2009). *The diary of Laura: Perspectives on a Reggio Emilia diary*. St. Paul, MN: Redleaf Press.
Elkind, D. (1990). Academic pressures—too much, too soon: The demise of play. In E. Klugman & S. Smilansky (Eds.), *Children's play and learning: Perspectives on policy implications* (pp. 3–17). New York, NY: Teachers College Press.
Elliot, E., Ashton, E., Hunt, A., & Nason, P. (2011). *Our youngest children: Learning with infants and toddlers*. Fredericton: University of New Brunswick Early Childhood Centre.
Ellsworth, E. (1997). *Teaching positions: Difference, pedagogy, and the power of address*. New York, NY: Teachers College Press.
Eyre, L. (2007). Whose ethics? Whose interests? The Tri-Council Policy and feminist research. *Journal of Curriculum Theorizing, 26*(3), 91–102.
Foucault, M. (1997). Polemics, politics and problematizations [Interview with P. Rabinow, May 1984]. In L. Davis (Trans.), *Ethics of essential works of Foucault* (Vol. 1). New York, NY: New Press. Retrieved from http://foucault.info/foucault/interview.html
Fraser, S. (2000). *Authentic childhood: Experiencing Reggio Emilia in the classroom*. Scarborough, ON: Nelson.
Friendly, M. (2006).*Canadian early learning and childcare and the Convention on the Rights of Children*. Toronto, ON: Childcare Research and Resource Unit, University of Toronto.
Freire, P., & Freire, A.M.A. (2004). *Pedagogy of hope*. London, England: Continuum.

Gandini, L. (1993). Educational and caring spaces. In C. Edwards, L. Gandini, & G. Forman (Eds.), *The hundred languages of children: The Reggio Emilia approach to early childhood education* (pp. 135–149). Norwood, NJ: Ablex.

Gleick, J. (1999). *Faster: The acceleration of just about everything.* New York, NY: Pantheon Books.

Grieshaber, S., & Cannella, G. S. (2001). *Embracing identities in early childhood education: Diversity and possibilities.* New York, NY: Teachers College Press.

Haraway, D.J. (1991). *Simians, cyborgs and women.* London, England: Routledge.

Haraway, D.J. (2008). *When species meet.* Minneapolis: University of Minnesota Press.

Hoffman, E. (2009). *Time.* New York, NY: Picador.

Holt, M. (2005). *The nature and purpose of education.* Berkeley, CA: Center for Ecoliteracy. Retrieved from http://www.ecoliteracy.org/publications/rsl/maurice-holt.html

Hughes, P., & Mac Naughton, G. (2000). Consensus, dissensus or community: The politics of parental involvement in early childhood educations. *Contemporary Issues in Early Childhood, 1*(3), 241–257.

Isaacs, S. (1930/1968). *Intellectual growth in young children.* New York, NY: Schocken.

Jones, E., & Nimmo, J. (1994). *Emergent curriculum.* Washington, DC: National Association for the Education of Young Children.

Katz, L., & Chard, S. (1989). *Engaging children's minds: The project approach.* Norwood, NJ: Ablex.

Lenz Taguchi, H.L. (2009). *Going beyond the theory/practice divide in early childhood education: Introducing an intra-active pedagogy.* New York, NY: Routledge.

Levine, R. (2006). *A geography of time: The temporal misadventures of a social psychologist, or How every culture keeps time just a little bit differently.* Oxford, England: Oneworld.

Mac Naughton, G. (2001). Beyond "othering": Rethinking approaches to teaching young Anglo-Australian children about Indigenous Australians. *Contemporary Issues in Early Childhood, 2*(1), 83–93.

Mac Naughton, G. (2005). *Doing Foucault in early childhood studies: Applying post-structural ideas.* New York, NY: RoutledgeFalmer.

Malaguzzi, L. (1993). History, ideas and basic philosophy. In C. Edwards, L. Gandini, & G. Forman (Eds.), *The hundred languages of children: The Reggio Emilia approach to early childhood education* (pp. 41–89). Norwood, NJ: Ablex.

Marshall, J. (2007). Michel Foucault: Educational research as problematization. In M.A. Peters & T. (A.C.) Besely (Eds.), *Why Foucault? New directions in educational research* (pp. 15–26). New York, NY: Peter Lang.

McCready, S. (2001). The triumph of the clockmakers: Counting the minutes and the seconds. In S. McCready (Ed.), *The discovery of time* (pp. 157–171). Naperville, IL: Sourcebooks.

McDonald, J.P., Mohr, N., Dichter, A., & McDonald, E.C. (2007). *The power of protocols: An educator's guide to better practice.* New York, NY: Teachers College Press.

Ministry of Education, New Zealand. (1996). *Te Whāriki.* Wellington, New Zealand: Learning Media Education.

Ministry of Education, New Zealand. (2005). *Kei Tua o tePae. Assessment for learning: Early childhood exemplars.* Wellington, New Zealand: Learning Media Education.

Montessori, M. (1912/1965). *The Montessori method.* New York, NY: Schocken.

Moss, G. (2003). Putting the text back into practice: Junior age non-fiction as objects of design. In C. Jewitt & G. Kress (Eds.), *Multimodal literacy* (pp. 73–87). New York, NY: Peter Lang.

Moss, P. (2009). *There are alternatives! Markets and democratic experimentalism in early childhood education and care.* The Hague, the Netherlands: Bernard Van Leer Foundation.

Oh, M. (2009). Contextualizing the watch episode of Laura: Its significance to Korean educators. In C. Edwards & C. Rinaldi (Eds.), *The diary of Laura: Perspectives on a Reggio Emilia diary* (pp. 97–106). St. Paul, MN: Redleaf Press.

Olsson, L.M. (2009). *Movement and experimentation in young children's learning: Deleuze and Guattari in early childhood education.* New York, NY: Routledge.

Orr, A.M., & Olson, M. (2007). Transforming narrative encounters. *Canadian Journal of Education, 30*(3), 819–838.

Pacini-Ketchabaw, V. (2010). Introduction. In V. Pacini-Ketchabaw (Ed.), *Flows, rhythms and intensities of early childhood education curriculum* (pp. ix–xviii). New York, NY: Peter Lang.

Pacini-Ketchabaw, V., & S checter, S. (2002). Engaging the discourse of diversity: Educators' frameworks for working with linguistic and cultural difference. *Contemporary Issues in Early Childhood, 2*(3), 400–414.

Penn, H. (2005). *Unequal childhoods: Young children's lives in poor countries*. New York, NY: Routledge.

Pinar, W., Reynolds, W., Slattery, P., & Taubman, P. (1995).Understanding curriculum: A postscript for the next generation. In W. Pinar, W. Reynolds, P. Slattery, & P. Taubman (Eds.), *Understanding curriculum* (pp. 847–868). New York, NY: Peter Lang.

Polakow, V. (1992).*The erosion of childhood*. Chicago, IL: University of Chicago Press.

Ramsey, P. (2004). *Teaching and learning in a diverse world: Multicultural education for young children*. New York, NY: Teachers College Press.

Rifkin, J. (1987). *Time wars: The primary conflict in human history*. New York, NY: Henry Holt.

Rinaldi, C. (1993). The emergent curriculum and social constructivism. In C. Edwards, L. Gandini, & G. Forman (Eds.), *The hundred languages of children: The Reggio Emilia approach to early childhood education* (pp. 101–111). Norwood, NJ: Ablex.

Rinaldi, C. (2006). *In dialogue with Reggio Emilia: Listening, researching and learning*. New York, NY: Routledge.

Rose, S., & Whitty, P. (2010a).*Communication and literacies*. Fredericton: University of New Brunswick Early Childhood Centre.

Rose, S., & Whitty, P. (2010b). "Where do we find the time to do this?" Struggling against the tyranny of time. *Alberta Journal of Educational Research, 56*(3), 257–273.

Tobin, J. (1997). *Making a place for pleasure in early education*. New Haven, CT: Yale University Press.

Wien, C.A. (1996). Time, work, and developmentally appropriate practice. *Early Childhood Research Quarterly,11,* 377–403.

Wien, C.A. (2004).*From policing to participation: Overturning the rules and creating amiable classrooms*. Washington, DC: National Association for the Education of Young Children. Retrieved from http://www.fcs.utah.edu/info/cfdc/5170/PolicingToParticipation.pdf

Wien, C.A., & Kirby-Smith, S. (1998). Untiming the curriculum: A case study of removing clocks from the program. *Young Children, 53*(5), 8–13.

Chapter Four

Addressing Divides and Binaries in Early Childhood Education

Disability, Discourse and Theory, and Practice in a Bachelor of Education Program

Luigi Iannacci & Bente Graham

This chapter explores understandings that teacher candidates had about young children with special needs or a learning disability prior to, during, and after a special education–focused course and a tutoring practicum they were required to complete as part of their bachelor of education degree. Discourses that informed their understandings are examined in order to critically assess theory/practice gaps in a teacher education context as they relate to disability, and to develop future special education curricula that destabilizes dominant and problematic discourses about disability.

Reconceptualist approaches to the professional development of early childhood educators stress the importance of deconstructing the ways in which dominant discourses shape student–teacher interactions in order to prevent the reinscription and furthering of inequitable and coercive relations of power (Cummins, 2001). This is a critical project that "invokes a tradition of curricular theorizing that sees as its goal the social transformation and reconstruction of educational institutions such as ECE [early childhood education]" (Iannacci & Whitty, 2009, p. 22). Reconceptualization is especially necessary at this point in time in ECE as the "hunt for disability" (Baker, 2002) and the fallout from this hunt have led to the "proliferation of categories of educational disability" (p. 676) and a subsequent significant increase in the number of young children assigned a "disability label at an earlier age than in the past" (p. 678). The "hunt" has been propelled by dominant discourses about disability that have shaped how practicing teachers relate to and teach young children with special needs[1] or a learning disability (Heydon & Iannacci, 2008). These "relations of ruling" (Smith, 1987, p. 3) have reinforced a disabled/abled binary and processes of pathologizing that manifest in limited and confining instructional practices and identity options (Cummins, 2005) being made available to these children (Heydon & Iannacci, 2008). This has specifically been demonstrated by a pedagogical determinism present in ECE, which has meant that learners with special needs or a learning disability are often assigned and resigned to fragmented, rote-oriented, context-reduced curricula (Barone, 2002; Delpit, 2003; Iannacci, 2008). Limited understandings of disability have also resulted in societies' denial of literacy and personhood for people perceived as disabled (Kliewer, Biklen, & Kasa-Hendrickson, 2006). Essentially these processes, confinements, and practices necessitate disruption and raise questions that require a critical examination of what prevents and is involved in fostering links between and blurring what has been deemed the "theory/practice divide in Early Childhood Education" (Lenz Taguchi, 2009) as it relates to understanding and responding to children who have special needs or a learning disability within ECE.

This chapter specifically explores teacher candidates' dominant understandings and constructions of children with special needs or a learning disability before and after they complete a bachelor of education (B.Ed.) degree that certifies them to teach in early and later childhood learning contexts (kindergarten–grade 6). The intention of this exploration is to identify how dominant discourses and notions shape teacher candidates' initial understandings of children with special needs or a learning disability. It also looks at the specific impact of a "special education"[2] course they take during their B.Ed. that is informed by critical disability theory and designed to aid them in supporting these learners during a tutoring practicum[3] in which they participate while taking the course. The purpose of this

1   Children who have not been formally identified as learning disabled but have been characterized in schools and in the education literature as "at-risk," "struggling readers," "non-readers," "reluctant readers," "cognitively, linguistically, culturally deprived," or "disadvantaged," etc. (McDermott & Varenne, 1995). As some of the learners the teacher candidates worked with had not been (and may never be) formally identified, the term "special needs" is used within this study to identify and distinguish these learners.

2   This was not the official name of the course. According to the Ontario Ministry of Education and Training's website: "Students who have behavioural, communicational, intellectual, physical or multiple exceptionalities, may require special education programs and/or services to benefit fully from their school experience. Special education programs and services primarily consist of instruction and assessments that are different from those provided to the general student population. These may take the form of accommodations (such as specific teaching strategies, preferential seating, and assistive technology) and/or an educational program that is modified from the age-appropriate grade level expectations in a particular course or subject, as outlined in the Ministry of Education's curriculum policy documents." Although this is a dominant understanding of special education, we believe that the special education curriculum/regular education divide, which has not been recognized by curriculum studies, is problematic. However, "special education" is a recognizable and identifiable area to readers, so we use "special education" to indicate our own course and practice that attempts to destabilize some of the problematic constructs, processes, and pedagogy associated with current understandings of special education.

3   The literacy tutoring practicum is an eleven-week placement aligned with the special education course. Teacher candidates have two hours a week of class and are required to tutor two students individually for

examination is to generate future curricula that provide teacher candidates with opportunities to address and blur the gap between theory and practice through a critical deconstruction and disruption of dominant and inequitable notions and practices as they relate to children with special needs or a learning disability. The questions we focus on in this chapter are as follows:

- What initial understandings do teacher candidates have about young children with special needs or a learning disability prior to beginning their B.Ed. program, a special education–focused course, and tutoring practicum that they are required to complete?

- What discourses inform these understandings?

- What is the impact of the course and the tutoring practicum aligned with the course on teacher candidates' understandings of children with special needs or a learning disability in relation to their initial understandings? How (if at all) has their thinking shifted?

- How can these understandings inform future special education curricula?

These questions are pursued with the hope that destabilizing dominant notions of disability allows teacher candidates to reevaluate and further develop their understandings and pedagogical orientations about children with special needs or a learning disability. Further, it is hoped that the process will reveal what curricular work needs to be done to further the above-mentioned goal. Answering these questions, informed by an understanding of disability as socially constructed, has been recognized as a goal for researchers and activists working within critical disability studies to pursue.

> Disability is politicized. While individual, medical, and deficit models continue to dominate thinking *about* disabled people, critical disability studies calls for counter-hegemony *with* disabled people. Alternative discourses. A reassessment of the dialectical split of (impaired) body/mind in society. . . . Clearly, then, an engagement with pedagogy involves a deconstruction of disabling pedagogies or pedagogies of exclusion. (Goodley, 2007, p. 319)

Unfortunately, these goals, aims, and foci have been neglected within educational research and practice and absent from the "discourses of critical pedagogy" (Gabel, 2002, as cited in Goodley, 2007, p. 318) as well. This chapter contributes to

---

forty-five minutes a session twice a week. They are therefore in schools two half days a week from September through December. The course is designed to assist teacher candidates in planning and implementing literacy instruction for students with special needs or a learning disability.

the growing body of reconceptualist-oriented literature that is beginning to work at destabilizing the monolith of disability as it appears in and is significant to educational contexts such as ECE.

Background/Context

Heydon and Iannacci (2008) have demonstrated how very few inroads have been made within the field of curriculum studies insofar as examining constructions of disability and children deemed disabled. They conducted a content analysis of ten years of issues of four prominent, peer-reviewed, international curriculum studies' journals and found that the journals merely included between one and five articles that directly and/or peripherally referred to issues of disability or to curriculum for disabled students. This minimal attention or exclusion "has meant that there are limited spaces in education that trouble what it means to be able or disabled or that question the curricula of disabled students" (p. 48). The field has therefore continued to support the special education–regular education binary that has led to unchallenged special education models and pedagogy.

A large-scale analysis of four major electronic databases searched using the term "reading disabilities" revealed similar gaps and absences and a view of learning disabilities as psychometric and biomedical in nature (Moffatt, 2006). There is a general dearth of work in the curriculum, critical pedagogy, and dis/ability fields that grapples with the social construction of disability, and the symbolic complex: a constellation of terms, concepts, practices (Danforth, 2009), and cultural analysis (McDermott & Varenne, 1995) required to fully consider issues related to disability within the context of ECE. Such thinking is at the preliminary stage of informing these fields as a result of the influence of reconceptualist perspectives that draw on a variety of perspectives including critical disability studies to form a theoretical pastiche intended to destabilize dominant discourses. However, the need for further work in this area is great considering the increasing number of young children in schools deemed disabled occurring internationally (Baker, 2002).

The "swarming effect"—the name that Baker (2002) gave "the hunt for and diagnosis of disability as a negative ontology that schools actively seek to name" (p. 679)—necessitates that research pay attention to how young children's ascribed disability labels are conceptualized, provided for, and understood as curriculum, relationships, and pedagogy have been primary factors in framing the ways that these students have been constructed and positioned within ECE (Triplett, 2007). As Heydon and Iannacci (2008) have pointed out, questions of disability are prerequisites for all educational conversations. Perspectives from critical disability theory are therefore helpful to draw on in reconceptualizing thinking about disability; what to teach or how to teach can never be adequately addressed without an understanding of who students are.

Theoretical Framing

As previously mentioned, this study and the special education course that participants took as they tutored students are theoretically informed by critical disability theory, which is situated within a postmodern paradigm. This paradigm has forwarded the notion that identities are socially constructed. Research from critical disability studies has specifically been concerned with interrogating the language used in relation to those identified as disabled and in the context of disability. This interrogation examines the impact of normative discourses (e.g., able/disabled binaries) and the ways in which these binaries reproduce/evoke/draw on other discourses (Pothier & Devlin, 2006). As such, disabilities are conceptualized as something created from what we as a society do, what we consider worthy of doing, and therefore "approached best as a cultural fabrication" (McDermott & Varenne, 1995, p. 323) rather than something inherent within people. Padden and Humphries (1988) argue that "being able or unable . . . does not emerge as significant in itself; instead it takes on significance in the context of other sets of meaning to which the child has been exposed" (as cited in McDermott & Varenne, 1995, p. 325). Thomas (2004) further explains, "Disability is a form of social oppression involving the social imposition of restrictions of activity on people with impairments and the socially engendered undermining of their psycho-emotional wellbeing" (p. 580). In short, "disabilities are less the property of persons than they are moments in a cultural focus" (McDermott & Varenne, 1995, p. 323). In terms of educational contexts, it stands to reason that "no student can have LD [learning disabilities] on his or her own. It takes a complex system of interactions performed in just the right way, at the right time, on the stage we call school" (Dudley-Marling, 2004, p. 489).

This repositioning of disability as a consequence of social/institutional rather than individual deficits has resulted in reconceptualized approaches to children with special needs or a learning disability within the context of ECE. These approaches have begun to forward asset-oriented (Heydon & Iannacci, 2008) ways of seeing and responding to these children and have rejected dominant deficit and "at-risk" discourses as they are committed to positioning children as "at-promise" (Swadener & Lubeck, 1995). An asset-oriented approach recognizes and builds on children's "funds of knowledge" (Moll, 1992) and views them as able, in possession of literacies and social, cognitive, artistic, emotional, cultural, linguistic, affective, epistemological resources rather than as deficient and lacking literacy. This approach is aware of the fact that "how students are discursively constructed has material effects" (Paugh & Dudley-Marling, 2011, p. 7). As such, language assigned to children with special needs or a learning disability (and the ways in which this language compromises their personhood and reifies and centers their identities in relation to their defined and measured deficiencies in learning contexts such as ECE) is a central concern of an asset-oriented approach.

Curricula informed by these theoretical perspectives and approaches were present within the special education course that teacher candidates participating in this study took. Prior to beginning this course and their B.Ed. (they began both at the same time), they were given a survey that accessed their initial knowledge of children with special needs or a learning disability. The course then provided them with opportunities to reevaluate these initial understandings as they examined case studies in order to identify and respond to assets that children possessed and discuss how and why these children have been positioned and read as deficient. Further, teacher candidates explored the history of special education and the dominant discourses that have shaped how disability has been conceptualized and how people with learning disabilities have been understood and provided for over time.

Throughout the course, teacher candidates were given opportunities to identify current agencies, texts, discourses, institutions, and processes that shape who is understood to be learning disabled and how they are constructed as a result of the factors they identify. Teacher candidates were also exposed to many documents and other forms of information that frame children with learning disabilities in limited and limiting ways (informed by medical and psychometric perspectives). Teacher candidates were asked to examine these constructions critically as they researched a variety of disabilities. One of the most important and continuous tasks that teacher candidates engaged in was assessing the learners assigned to them (usually grade 2 and 3 students, a few in grade 1) in ways that identified their assets and capitalized on these assets as they planned individualized literacy-focused sessions for these learners. Throughout the course teacher candidates also examined the variety of semiotic forms learners use to create and understand texts and their surroundings. These texts were discussed in relation to the texts that schools privilege and sanction in terms of knowledge demonstration (e.g., print texts).

Methodology and Design

Methodologically, the study is informed by critical discourse analysis (CDA) and focused on providing a deconstructive reading and interpretation of the way that social power, dominance, and inequity are enacted, reproduced, and resisted by text and talk in social/political contexts (Van Dijk, 2001). CDA is commensurate with the theoretical approach of the study as language use is understood and positioned as a social action; as situated performance; and as tied to social relations and identities, power, inequity, and social struggles. CDA acts as an inroad into understanding social phenomena (Slembrouck, 2007), which in the case of this study means providing insights into the social phenomenon known as disability. Importantly, discourse (much like text) is not confined to one semiotic form and, as such, is not only a way of talking and writing, but a way of thinking and acting. Discourse is

> embedded in the worldview of particular social groups and is therefore tied to a set of values and norms. As people apprentice into new social practices, they become complicit with this set of values and norms, this worldview. (Gee, 1990, p. X)

The discourse specifically being analyzed, and thus the social phenomena being critically examined in this chapter, focuses on teacher candidates' initial understandings (collected prior to beginning the B.Ed. and the course discussed in this chapter) and subsequent understandings (collected after the course as well as after most of the B.Ed. degree had been completed) of students with special needs or a learning disability.

Again, the first form of data that teacher candidates completed prior to commencing their B.Ed. program and the special education–focused course was an online survey. The survey accessed their initial background knowledge regarding students with special needs or a learning disability. Once research participants completed the course and the tutoring program described above, they were asked to complete a similar online survey that asked them once again to articulate their understandings about students with special needs or a learning disability. Only surveys by teacher candidates who agreed to participate in this study were collected and analyzed. Analysis of these data took place ten months after they had graduated.

Three months after participants completed their course work and fulfilled most of the practicum requirements of the B.Ed., they attended a focus group session in which they were asked the following:

- What do you now understand about children with special needs or children with a learning disability?

- What impact did the course have on your understanding of children with special needs or a learning disability?

- Provide an example from your tutoring placement or a personal learning experience that informed your understandings about children with special needs or a learning disability (e.g., a moment or interaction that either furthered or consolidated your learning or led to an asset-oriented way of thinking about these children)?

Essentially, teacher candidates were given an opportunity to share narratives from their tutoring placement, classroom placements, and/or personal learning experiences from the course that spoke to their understandings about children with special needs or a learning disability. Again, researchers began to analyze these data ten months after participants had graduated.

When both sets of surveys and audiotaped focus group conversations were analyzed they were triangulated in order to identify recurring and central themes and dominant discourses present within the data. Once these themes and discourses were identified, they were reexamined in order to ensure that inconsistencies and contradictions were apparent rather than being concealed. Triangulation, therefore, not only served to compare information to determine corroboration and further a process of cross-validation (Oliver-Hoyo & Allen, 2006), but also to make explicit complexities within data (i.e., competing and contradictory discourses). Data were then analyzed in relation to larger social contexts (i.e., contextualizing or "nesting") (Clandinin & Connelly, 2000) by looking at various macro factors in relation to initial teacher candidates' understandings of students with special needs or a learning disability. This level of analysis revealed factors that facilitated and constrained how influential course theory was in informing teacher candidates' understandings and practices in relation to students with special needs or a learning disability as well as what curricular changes needed to be made to the course to further address and coalesce theory/practice gaps.

Participants

Of the 240 teacher candidates enrolled in the Primary/Junior B.Ed. program during the year this study was conducted, 61 (49 female, 12 male) agreed to participate (a 25% participation rate) by signing a consent form that was attached to a letter given to them during an initial information session in August. Teacher candidates took the form and letter away with them in order to reread the information and contemplate participation and then submitted their forms to their instructors during subsequent classes. Not all of the course instructors were researchers[4] and the form allowed teacher candidates to indicate whether they were or were not willing to be involved in the study in order to avoid any public pressure to agree to participate. Consent forms were submitted by mid-September to give teacher candidates time to make an informed decision about participation. Almost all of the nonparticipants simply did not return forms. As the participants were enrolled in a consecutive B.Ed. program, they had already achieved an undergraduate (usually honors) degree as this is an admission requirement to the program, and had accomplished academic records as admission is capped at 150 (despite there being 1,000 applicants who seek entrance into the program).

---

4 Within this chapter "researchers" refers only to Luigi Iannacci and Bente Graham. The study did not employ research assistants.

Further, acceptance into the B.Ed. is contingent on a strong background that requires applicants to describe their experiences (volunteer or otherwise) and how these relate to teaching. It is therefore not surprising that teacher candidates enrolled in the program and who agreed to participate in this study are generally in their late twenties. The study received university ethics approval and is in full accordance with the *TriCouncil Policy Statement* regarding research ethics. Every effort was made to foster collaborative power relations and ensure that results and participation were not biased. For example, several measures were used to ensure that participants understood that they had complete freedom to decline participation. During the information session, it was made clear that the project was by no means mandatory and that not participating would have no effect on grades. Further, teacher candidates were clearly told orally and in writing that data generated from the study would be given to a researcher who was not their instructor and that he or she would then assign a pseudonym to each participant so that their identities would be completely protected. Focus groups were also organized so that they were conducted by a researcher who was not the teacher candidates' course instructor. Once again, this instructor assigned participants' pseudonyms during survey data collection, organization, and analysis. Focus group sessions took place after the course had ended and final grades had been submitted. Focus group data were given to an independent transcriber who did not know the participants and had no affiliation with the B.Ed. program. Formal data analysis began ten months after teacher candidates had graduated from the program.

As previously mentioned, teacher candidates involved in this study completed a practicum placement that required them to tutor two students who had special needs or a learning disability as they took a course grounded in critical disability theory. This was designed to provide them with continuous opportunities to apply and make sense of theory and practice explored in the course. Participating schools nominated young children from grade 1 to grade 3 to participate in the tutoring program and acquired parents'/guardians' permission in order for their children to take part.

Findings

Preliminary Survey
The survey that teacher candidates completed prior to beginning the B.Ed. program revealed print- and decoding-centric conceptualizations of literacy. Many teacher candidates specifically wrote about reading as being about sounding out words and decoding print. This is significant, as a learning disability was often conceptualized as synonymous with print literacy decoding difficulties and deficits. Children who had special needs or a learning disability were synonymously understood as having difficulty with phonics and poor phonological awareness.

The dominant view of a learning disability was deficit oriented and conflated with attention deficit hyperactive disorder (ADHD), attention deficit disorder (ADD), and dyslexia and also attributed to English as a second language (ESL) learners. Teacher candidates often used words such as "delayed," "challenged," and "at risk" to describe learners who had special needs or in reference to a learning disability. A learning disability was also frequently defined as a disorder, an obstacle, an impairment, and an inability. Further, it was understood to be the result of (in descending order) physical, neurological, biological, genetic, motivational, behavioral, emotional, familial, social, and economic factors. When familial factors were mentioned as something that resulted in a learning disability, they included (in descending order) the amount of reading supported and encouraged at home, changes in family life such as divorce or new living arrangements, emotionally abusive parents, a child having witnessed a traumatic event, abusive family relationships, and last (albeit very infrequently) poverty/hunger. A learning disability was also understood as being about a child's slower pace in learning things and poor performance compared to the norm. The norm was often characterized as being the rest of the children of the same age and grade.

The support that teacher candidates anticipated having to provide learners with special needs or a learning disability focused on instructional responses that were quantitatively focused. Children with special needs or a learning disability were understood as being in need of more of everything, which included the following: more time, more one-to-one instruction, more attention, more support, and more instruction from the teacher. Teacher candidates' anticipated instructional responses also focused on the affective qualities of the teacher. They often cited the need for teachers to be patient, to be positive, to encourage, to go above and beyond, and to be committed to helping children with special needs or a learning disability succeed.

Final Survey
The survey that teacher candidates completed at the end of the special education–focused course after the tutoring and two-thirds of their classroom practicum placements were completed revealed different conceptualizations of literacy that were now meaning-making focused. Teacher candidates understood that meaning making involved a variety of resources to which the students had recourse. These were often defined as a variety of cueing systems (e.g., semantic, syntactic, critical, graphophonemic, pragmatic) that students used when reading texts. Texts were no longer exclusively print in nature, but recognized and understood as being beyond written formats (i.e., not just about books). This is significant to their understandings of what having a disability means because teacher candidates no longer characterized a learning disability as synonymous with print literacy decoding difficulties and deficits as they had in the first survey. A learning disability was

often conceptualized as a "learning difference" as opposed to a difficulty with phonics and poor phonological awareness. However, deficit-oriented language taken from the *Ontario Curriculum Unit Planner* (OCUP): *Special Education Companion* (Ontario Ministry of Education, 2002) that defined a variety of exceptionalities was often used to qualify statements. As such, the learning difference that teacher candidates referred to was still defined as an impairment, a deficit, and/or a disorder. The contradictory conceptualization and language regarding disability were further pronounced in the survey as, interestingly, asset-oriented perspectives were more present. Teacher candidates were more aware of students' funds of knowledge than they had been in the first survey, but often named assets as strengths that were primarily cognitive in nature (e.g., reading strategies). The understanding of a learning disability as synonymous with ADHD, ADD, and dyslexia and being attributed to ESL learners was significantly less prevalent.

Although a learning disability was now being understood as multifaceted and about different ways of learning, teacher candidates named the same factors when they mentioned reasons for the existence of a learning disability. These factors also follow the same order of dominance found in the first survey. As such, physical and neurological bases for having a learning disability were cited most often. The understanding that a learning disability is about learning at a slower pace was not as prevalent as it was in the first survey. However, teacher candidates were more apt to focus on discussing a learning disability in comparison with norms that were linked to the Ministry of Ontario's grade level curriculum expectations; school board–mandated evaluations such as a commercially prepared and mass-purchased reading running-record system that defined what levels of student achievement are normal for each grade; and standardized, province-wide testing as required by an "arm's-length agency of the provincial government" within Ontario known as the Education Quality Accountability Office (EQAO).

Teacher candidates no longer focused on quantity of instruction as it related to supporting children with special needs or a learning disability, but rather on the quality and nature of instruction insofar as it is able to capitalize on learners' assets. They demonstrated this by specifically discussing the need to address various modes that students have access to when learning and providing them with individualized accommodations to allow them to use these modes to demonstrate knowledge. However, as in the first survey, there was very little engagement with the social construction of disability, as a learning disability remained something that was identifiable in relation to norms.

Focus Groups
Audiotaped interviews with focus groups conducted three months after the course and most of the teacher candidates' practicum placements had ended revealed the overarching theme that was present in both the first and second survey, namely,

limited engagement with the social construction of disability. Teacher candidates continued to conceptualize a learning disability as a learning difference, but beyond this, their responses tended to focus on instructional strategies. When cued and prompted about the nature of a learning disability, they often defaulted to focusing on physical, cognitive, and genetic factors that they felt determined a learning disability.

Teacher candidates were asked questions during the focus group sessions that required them to address what they understood about children with special needs or a learning disability. However, even after taking the special needs–focused course teacher candidates' responses were most often not about the students but rather about what they did and what the teaching profession and school system does/can do to what some of them referred to as "fix" students. Their responses regarding students fell into three categories. Focusing on deficits was most often cited within responses that addressed a learner or learners whom teacher candidates encountered. The following example is indicative of this focus:

> My first classroom only had two kids that were identified and had difficulties, and the rest of the kids were pretty good. Then I went to a grade 6 classroom where they were *everywhere*. Like everybody needed something . . . this class had a lot of behavioral issues.

Some of the responses attempted to identify a child's assets. This was often demonstrated as teacher candidates discussed their practicum placement experiences:

> My first placement was in a grade three 3 classroom and there was only a few special needs, but this one student who had a learning disability and it was processing information I think. He was doing a test and I was scribing for him and I suddenly realized that he knew *everything*. He couldn't write it down and he needed someone to write it and I was just blown away. And I was like, "this is what a learning disability is." Like he had the information and he just couldn't get it out on paper. And that was a really big moment to see what it really is.

The rest and majority of the responses focused on what teacher candidates did instructionally, but it was not always clear how this instruction was responsive to an asset that they may have previously identified. The following quote demonstrates this unclear connection and also how teacher candidates' responses were sometimes structured in ways that combined the previous two types of responses as they began by focusing on deficits, then attempted to identity an asset before an unclear instructional connection to an asset was discussed.

> One of the girls I was tutoring, she had a lot of trouble at first. Working with her the first day, she told me she hated reading. She didn't want to do anything. You know it took a while to hook her into . . . she was *very* fidgety and would move around a lot. She liked humor a lot. . . . I would make some cards and

we would walk around the school and I would be like, "find the card, then read them to me." . . . I don't know what you call it . . . hide the thing around the school [scavenger hunt].

Although humor is identified as an asset that the teacher candidate student possessed, it is not clear how a scavenger hunt instructionally responded to or was used to capitalize on the learner's asset.

When on occasion teacher candidates critically contemplated a learning disability, they quickly defaulted toward institutional discourses and redirected their responses toward the Ontario Ministry of Education's definition of learning disability. The following interaction between four teacher candidates during one of the focus group sessions demonstrates how this default option prevented discussion from pursuing critical interrogations of the nature of disability.

> Francesca:[5] A learning disability according to who or to what? What is the standard of people that don't have a learning disability?
> Sue: Yeah.
> Margaret: That's why I use the words traditional learner . . .
> Sue: Yeah, yeah.
> Margaret: And I don't like, "Sit at your desk, be quiet, write on your sheet," type thing like, "Read that" and I don't know, that's to me the traditional . . .
> Sue: Uh huh.
> Margaret: type and I think more and more I don't think most kids learn that way, at all. I know I didn't. I hated doing it. I think I coped. I got through it but I didn't learn as if I was doing it. I don't know, I'm getting off topic. . . .
> Jeff: I'm confused about the Ministry category. I don't know that I know what the definition is. What the Ministry . . .
> Sue: Yeah. I don't think . . .
> Jeff: definition, says the definition is.
> Sue: I don't think I know it either.
> Francesca: I know what I think it is now. I mean I have a general idea but if someone wants the Ministry definition I would have to go to the book [*OCUP: Special Education Companion*, 2002] . . .
> Sue: Yeah.
> Francesca: and find it out. I don't know the Ministry definition.

During the focus groups it also became clear that institutional discourses mediated the degree to which theory became manifest in practice. Practices that accommodated learners, for example, were viewed suspiciously as a result of misunderstandings and misnomers about ministry and school board policies, practices, protocols, and procedures regarding disability and the *Individual Educational Plan (IEP)* (Ontario Ministry of Education, 2004). Just prior to the conversation in the following transcript, Sarita, a teacher candidate, mentioned that one of her students would benefit from using a calculator. She explained

---
5   All names are pseudonyms.

that the student could successfully complete problem-solving questions on a test but would spend so much time on each question that she couldn't complete the test. Although she would forget computational procedures, she understood which computations were necessary for solving the problem. The teacher candidate wanted to provide this student with a calculator, but questioned whether it was appropriate to do so.

> Sarita: I asked the teacher, but she said unless she's on an IEP I can't give her one because she's not on an IEP and she said, . . . "If you are on an IEP. There are a couple of students that are, and they *can* use calculators. But she's *not* on one." So she said that she can't have one.

Throughout the focus groups there was much discussion about how schools where the teacher candidates were placed during their practicum were focused on improving students' abilities to infer (a skill that comes up frequently in reference to the EQAO literacy test that children are required to complete in grades 3 and 6 in Ontario). In speaking about this focus on inferring, teacher candidates raised concerns regarding the amount of importance placed on demonstrating inferences through writing.

> Tasha: I find a lot of school was really focused on inferring. And in most classes that I was in, the students could do it verbally extremely well, but when it came to writing it was a huge challenge. I know probably it's just practice and practice. It was interesting when I was in the placement to note. I felt like everyone kept saying [to students], "You know you do it verbally really well, but we need you to practice the writing element of inferring." Like them being able to *write* down their inferences. You shouldn't have to be like that right? It shouldn't have to be.

Discussion

Tensions in the data between competing and contradictory discourses and critical engagement with the construct of disability speak to the complexity of addressing the theory/practice divide within programs designed to prepare and accredit teachers to work in early childhood education classrooms. This complexity extends well beyond notions of the divide that conceptualize theory/practice as a binary. For example,

> the theory-practice connection is no better served than when it is lived. . . . Our challenge is to create a community that educates all of us, those in the university and those in the schools, a community that expands our relationships with one another and, in so doing, our knowledge and our effectiveness. (Lieberman, 1992, p. 11, as cited in Pinar, Reynolds, Slattery, & Taubman, 1995, p. 790)

This binary, which assigns geographic positions to where theory and practice are located, is insufficient in recognizing how a variety of discourses mediate the divide and, therefore, the ways in which power influences how, when, and why theory/practice is lived, subjugated, perpetuated, and controlled. Conceptualizations of disability expressed by teacher candidates in the first survey and reiterated by them in the second survey and focus groups, for example, reflect dominant discourse about disability that locates disability within persons deemed disabled. This idea has historical roots in the field of learning disabilities, as it has constructed childhood learning difficulties as "expressions of faulty internal psychology and/or neurology" (Danforth, 2009, p. 19). As evidenced by the data in our study, these notions continue to prevail even when critically interrogated within the scope of a course designed to encourage this interrogation.

Some of the factors that perpetuate this discourse can be explained by the prevalence of these ideas in information aimed at teachers (both pre-service and experienced). A key example is the *OCUP: Special Education Companion* (Ontario Ministry of Education, 2002) that teacher candidates used throughout the year. Although their course work prepared them to critically interrogate the discourse embedded in this document, its official status and power as a text defining disability made it a reference point for them, particularly when they experienced the uncertainty that comes with critically contemplating and destabilizing notions of disability. This was most apparent in the interaction between Francesca, Sue, Margaret, and Jeff.

As teacher candidates researched exceptionalities, they also accessed a variety of special education texts. Again, although they were provided with several opportunities to critically examine notions that conceptualized disability from a medical, psychometric, and deficit orientation, the majority of these special education texts are informed by these perspectives. Research and theory coming from educational psychology available to teachers remain steeped in traditions and notions that inadequately theorize disability and problematically position people with disabilities as deficient in their ability to meet norms. The limited understandings of disability present in this literature continue to dominate theory and practice as they relate to ECE and children with special needs or a learning disability. Theory is clearly shown *not* to be value free, inherently good, and something that can be transferred from one site to another in the interest of expanding knowledge and effectiveness.

Ultimately, contextualizing what a learning disability is and who children with special needs or a learning disability are is missing from the learning disabilities field. As Moffatt's (2006) findings demonstrated at the beginning of this chapter, it has also been missing from educational research in general as it too has constructed learning disabilities as predominantly psychometric and biomedical in nature. Further, as stated above, Heydon and Iannacci (2008) pointed out that the curriculum studies field has been remiss in addressing disability.

Perspectives that contextualize and destabilize the notion of disability continue to have marginal status and visibility within the field of education. The lack of attention placed on child poverty, for example, as a factor that contributes to who is deemed disabled and why disability presents itself received inconsequential attention in both of the surveys and educational research concerning disability. This is occurring at a time when "over one million Canadian children live in unsafe housing, face hunger or poor health, and have limited opportunities" (Ferguson, 2007, p. 2). Instead, what remains is an understanding of disability as something innate that presents itself when deviations from culturally bound so-called normal abilities that are psychological, neurological, and measurable occur. This tautology, with its circular and flawed logic, will be destabilized only when the complex cultural analysis reviewed above becomes part of our understandings of disability.

Another level of power relations was operating in the maintenance of dominant views of disability. As was clear in the situation described by Sarita, above, disability is constructed and recognized within official documents and by policy. The use of teaching and learning aids such as calculators is viewed as a form of cheating if such aids are made available to those who have not been documented as being in need or disabled. This furthers the positioning of instructional responsiveness toward students with special needs or a learning disability as subordinate to "normal," as opposed to a way of enabling students to demonstrate knowledge in ways that are respectful of and responsive to the various processes, modes, and semiotic forms that students engage in to demonstrate knowledge. This sense of what are privileged and sanctioned ways of demonstrating knowledge was also evident in the limited ways that children were expected to demonstrate their ability to develop inferences, as noted by teacher candidate Tasha. This may help to explain why teacher candidates were able to be much more asset oriented in their discourse within the second survey and the focus groups, but tended to focus on and privilege assets that were cognitive in nature.

Although these messages were being communicated to teacher candidates by associate teachers,[6] it is essential to note that these practices and notions are not inherently located within associate teachers. They too receive strong messages about who is disabled, what they are "allowed," what knowledge is valued, and what modes are privileged in demonstrating knowledge. Practices and discourses used by associate teachers are, however, often replicated by teacher candidates, who understand that their success in the placement depends in large part on the associate teachers' evaluation. These power dynamics also contribute to how dominant discourses and problematic practices regarding disability are reproduced.

---

6   Classroom teachers that teacher candidates worked with during their practicum.

In analyzing teacher candidates' notions of disability, we began to take a more focused look at and question our own practices, course content, assignments, and curricula designed to help teacher candidates develop a critical understanding of disability and to respond to students with special needs or a learning disability. What we discovered was that our own practice in relation to a major assignment that teacher candidates were expected to complete in the course both replicated dominant practices in the field of special education and notions of disability. Despite our focus on an asset-oriented approach, the assignment called for teacher candidates to research an exceptionality, to look at multiple definitions of the exceptionality, to critically discuss how differing definitions contribute to the idea that disability is socially constructed, to communicate the variance of the exceptionality, and to identify what assets students who have been identified with this exceptionality may bring to classrooms. Further, we asked that teacher candidates demonstrate environmental, instructional, and assessment accommodations that students identified with the specific exceptionality they were researching may require.

As we analyzed the data and the gaps inherent in the theory/practice we engaged in with teacher candidates, we discovered that this assignment contributed to rather than destabilized dominant notions of disability by ensuring that the teacher candidates' gaze was focused on a decontextualized definition of disability as opposed to what the disability means and its significance to a child. The abridged, reduced, static, two-dimensional, generic, reified, stereotyped, textbook depiction of a learning disabled child dominant in the field of learning disabilities and education (Danforth, 2009) was exactly what we were propagating through this assignment. To some teacher candidates' credit, they still managed to remain asset oriented and critically engage depictions of disability within the material they read and used for their presentations. However, without significantly revising this assignment, it would be impossible to expect teacher candidates to critically engage in the social construction of disability.

We have, therefore, redesigned the assignment so that teacher candidates are creating case studies that focus on a child who has a disability. As such, researching the disability is still important, but teacher candidates will critically assess and use the information to consider a variety of factors when writing their case study, which focuses on a child with the disability and so requires that they contextualize the child about whom they are writing. Teacher candidates will be specific about what this exceptionality looks like and means in relation to the child. From this information, they will determine what assets the child has and link programming and accommodations in ways that fully consider and capitalize on these factors and assets. The teacher candidates' gaze will remain on the child rather than on some obscure notion of his or her disability and reified identity.

Conclusion

Although this research project has contributed to our ability to address theory/practice gaps in our context, we know that this process and the knowledge it has produced are transferable to other teacher education contexts that also focus on developing future ECE teachers' understandings of disability and the knowledge of how to respond to children who have special needs or a learning disability. As stated throughout this chapter, we realize that these perspectives and approaches have yet to destabilize dominant discourses and beliefs about disability, but are beginning to be recognized. Interestingly, a study by Paugh and Dudley-Marling (2011) that was conducted during the same time frame as this study also revealed how difficult it was for novice teachers to "challenge the powerful discourse of schooling that situates school failure—and success—in students and their families" and to resist "the deficit language that dominates the discourse of school failure" (p. 13), despite the fact that over the course of a year these novice teachers participated in several biweekly inquiry group meetings designed to help them shift from a deficit to an asset-oriented gaze regarding students who struggle. Paugh and Dudley-Marling concluded that it was necessary for teacher education to "raise awareness about discourse, [and] help teachers to use such knowledge to assume positions of authority and provide tools for challenging, rather than defaulting to, deficit discourses surrounding learning diversity" (p. 14).

We also urge fellow teacher educators to engage in dialogue about the complex nature of disability and experiment with practices in their courses and programs that reconceptualize how it is constructed and responded to. Special education curricula for teacher candidates must be informed by and commensurate with sociocultural and critical disability perspectives in order to challenge, resist, and disrupt dominant and taken-for-granted discourses that have affected how children with special needs or a learning disability have been understood, positioned, and provided for in ECE. Considering the power dynamics and tensions that have been documented throughout this chapter, it is also imperative that these theoretical perspectives not remain the domain of one geographic location (i.e., the university). Limited and limiting notions of disability and their effect on children in ECE contexts and many other learning environments necessitate that faculties of education have far more influence in reconceptualizing ministry and school board policies, procedures, protocols, and curricula because it is the current gap between these worlds and the power relations it fosters and sustains that are by far the most profound and difficult to address.

References

Baker, B. (2002). The hunt for disability: The new eugenics and the normalization of school children. *Teachers College Record, 104*, 663–703.

Barone, D. (2002). Literacy teaching in two kindergarten classrooms in a school labeled at-risk. *The Elementary School Journal, 102*(5), 415–441.
Clandinin, J., & Connelly, M. (2000). *Narrative inquiry: Experience and story in qualitative research.* San Francisco, CA: Jossey-Bass.
Cummins, J. (2001). *Negotiating identities: Education for empowerment in a diverse society.* Covina, CA: California Association for Bilingual Education.
Cummins, J. (2005, April). *Diverse futures: Rethinking the image of the child in Canadian schools.* Paper presented at the Joan Pederson Distinguished Lecture Series, University of Western Ontario, London, ON.
Danforth, S. (2009). *The incomplete child: An intellectual history of learning disabilities.* New York, NY: Peter Lang.
Delpit, L. (2003). Educators as "seed people" growing a new future. *Educational Researcher, 32*(7), 14–21.
Dudley-Marling, C. (2004). The social construction of learning disabilities. *Journal of Learning Disabilities, 37*(6), 482–489.
Education Quality and Accountability Office (EQAO). (2008). *About EQAO.* Toronto, ON: Queen's Printer for Ontario. Retrieved from http://www.eqao.com/AboutEQAO/AboutEQAO.aspx?status=logout&Lang=E
Ferguson, C. (2007). Living below the poverty line: Canadian children in poverty (2007). World Vision Canada Programs. Retrieved from http://www.worldvision.ca/Programs-and-Projects/CanadiaPrograms/Documents/Living%20Below%20the%20Line.pdf.
Gee, J. P. (1990). *Social linguistics and literacies: Ideology in discourses.* London, England: Falmer Press.
Goodley, D. (2007). Towards socially just pedagogies: Deleuzoguattarian critical disability studies. *International Journal of Inclusive Education, 11*(3), 317–334.
Heydon, R., & Iannacci, L. (2006, May). Biomedical approaches to literacy: Two curriculum teachers challenge the treatment of dis/ability in contemporary early literacy education. *Language and Literacy* [Special print edition], 32–39.
Heydon, R., & Iannacci, L. (2008). *Early childhood curricula and the de-pathologizing of childhood.* Toronto, ON: University of Toronto Press.
Iannacci, L. (2008). The pathologizing of culturally and linguistically diverse students in early years classrooms. In R. Heydon & L. Iannacci, *Early childhood curricula and the de-pathologizing of childhood.* Toronto, ON: University of Toronto Press.
Iannacci, L. & Whitty, P. (Eds.) (2009). *Early childhood curricula: Reconceptualist perspectives.* Calgary, AB: Detselig Press.
Kliewer, C., Biklen, D., & Kasa-Hendrickson, C. (2006). Who may be literate? Disability and resistance to the cultural denial of competence. *American Educational Research Journal, 43*(2), 163–192.
Lankshear, C., & Knobel, M. (2003). *New literacies: Changing knowledge and classroom learning.* Buckingham, England: Open University Press.
Lenz Taguchi, H. L. (2009). *Going beyond the theory/practice divide in early childhood education: Introducing an intra-active pedagogy.* New York, NY: Routledge.
McDermott, R., & Varenne, H. (1995). Culture as disability. *Anthropology and Education Quarterly, 26*, 323–348.
Moffatt, L. (2006). *(Dis)abling readers: Discourses of literacy and learning in research on "reading disabilities" 2000–2005* (Unpublished dissertation comprehensive exam). University of British Columbia, Vancouver.
Moll, L. (1992). Funds of knowledge for teaching: Using a qualitative approach to connect homes and classrooms. *Theory Into Practice, 31*(2), 132–141.
Oliver-Hoyo, M., & Allen, D. D. (2006). The use of triangulation methods in qualitative educational research. *Journal of College Science Teaching, 35*(4), 42–48.

Ontario Ministry of Education. (2002). *Ontario curriculum unit planner: Special education companion.* Toronto, ON: Queen's Printer for Ontario. Retrieved from http://www.edu.gov.on.ca/eng/policyfunding/ocup/

Ontario Ministry of Education. (2004). *The individual education plan (IEP): A resource guide.* Toronto, ON: Queen's Printer for Ontario.

Ontario Ministry of Education. (2007). *Overview: An introduction to special education in Ontario.* Toronto, ON: Queen's Printer for Ontario. Retrieved from http://www.edu.gov.on.ca/eng/general/elemsec/speced/ontario.html

Paugh, P. C., & Dudley-Marling, C. (2011). "Speaking" deficit into (or out of) existence: How language constrains classroom teachers' knowledge about instructing diverse learners. *International Journal of Inclusive Education, 15*(8), 817-833.

Pinar, B., Reynolds, W. M., Slattery, P., & Taubman, P. M. (1995). *Understanding curriculum.* New York, NY: Peter Lang.

Pothier, D., & Devlin, R. (2006). Introduction: Toward a critical theory of dis-citizenship. In D. Pothier & R. Devlin (Eds.), *Critical disability theory: Essays in philosophy, politics, policy, and law* (pp.1–22). Vancouver: University of British Columbia Press.

Slembrouck, S. (2007). *What is meant by "discourse analysis"?* Retrieved from http://mark.degrassi.ca/papers/ma/discourse-analysis/dis26.htm

Smith, D. E. (1987). *The everyday world as problematic: A feminist sociology.* Hanover, NH: University Press of New England / Northeastern University Press.

Swadener, B. B., & Lubeck, S. (1995). (Eds.). *Children and families "at promise": Deconstructing the discourse of risk.* Albany, NY: SUNY Press.

Thomas, C. (2004). How is disability understood? An examination of sociological approaches. *Disability & Society, 19*(6), 569–583.

Titchosky, T. (2007). *Reading and writing disability differently.* Toronto, ON: University of Toronto Press.

Triplett, C. F. (2007). The social construction of "struggle": Influences of school literacy contexts, curriculum, and relationships. *Journal of Literacy Research, 39*(1), 95–126.

Van Dijk, T. A. (2001). Critical discourse analysis. In D. Tannen, D. Schiffrin, & H. Hamilton (Eds.), *Handbook of discourse analysis* (pp. 352–371). Oxford, England: Blackwell.

Chapter Five

An Early Childhood Professional's Authority

How Can It Be Used for Influencing and Instigating Action for Social Goods?

Rachel Langford

It is often stated that an early childhood educator should not "be an expert" and it does seem reasonable to say that early childhood educators should not use expertise to assume authority and power over others. Rather, authority should be shared with others who are disempowered through educational processes (Novinger, O'Brien, & Sweigman, 2005). Dahlberg, Moss, and Pence (2007) articulated this position in their description of pedagogical work:

> Such practice would not rely on "one best way" and the authority of the early childhood worker but would seek instead to bring multiple perspectives—of children, parents and others in the community—to the task of understanding or making meaning of pedagogical work with young children and engaging in on-going dialogue about what we want for our children. (p. 178)

Conversely, it is also reasonable to say that early childhood educators are both powerful and powerless. In this chapter, I explore this quandary of an early childhood educator's authority as a professional in the classroom and in society. Drawing on a range of feminist educational philosophers and critical pedagogy and early childhood theorists as well as postfoundational researchers focusing on authority and teacher identity formation (e.g., Applebaum, 1999; Dahlberg & Moss, 2005; Hanrahan & Antony, 2005; Luke, 1996; Maher, 2001; Moss, 2006; Munro, 1998; Ryan & Ochsner, 1999), I examine a traditional understanding of authority within the classroom and profession and its limitations. I then draw upon alternative understandings of authority that may make it possible for authority to be explicitly taken up and taken back by early childhood professionals as a legitimate teacher behavior. I propose that this authority can be used for influencing and instigating action for social goods. For the purposes of this chapter, social goods are understood to be what we want for children, families, early childhood educators, and our society. These social goods are collectively negotiated, renegotiated, defined, and redefined by multiple participants and in multiple sites at the local, state, and global levels. I contend that early childhood educators need authority to address three interrelated social goods: social equity in the classroom; sector professionalization that represents the interests of early childhood educators; and the provision of a comprehensive, accessible, and affordable early childhood care and education system. My general argument will be that a denial of an early childhood educator's authority in the classroom and beyond has "several potentially disabling consequences" (Luke, 1996, p. 284) for early childhood educators themselves and for the social changes envisioned by many of them.

There has been a long history of activism in the field of early childhood education (Cannella & Bloch, 2006). In the 1960s and 1970s, for example, feminist educators endorsed child-centred pedagogy as a liberal democratic initiative to bring equality into curriculum projects in classrooms. Since the 1960s, Canadian women's, labour, and child-care advocacy groups have fought for a national comprehensive and cohesive early childhood education and care (ECEC) system (Friendly & Prentice, 2009; Penn, 2010; Prentice, 2001). In 2011, Canada still lags significantly behind other countries in the provision of this system. Thus there is still much work to be done by advocates, including early childhood educators (Mahon, 2009). There has also been a long history in Canada of the marginalization of the early childhood education sector as a secondary labour market (Langford, 2010). The Canadian Child Care Human Resources Sector Council (2002) has called on early childhood educators to act on the problems of professional status and lack of respect in ECEC by becoming strong and vocal advocates.

Sector professionalization is currently being debated as a means of bringing early childhood educators the necessary symbolic (i.e., status and authority) and material rewards they need and deserve (Osgood, 2009; Urban, 2008, 2010). Professionalized occupations are distinguished by expertise, education and training, autonomy, values, power, reward, and status (Adams, 2010; Brock, 2006). Some scholars maintain that professionalism is important for the sector. Moss (2010), however, has wondered "what [it is] we gain by the focus on 'professionalism'" when the focus could be "on education and the educator; the purpose of the former and the requirements of the latter" (p. 17). I will argue in this chapter that in Canada, given the trend toward professionalism in a highly gendered occupation, we need to expose and make explicit how the particular processes of professionalization can both expand and limit the authority of early childhood educators and their capacity to engage in actions for social goods.

My underlying premise is that an early childhood educator's authority is grounded in an understanding of the teacher as subject and agent in the theoretical and discursive formation of a teacher and professional identity. Educational researchers working from a postfoundational standpoint reject a universal, unitary, static, coherent, and complete notion of *teacher* and *professional* (Grieshaber, 2001; Moss, 2006). Rather, they view identity as gendered, classed, racialized, particular, multiple, dramatic, incoherent, and incomplete to emphasize the complexities of identity formation. Some of these researchers have explicitly linked identity formation with the issue of female authority. In an earlier study on women teachers, Munro (1998) explored both the impossible "fictions" of teaching that female teachers have been subjected to (i.e., to be a teacher one must possess authority, knowledge, and power within a transmission pedagogy, but as a woman one cannot possess any of these), and teachers' individual "fictions" or stories about their working lives created within the condition of being a subject on the margins of school life. Here the teacher is seen as active, embodied with agency or as an actor engaged in creating a dramatic teaching life story. In her critical ethnographic study, Britzman (1992) used the notion of subjectivity to contend that "it is within our subjectivities" that teachers make sense of "competing conditions even as these competing conditions 'condition' our subjectivity in contradictory ways" (p. 57). Britzman used Bakhtin's (1986) concept of "heteroglossia" to describe "the polyphony in the schools and surrounding culture" that shapes how we become and identify as teachers (Britzman, 1992, p. ix). Britzman also distinguished between Bakhtin's explanation of authoritative (dominant knowledge structures) and internally persuasive discourses (alternative ways of seeing and knowing things) to examine the contradictory realities in the experiences of teachers. In the following sections I use these realities, complexities, and difficulties of teaching and being a professional to guide my work through the quandary of an early childhood professional's authority to reclaim it for advancing social goods.

Authority in the Classroom and Profession

The Penguin English Dictionary (2003) defines "authority" as "1) the power to issue directives accompanied by the right to expect obedience; 2) the position of a person who has such power: *those in authority*" (p. x). In this definition, then, an individual person with authority has a strong influence, power, and control over others who must obey, and this authority can be justified on the basis of institutional position or disciplinary and professional expertise alone. Criticisms of traditional authority have come from various quarters. In critical pedagogy, traditional authority is closely linked to a transmission model of teaching or to "banking education" (Freire, 1998, p. 56). Freire described five oppressive operations that are enforced by the impersonal authority of the "banking instructor":

(1) teaching methods make students passive learners; (2) the student mind is considered empty, to be filled by the teacher's knowledge; (3) students are required to regurgitate predigested (by the teacher) knowledge; (4) students accept received knowledge as the truth; and (5) the student's worldview becomes the teacher's rather than one's own (Freire, 1998). In these operations, diversity among the students (e.g., learner differences) and relationships between the teacher and students are not of primary importance (Applebaum, 1999, p. 308). In the field of early childhood education, Dahlberg and Moss (2005) described the connection between the child and teacher in transmission pedagogy: "The lacking child requires a teacher who is the privileged voice of authority" (p. 103).

Liberal feminist theorists maintain that in both public and private social life, men exercise authority or are granted authority on the basis of perceived superior qualities. Thus, authority is seen as patriarchal and coinciding with a hierarchical system, objectivism, and competitive individualism (Luke, 1996). Traditional teacher authority has been considered particularly problematic because it is exercised at the expense of the learner's freedom (Bingham, 2002; Maher, 2001). To counter these problems, feminist educational philosophers as well as critical pedagogy scholars have emphasized avoiding "masculinist power and control over students" (Applebaum, 1999, p. 307) and instead have focused on "sharing power with or empowering students in an effort to distribute classroom authority more evenly and to diminish potentially negative effects of traditional classroom hierarchies" (Ropers-Huilman, 1997, p. 336). For some, feminist pedagogy meant rejecting power and authority altogether to commit to pedagogies of nurturance and caring (Applebaum, 1999). Although authority as a teacher behavior may be rejected, Luke (1996) has suggested that it is often present in practice but camouflaged as something else. This is because "everyone is not only affected by power, but also to some extent exercises it; we are governed but also govern ourselves and may govern others, to a greater or lesser extent" (Dahlberg et al., 2007, p. 29).

Ryan and Ochsner (1999) noted that "early childhood teaching tends to be reduced to two dominant stereotypes: that of the good sensitive, and nurturing developmentally appropriate educator, or his/her antithesis, the autocratic developmentally inappropriate educator" (p. 14). McArdle and McWilliam (2005) have suggested that it is not necessary to create a binary in which educators have to camouflage their authority because a nurturing educator does not use authority. This contrasting "disallows the investigation of pedagogy as a more complex field of practice, one that is inevitably riddled with unresolved and unresolvable contradictions and tensions" (p. 324). McArdle and McWilliam drew on Haraway's (1991) use of ironic categorization, which examines the tensions within the propositions inside the categories of analysis rather than setting these up as discursive oppositions. This allowed McArdle and McWilliam (2005) to take up "the challenge of locating a space for thinking and speaking and enacting practice that might incorporate both 'freedom' *and* 'structure,' both 'facilitating' *and* 'teaching'. . . by insisting that both of the opposing terms of the binaries are necessary for speaking the truth about. . . education" (p. 328). "Teacher-directed, child-centred pedagogy" could be described as one of these ironic categories and may reflect what happens in the formation of a teacher identity and the experiences of early childhood educators (McArdle & McWilliam, 2005, p. 328). Articulating these difficult and complex expressions of authority in teaching is an important step in reclaiming an early childhood educator's authority.

A more traditional understanding of authority is also evident in the accepted definition of a profession as having a unique body of knowledge, a protected identity, and restricted access through the establishment of a regulatory body (Musgrave, 2010). Many highly gendered "caring" fields (i.e., nursing, social work, early childhood education [ECE]) have sought this authority and legitimacy through professionalization. For example, members of the ECE community in Ontario pressured the provincial government to legislate a regulatory professional college in the hope that the college would bring greater recognition and status to ECE members. In Manitoba and Alberta, members of the ECE sector proposed a child-care program accreditation model that would identify and elevate high-quality programs and their staff. But professionalization presents a quandary. Professional institutions and processes can be top-down expert systems concerned with quality control, which increasingly define and regulate the early childhood educator who may become more distant from understanding the possibilities of his or her own authority and capacity to influence social policy. Adams (2010) has recently noted that, in Canada, "new professional groups [that] are being created . . . [have] less autonomy and authority than did their predecessors" (p. 50) as a result of trends toward greater public accountability and professional standardization. Dillabough and Acker (2002) have remarked that within neoliberal states, teachers may abdicate professional autonomy for greater responsibility as caretakers of the state's children within a stratified gendered labour market instead of becoming "professionals in their own terms" (p. 238).

Taking Authority Back as an Early Childhood Professional

Despite the alignment of authority and patriarchy, some scholars have questioned feminist and critical pedagogy's overreliance on the notions of nurturance and caring and seek to take authority back by removing the "undesirable characteristics of traditional authority" (Applebaum, 1999, p. 308). "Unconditional giving and selfless support," two characteristics of the maternal image of nurturance, have been found to be particularly problematic for female teachers and, by extension, for those who engage in social action (Applebaum, 1999, p. 311). Woodrow and Busch (2008) have added that "although these 'Mary Poppins' images are now outdated and perhaps whimsical, the values of caring and nurturing are still perpetuated in the [early childhood] profession's discourses" (p. 89). These characteristics of caring and nurturing have been linked to welfare-state discourses that produce essentialized identities in order for the welfare state to be legitimized. In these discourses, women are given the moral authority and the roles of caretakers and midwives of public welfare within the private and domestic domains of home and schools and not the role of professionals and activists within the public domain of social policy and change (Dillabough & Acker, 2002).

Luke (1996) explored the epistemological and pedagogical consequences resulting from a feminist pedagogy that eschews all claims to power and authority to be loyal to commitments to nurturance and caring. Luke's conclusion was that feminists have to stand on one side or the other side of the nurturance/authority binary. Luke recommended "progressive" educators "disengage from their anxieties about authority and power," stating, "We do need to take authority—or at least, make explicit that we already embody and exercise authority even in its camouflage of pastoral nurturance. Second, we do need to acknowledge and theorize the power we variously exercise" (p. 302).

In her response to Luke's recommendation, Applebaum (1999) maintained that it is possible, at least in her role as an educational philosopher and an educator, for feminist pedagogy to embrace both nurturance and authority. She described a "relational authority" that "can dissolve the sharp dichotomy between nurturance and authority" (1999, p. 308). To build her theory of relational authority, she tackled the notions of nurturance (maternal and caring) and authority, finding in both a narrow understanding. In contrast to viewing authority based on power, control, and enforcement, Applebaum maintained that authority can be "the power to influence and inspire action, opinion and beliefs" and it can be "mixed with a nurturance in which relations and connectedness do not have implicit demands of selflessness and unconditionality"(1999, p. 314). For Applebaum, the concept of relational authority implies "reciprocal experiences and relationships" (1999, p. 314), and a teacher's knowledge and authority that takes relationships with students seriously has to be "demonstrated" to students so that they can see what is of value. In the relational notion of authority the teacher asks, Who am I? Who are the learners? Applebaum concluded that feminist authority is not an oxymoron and that it is possible to have *authority with* as opposed to *authority over* students.

In ruminating on the male educators who inspire her own teaching, Maher (2001) found they possess authority but "their authority is a kind of magic; early failures are overcome through the teachers' idealistic commitments to the students" (p. 14). In contrast, female teachers with authority were viewed as villainous and "archetypical spinsters" (p. 14). At the same time, Maher suggested that the teacher who is solely committed to nurturance often fails to recognize the unequal power relations that exist within the classroom; "The teacher's relative passivity in the name of facilitation actually leaves in place and reinforces the power relations brought into the classroom from the outside society" (p. 27). Maher maintained that thinking about differences (i.e., sex and race) as forms of unequal power relations can help reframe the grounds for the teacher's authority and for the teacher's "active intervention in the power dynamics of the classroom" (p. 28). In other words, Maher argued that if teachers do not possess the authority to intervene, then, in practice, social inequities in the classroom are perpetuated. Thus,

> the teacher's authority is not set in opposition to the child's 'freedom', but seen as a set of relations that can be acknowledged, as grounded in teachers' and students' evolving (and various) connections to each other, the curriculum, and the classroom and societal setting. (p. 28)

Similarly, in his analysis of Freire's "banking instructor" Bingham (1998) concluded that authority can be "on the side of freedom" (p. 463) when there is dialogue between the teacher who can also be a student and a student who can also be a teacher. Drawing on the psychoanalytic work of Benjamin (1995), Bingham described how an authoritative balance can function so that authority does not "succumb to the unwanted psychic extremes of domination and submission" (p. 448) but rather remains a dynamic and intersubjective process in which conditions of authority, vulnerability, and excess are sometimes practiced by the teacher and sometimes by the student.

Feminist philosophers Hanrahan and Antony (2005) also distinguished legitimate authority from objectionable authoritarianism and argued that the "exercise of authority should be preserved" because "it enables feminists to coordinate their efforts to achieve larger social goods" (p. 59). As workers in a highly gendered field, early childhood educators are given very little legitimacy, expertise, authority, and status. In the 1980s, Finklestein (1988) described how early childhood educators throughout their history have lacked the authority to promote system changes:

> On the one hand, a small number of high-status, well-paid experts—paediatricians, child psychiatrists and psychologists, university professors in education departments and in faculties of human development—legitimately claim a sophisticated body of theoretical knowledge about child development. On the other hand, the practitioners of early childhood education—nursery school and kindergarten teachers, day-care workers, and mothers—have been unable to assert "clinical authority", much less transform it into political, economic, or social legitimacy for themselves. (p. 11)

Hanrahan and Antony (2005) almost two decades later questioned (in reference to higher education) "the motives [of those] most vociferous in their assaults on the notion of pedagogical authority," particularly for female teachers (p. 61), at a time in which women were more broadly in society acquiring greater rights. Hanrahan and Antony described their feminist theory of authority as follows:

> Authority is legitimate when it is constructed by means of a substantively grounded, procedurally proper system of authorization—that is one involving a marking system that tracks satisfaction of the grounding conditions and that is bound by procedural mechanisms permitting complaint and redress. Authority structured in this way . . . should enable us to reap the benefits of collectivity, without the risk of authoritarian abuse. Women should persuade themselves that legitimate authority is possible and summon the courage to claim it. (p. 78)

Ryan and Ochsner (1999) illustrated this legitimate authority in their examination of the gender equity practices of two American kindergarten teachers. These teachers moved beyond the dichotomy of the nurturing/autocratic early childhood teacher to find an image of the teacher who takes "a proactive and explicit political stance with children against social inequalities" (p. 14). One of the teachers stated:

> I use my power and authority as the teacher to hold issues about gender up to the light for students to see. It's amazing to me that thinking and talking about something is a form of social action. And what you put out there to think about and talk about during workshare is powerful. (p. 17)

How can an early childhood educator take back authority within his or her profession? Osgood (2009), Stronach, Corbin, McNamara, Stark, and Warne (2003), and Urban (2008) have offered possibilities for understanding a profession that manages and moves beyond traditional notions of authority. Stronach et al. (2003) described an "insider" construction of professionalism for teachers formed within communities of practice and from personal and professional subjectivities and in-depth knowledge of everyday practices. Osgood (2009) set her alternative form of professionalism against a model of professionalism "that is characterized by regulation and control through a standards agenda and adherence to mechanistic reductionism—so that the power elite (government and its agencies) act as a regulator of the behaviours of the subordinate (the ECEC workforce)" (p. 740). For Osgood, early childhood educators need "space and opportunity to explore and act upon 'professionalism' as a highly politicized construct . . . [and] to reach critical understanding of the ways in which they are positioned within discourse" (p. 747). Finally, Urban (2008) conceptualized professionalism as "a complex ecology of the profession" in which there are reciprocal relationships and spaces for dialogue and for asking critical questions "between the various actors and their roles at different layers of the system" (p. 149). It can be argued that inherent in these forms of professionalism is an understanding of a relational authority in which various actors have legitimacy (Hanrahan & Antony, 2005) and "the power to influence and inspire action, opinion and beliefs" of others (Applebaum, 1999, p. 314).

Authority Reclaimed by Early Childhood Professionals

Having explained a range of scholars' views on authority in the previous section, I now build an argument that proposes we reclaim, make explicit, and render visible an early childhood professional's authority. I agree with Osgood (2009) that reclaiming an early childhood educator's authority is particularly important in a neoliberal social and political climate in which the ECE workforce is increasingly constructed in research and policy as deficient and incompetent, evidenced by the "poor quality" of their programs. We appear to be at a critical point in time in which early childhood professionals need to assert their authoritative stance on who they are and what they do.

I examine in this section what this authority would look like at the level of teacher–child interactions and at the broader level of what it means to be an early childhood professional and an advocate for system changes. In previous sections, I described what this authority might be like. It should not be authority over others and it can be distinguished from the objectionable authoritarianism described by Hanrahan and Antony (2005) and from the banking model described by Freire (1998). This authority, mixed with nurturance and caring, and based on respectful and trusting relationships (Applebaum, 1999) would be exercised to address social inequities, take social actions, and promote social goods. Thus, the quandary for early childhood educators is no longer whether "to have or not to have authority," as McArdle and McWilliam (2005) explain, but rather understanding "how . . . an authority mixed with nurturance and caring [can] be practiced" while recognizing that this practice will be "riddled with unresolved and unresolvable contradictions and tensions" (p. 324). Thus, authentic, internally persuasive discourses of an early childhood educator's authority as a professional are coordinated with dominant knowledge structures of authority and professionalism to produce particular and multiple teacher identities that are highly complex.

But what does this reclaiming and assertion of authority on one's own terms mean to early childhood educators in practice, particularly as they become increasingly professionalized? I have found Smith's (1999) description of the three properties individual and collective subjects (and agents)—knowledge, judgement, and will—useful for understanding how an early childhood educator might practice authority in relations with others. These properties are particularly useful because they can be located inside the actualities of an early childhood educator's everyday experiences or, as Smith has described, from the standpoint of educators. It is important to note that the enactment of relational authority within a professional environment is, in reality, a collective practice because it involves relationships with others: children, families, colleagues, policy makers, and regulators who bring multiple perspectives on the practice. For example, when educators co-construct with children understandings of human differences, when they work with children on social justice projects, and when they advocate with others for public funding for an early childhood system, they engage in collective enactments of authority. Inherent in this collective and professional work are the complexities in determining what are social goods and actions and the processes of decision making and conflict.

Knowledge

Early childhood educators have authority when they are knowledgeable. Their knowledge consists of information, understanding, or skills acquired through learning or the experience of becoming and being an early childhood educator and a professional. In my view, acknowledgement of this authoritative knowledge and expertise is critical for making the pedagogical and advocacy work of early childhood educators visible and legitimate. Miller (1996) put it succinctly: the knowledge and skills of teachers must not be considered simply a reflection of "instinctive, innate capacities in women" (p. 106). Furthermore, without this authoritative knowledge, which can consist of knowledge about, for example, the everyday experience of caring for and teaching young children, children's competencies, early childhood policies, and activist strategies, early childhood educators cannot "coordinate . . . efforts to achieve larger social goods" (Hanrahan & Antony, 2005, p. 70). As Hanrahan and Antony have stated, we need the courage *to claim* this knowledge as legitimate in order to advance what it is we want for children, families, ourselves, and our society.

In my view, what is really at issue is the nature of this knowledge—for different knowledge bases claimed by different "experts" produce different kinds of authoritative early childhood educators. Moss (2006), for example, has described the connection between technology of quantification as a modernist professional discourse and the image of the early childhood worker as a professional technician:

> Their role is to apply a defined set of technologies through regulated processes to produce pre-specified and measurable outcomes. The technologies and processes include working with detailed and prescriptive curricula (or similar practice guidelines), programmes and similar procedures to regulate methods of working, and using observation and other methods to assess performance against developmental norms and other standardised outcome criteria. (p. 35)

It is clear from Moss' description that an early childhood educator as a professional technician does not produce and possess his or her own authoritative knowledge; he or she simply translates (Finklestein, 1988) other experts' theories into practice. One of the characteristics of a profession is that it has an effective means of producing and managing the professional and particular body of knowledge (Urban, 2008). Use of theories of developmental norms and other standardized outcome criteria as dominant knowledge structures of professional authority can result in an educator assuming taken-for-granted knowledge. However, the educator as a technician may question and resist various processes that regulate his or her teaching practices and assert authoritative knowledge based on his or her own and others' experiences within the local early childhood setting.

In contrast to the teacher as technician, Moss (2006) described the teacher as a "researcher who is constantly seeking a deeper understanding of existing knowledge and new knowledge, in particular of the child and the child's learning processes" (p. 36). The teacher's research is part of everyday practice and new knowledge emerges out of "creating knowledge in relationship with others and also with theories, concepts and analyses from many different fields" (p. 36). An early childhood professional's knowledge as a researcher is not fixed but changes and grows as a result of coordinated interactions with others, multiple perspectives, and different social and historical contexts. The authoritative knowledge of a teacher as a researcher is different from that of a teacher as a technician. Unlike the technical teacher, the researching teacher possesses knowledge co-constructed with others out of the particular social and historical circumstances of the early childhood setting. Dahlberg and Moss (2005) described a teacher's complex role in "creating complexity in the child's environment and by introducing new theories, concepts, languages and materials, as tools for children's theorizing and meaning making" (p. 104).

While claims to teacher knowledge can contribute to power imbalances in various social interactions (e.g., teacher–family), an early childhood educator's claim that he or she does "not know" and "is not an expert" works against the ability to advance social goods within the early childhood setting and in the broader society. In other words, early childhood educators need intelligence; expertise and authority; and "the power to influence and inspire action, opinion and beliefs" (Applebaum, 1999, p. 314). Moreover, when an early childhood educator denies his or her knowledge achieved through education, ongoing practice, experiences in concert with others, and reflection on practice and experiences, then I would argue that his or her behaviour becomes inauthentic or a "performance." This lack of authenticity is particularly evident when teachers as technicians enact other experts' knowledge or professional standards. Osgood (2009) has referred to this enactment as "a tick-box culture of performativity that obscures more opaque aspects of professionalism" (p. 743). Many of us have visited early childhood settings in which the language and interactions between teachers and children seem mechanical and routinized as the teacher becomes increasingly removed from his or her own "teaching self." Under this condition of inauthenticity, early childhood educators cannot truly engage in critical reflective practice, which Mac Naughton (2005) described as the ability "to analyse their implication in oppressive and inequitable power relationships with students and then use their analysis to work against that oppression and inequity" (p. 7). Fenech, Sumsion, and Shepherd (2010) have similarly argued that "normalized, technical practices fail to recognize early childhood university-qualified teachers as experts, and accordingly limit their capacity to work autonomously and exercise professional judgement in the interests of children and families" (p. 91). These scholars have proposed a "resistance combined with activism-based teacher professionalism" in which early childhood teachers "produce alternative knowledges about quality ECE and the integral role teacher professionalism plays in this" (p. 91). Ryan and Ochsner maintained that "reconstructing the knowledge base to expand our definitions of what constitutes good teaching" (p. 15) is required. The good and professional teacher redefined, then, can engage in social action with a sense of authority and legitimacy.

Judgement
Early childhood educators exercise their authority when they make judgements, which are opinions and evaluations to reach decisions on their pedagogical and advocacy practices. Early childhood educators make these judgements regularly throughout the day during transitions and routines, in planning activities, in their interactions with children and families, and with policy makers. These judgements are always part of ordinary practices and many of these practices involve negotiating social goods in and beyond the early childhood setting. However, as Dahlberg et al. (2007) have pointed out, these judgements should not be seen as personal or expert judgements but rather as collective ones. Personal judgements are individualistic and made in isolation of others, children, families, teaching colleagues, and advocacy allies. Expert judgements are frequently divorced from early childhood educators' local knowledge and experiences with others. Moreover, Jones (1999) has described what technical notions of authority intend to do: "suspend the process of judgement and decision-making as an on-going, conflicted, and collective process, and locate it in one, ultimate, sovereign point" (p. 108).

Dahlberg et al. (2007) contend that early childhood educators' foremost task is "constructing and deepening *understanding* [emphasis in original] of the early childhood institution and its projects, in particular the pedagogical work—to make meaning of what is going on" (p. 106). They further explained:

> From constructing these understandings, people may choose to continue to make judgements about the work, a process involving the application of values to understanding to make a judgement of value. Finally, people may further choose to seek *some agreement with others* about these judgements—to struggle to agree, to some extent, about what is going on and its value. (p. 106; emphasis in original)

In judging their practices and the authority inherent in them, early childhood professionals may assume responsibility for their judgements. Teachers working in the mode of a professionalized technician are more likely to locate responsibility for their pedagogical judgements and decisions in the "experts" who communicate what is best for children and families on the basis of standards and other quantitative measures. Moyles (2001) has also described how authoritative professional discourses tend "to engender a sense that responsibility and power lie outside the domain of the practitioner" (p. 82). Conversely, the teacher who is a researcher works explicitly with authoritative knowledge from inside and outside of the early childhood setting and co-constructed with others, and thus claims and takes responsibility for his or her own judgements. Dahlberg et al. (2007) wrote that "judgements should be delivered not as a statement of fact but precisely as a judgement and be judged by others in turn" (p. 113). Drawing upon Lenz Taguchi's (2006) "ethic of resistance" in which taken-for-granted truths are continually reconstructed as judgements, Fenech et al. (2010) considered "resistance-based professionalism" to be critical for producing alternative knowledges of what is means to be a professional (p. 92).

Will

Early childhood educators exercise their authority through an expression of their will in relation with others. Will is defined as a desire, wish, intention, determination, or inclination, and uses of the term can have positive (e.g., will-power) or negative (e.g., wilful-power) connotations. This understanding of an early childhood professional's will requires us, as Luke (1996) has indicated, "to acknowledge and theorize the power we variously exercise" (p. 302). In explaining her theory of relational authority, Applebaum (1999) wrote:

> In order to influence action, opinion and belief, and especially to inspire others, there must be a bilaterally active relationship; someone who inspires and someone who is inspired. To be inspired is not a passive state but rather, a transaction in which the one inspired actively relates with the one who inspires, and moreover, is altered in a deep sense by the relationship. (p. 134)

Thus an authoritative early childhood educator can influence, for example, the ways in which children view and interact with one another and the ways in which governments produce policies. But he or she considers how this exercise of will is responsible, ethical, and works toward collective social good. Dahlberg and Moss (2005) have vitalized the place of ethics in the preschool, arguing for ethical approaches that foreground responsibility and relationships to others and that "require listening, reflection, interpretation, confrontation, discussion, and judgements open to question" (p. 13).

An explicit articulation of authority as will reveals that behind concepts like facilitation, free choice, and "power-sharing," early childhood educators do exercise their will. A teacher's will is evident in the scheduling and routines, at group times, and in other teacher-led/directed activities. Children know that this will is lodged in adults in the classroom. There is no escaping that teachers lead and coordinate these daily events, so the question is not whether they do or do not, but rather how they carry them out for promoting collective and social goods. This new question ensures that an early childhood educator's will is consciously and critically constructed out of experiences within a local and particular social, cultural, and political community in which teachers, children, families, advocacy allies, and policy makers exist. The question also requires a distinction to be made between reflective practice and critical reflective practice that Mac Naughton (2005) has described: "Inserting the 'critical' into reflective practice . . . links education to a wider social project to create social justice and emancipation, and freedom of all through education" (p. 9). Sachs (2003) has similarly described a transformative activist professionalism that is based on critical reflection, collective action, and the principles of equity and social justice. Critical reflection of an early childhood professional's authority as knowledge, judgement, and will is a starting point for examining how Canadian early childhood educators can manage the emergence of sector professionalization. As noted in an earlier section, early childhood educators in Alberta, Manitoba, and Ontario have recently pursued program accreditation and a regulatory college to enhance their status as professionals. On-going dialogue within and between sector levels (i.e., teachers, professional associations, regulatory bodies, government ministries) that addresses the "complex ecology of the profession" (Urban, 2008, p. 149) and integrates the ideas examined in this chapter may offer an opportunity to broaden the possibilities for sector professionalization in Canadian provinces.

Conclusion

In this chapter, I have maintained that early childhood professionals need authority in order to pursue social goods at this "perilous moment of humankind's history" (Moss, 2010, p. 9). In Canada, after a turbulent period of social, political, and economic high and lows of early childhood policy, some provincial governments have begun to take steps to change their early learning system in the absence of leadership at the federal level. At these provincial levels, the ECE sector has also experienced varying degrees of professionalization that may provide an opportunity for early childhood educators to authoritatively articulate what they want for an early childhood system. In Canada, issues of diversity and inclusion are the forefront of a vision for an early childhood system. At this critical moment in the history of early childhood education in Canada, I have questioned and reformulated the nature of an early childhood professional's authority drawing on the views of feminist educational philosophers and critical pedagogy and early childhood theorists. I have proposed that early childhood educators reclaim and articulate a relational authority expressed in practice as knowledge, judgement, and will. I have also argued that there are forms of professionalism that are better aligned with this reformulation of authority. I have not disputed that there are benefits to professionalizing the ECE workforce; in my view, it is possible for early childhood educators to harness the acquisition of greater recognition, authority, and status for promoting social goods, and as Luke (1996) has put it, "stake [a] public claim on the knowledge domains and institutional practices we want to transform" (p. 302). At the same time, this authority cannot be taken for granted within a neoliberal state and the pervasive influence of government discourses of quality assurance, regulation, and surveillance (Osgood, 2009, p. 741). But early childhood educators who claim their own authority built from the practices of knowledge, judgement, and will, may be able to work more successfully with the regulatory frameworks and licensing regimes in which they operate. The third cornerstone of a professional system in early childhood education articulated by Urban (2008) is a Freirean concept of hope, which implies "encouraging and empowering actors at all layers of the system to engage in an exploration of possible futures" (p. 149). It is my hope that, in this chapter I have explored the possibility that the expression of an early childhood professional's authority has the capacity to influence and instigate social goods.

References

Adams, T. L. (2010). Profession: A useful concept for sociological analysis? *Canadian Review of Sociology, 47*(1), 49–70.
Applebaum, B. (1999). On good authority or is feminist authority an oxymoron? In R. Curren (Ed.), *Philosophy of education* (pp. 307–317) Urbana-Champaign, IL: Philosophy of Education Society.
Bakhtin, M. (1986). *Speech genres and other late essays* (Vern W. McGee, Trans.). Austin: University of Texas Press.
Benjamin, J. (1995). *Like subjects, love objects*. New Haven, CT: Yale University Press.
Bingham, C. (2002). On Paulo Freire's debt to psychoanalysis: Authority on the side of freedom. *Studies in Philosophy and Education, 21,* 447–464.
Britzman, D. P. (1992). *Practice makes practice*. Albany, NY: SUNY Press.
Brock, A. (2006). *Dimensions of early years professionalism: Attitudes versus competencies? Reflecting on early years issues, training, advancement and co-operation in teaching young children*. Association

for the Development of Early Years Educators (TACTYC). Retrieved from http://www.tactyc.org.uk/reflections_papers.asp

Canadian Child Care Human Resources Sector Council. (2002). *Our child care workforce.* Ottawa, ON: Government of Canada's Human Resources Partnerships Directorate.

Cannella, G. S., & Bloch, M. (2006). Social policy, education, and childhood in dangerous times: Revolutionary actions or global complicity. *International Journal of Educational Policy, Research and Practice, 7,* 5–20.

Dahlberg, G., & Moss, P. (2005). *Ethics and politics in early childhood education.* London, England: RoutledgeFalmer.

Dahlberg, G., Moss, P., & Pence, A. (2007). *Beyond quality in early childhood education and care: Languages of evaluation.* New York, NY: Routledge.

Dillabough J., & Acker, S. (2002). Globalization, women's work and teacher education: A cross-national analysis. *International Studies in the Sociology of Education, 12*(3), 227–260.

Fenech, M., Sumsion, J., & Shephard, W. (2010). Promoting early childhood teacher professionalism in the Australian context: The place of resistance. *Contemporary Issues in Early Childhood, 11*(1), 89–105.

Finkelstein, B. (1988). The revolt against selfishness: Women and the dilemmas of professionalism in early childhood education. In B. Spodek, O. Saracho, & D. Peters (Eds.), *Professionalism and the early childhood practitioner* (pp. 11–27). New York, NY: Teachers College Press.

Freire, P. (1998). *Pedagogy of the oppressed.* New York, NY: Continuum.

Friendly, M., & Prentice, S. (2009). *About Canada: Childcare.* Halifax, NS: Fernwood.

Grieshaber, S. (2001). Advocacy and early childhood educators: Identity and cultural conflicts. In S. Grieshaber & G. S. Cannella (Eds.), *Embracing identities in early childhood education: Diversity and possibilities* (pp. 60–72). New York, NY: Teachers College Press.

Hanrahan, R., & Antony, I. (2005). Because I said so: Toward a feminist theory of authority. *Hypatia, 20*(4), 59–79.

Haraway, D. (1991). *Simians, cyborgs and women: The reinvention of nature.* New York, NY: Routledge.

Jones, K. (1999). The trouble with authority. *Differences: A Journal of Feminist Cultural Studies, 3*(1), 104–127.

Langford, R. (2010). Critiquing child-centred pedagogy to bring children and early childhood educators into the centre of a democratic pedagogy. *Contemporary Issues in Early Childhood, 11*(1), 113–127.

Lenz Taguchi, H. (2006). Reconceptualizing early childhood education: Challenging taken-for-granted ideas. In J. Einarsdottir & J. Wagner (Eds.), *Nordic childhoods and early education: Philosophy, research, policy and practice in Denmark, Finland, Iceland, Norway and Sweden* (pp. 257–287). Greenwich, CT: Information Age.

Luke, C. (1996). Feminist pedagogy theory: Reflections on power and authority. *Educational Theory, 46*(3), 283–305.

Mac Naughton, G. (2005). *Doing Foucault in early childhood studies: Applying poststructural ideas.* London, England: Routledge.

Maher, F. (2001). John Dewey, progressive education, and feminist pedagogies: Issues in gender and authority. In K. Weiler (Ed.), *Feminist engagements: Reading, resisting, and revisioning male theorists in education and cultural studies* (pp. 13–32). New York, NY: Routledge.

Mahon, R. (2009). Canada's early childhood education and care policy: Still a laggard? *International Journal of Child Care and Education Policy, 3*(1), 27–42.

McArdle, F., & McWilliam, E. (2005). From balance to blasphemy: Shifting metaphors for researching early childhood education. *International Journal of Qualitative Studies in Education, 18*(3), 323–336.

Miller, J. (1996). *School for women.* London, England: Virago.

Moss, P. (2006). Structures, understandings and discourses: Possibilities for re-envisioning the early childhood worker. *Contemporary Issues in Early Childhood, 7*(1), 30–41.

Moss, P. (2010). We cannot continue as we are: The educator in an education for survival. *Contemporary Issues in Early Childhood, 11*(1), 8–19.

Moyles, J. (2001). Passion, paradox and professionalism in early years education. *Early Journal of International Research and Practice, 21*(2), 81–95.

Munro, P. (1998). *Subject to fiction: Women teachers' life history narratives and the cultural politics of resistance.* Philadelphia, PA: Open University Press.

Musgrave, J. (2010). Educating the future educators: The quest for professionalism in early childhood education. *Contemporary Issues in Early Childhood, 11*(4), 435–442.

Novinger, S., O'Brien, L., & Sweigman, L. (2005). Challenging the culture of expertise: Moving beyond training the always already failing early childhood educator. In S. Ryan & S. Grieshaber (Eds.), *Practical transformations and transformational practices: Globalization, postmodernism, and early childhood education* (pp. 217–241). Amsterdam, the Netherlands: Elsevier.

Osgood, J. (2009). Childcare workforce reform in England and "the early years professional": A critical discourse analysis. *Journal of Education Policy, 24*(6), 733–751.

The Penguin English Dictionary (2nd ed.). (2003). London, England: Penguin Books.

Penn, H. (2010). *International perspectives: Canada—a brave campaign for state provision.* Childcare-Canada.org. Retrieved from http //action.web.ca/home/crru/rsrcs_crru_full.shtml?x=129663

Prentice, S. (Ed.). (2001). *Changing child care: Five decades of child care advocacy and policy in Canada.* Halifax, NS: Fernwood.

Ropers-Huilman, B. (1997). Constructing feminist teachers: Complexities of identity. *Gender and Education, 9*(3), 327–343.

Ryan, S., & Ochsner, M. (1999). Traditional practices, new possibilities: Transforming dominant images of early childhood teachers. *Australian Journal of Early Childhood, 24*(4), 14–20.

Sachs, J. (2003). *The activist teaching profession.* Buckingham, England: Open University Press.

Smith, D. (1999). *Writing the social: Critique, theory and investigation.* Toronto, ON: University of Toronto Press.

Stronach, I., Corbin, B., McNamara, O., Stark, S., & Warne, T. (2003). Towards an uncertain politics of professionalism: Teacher and nurse identities in flux. *Journal of Education Policy, 17*(1), 109–128.

Urban, M. (2008). Dealing with uncertainty: Challenges and possibilities for the early childhood profession. *European Early Childhood Education Research Journal, 16*(2), 135–152.

Urban, M. (2010). Rethinking professionalism in early childhood: Untested feasibilities and critical ecologies [Editorial]. *Contemporary Issues in Early Childhood, 11*(1), 1–7.

Woodrow, C., & Busch, G. (2008). Repositioning early childhood leadership as action and activism. *European Early Childhood Education Research Journal, 16*(1), 83–93.

Chapter Six

When Queer Enters Early Childhood Teacher Training

What's So Inappropriate about That?

Zeenat Janmohamed

This chapter challenges the heteronormative nature of early childhood teacher training by arguing for a more complex understanding of diversity that includes queer parents and their young children. Through a queer reading and feminist analysis, this chapter uncovers dominant assumptions of universality underlying the heteronormative discourse of developmentally appropriate practice that pervades postsecondary programs in early childhood training and its implications for practice.

Why We Need Queer Identity in Early Childhood Training

The narrative of queer families or queer identity is not common to early childhood research or practice. Nor is it common in professional preparation programs. Although issues of diversity, equity, and inclusion have evolved in the early childhood profession, there remains a heavier emphasis on families that are immigrants, children who are raised in families led by one parent, or children who may be adopted or fostered. The story of inclusion is often recognized through the individual needs of adult learners, and this also plays a significant role in how early childhood educators discuss diversity and difference.

In an effort to create climates of "inclusion," issues facing parents who may come from other cultures, children who are English language learners, and the needs of families living in poverty are explored by a variety of scholars (Freiler, Rothman, & Barata, 2004; Janus & Duku, 2007; Tyyskaa, 2001). All of this is important and not to be discounted because the reality of immigrants and refugees is critical to the knowledge that educators need to have, as are the needs of children growing up in families at risk. However, my goal is to infuse more complexity into how diversity, equity, and inclusion are explored in early childhood education in ways that cut across modes of differentiation and open up new possibilities for understanding the multiplicity of diversity and difference.

This chapter begins by looking at how early childhood education has moved from being a private matter to an area of public policy interest, and how the education and training of early childhood educators are situated within this context. I then explore how early childhood educators are prepared to support queer families and consider how the singular construct of child development in early childhood can be challenged by queer theory. I present preliminary findings of my research study that documents the dominant infusion of developmentally appropriate practice and its underlying injection of heteronormative construction of family engagement in early childhood practice.

My research explored how early childhood studies prepares educators to establish meaningful relationships with queer parents by analyzing course outlines, core foundational textbooks, and readings in courses related to child development and working with families. I explored these materials at four colleges in Ontario located in communities where I conducted my study. I conducted semi-structured interviews with queer parents and developed connections between what early childhood educators learn about families and what families experience in early childhood programs. In pursuing further research, I was interested in rupturing the dominant discourse of heteronormativity, and the propensity to silence queer identity in early childhood settings. I am interested in moving "queer" from a position of other to one that is more apparent in early childhood, affecting educators, parents, and children. I see the possibility and necessity to infuse queer perspectives into traditional child development to bridge a gap that could lead to a deeper understanding of inclusion instead of perpetuating research and practice that I believe continue to be responsible for a traditional and monolithic view of childhood development. One of the research questions I addressed in my study was, how does the notion of developmentally appropriate practice influence the dominant and heteronormative discourse in early childhood curriculum and practice?

In the context of the early childhood professional preparation program, the pedagogical approach to understanding diversity and difference is often laid out in environmental scans that enable one lecture to focus on immigrants and refugees, the next on children being raised by grandparents, and the next on the needs of English language learners. The *Early Childhood Education* (ECE) *Program Standards* of the Ontario Ministry of Training, Colleges and Universities (2000) sets expectations that early childhood educators will graduate with knowledge about diversity and equity. However, the approach in early childhood training is focused more on helping families with diverse backgrounds with transitions into early childhood programs rather than dwelling more deeply on the social and pedagogical differences of the individual family construct. This approach assumes commonality in the traditional conceptual framework of family and is in fact extended to "same-sex" families. If that same-sex coupling is married, it is given more legitimacy—somehow, the symbolic nature of marriage, and its heteronormative promise, softens the image that queers don't just have sex all the time. They also raise children, spend time at the grocery store, negotiate school dropoffs and pickups, and generally operate in the heteronormative framework of a nuclear family unit. This construct also perpetuates a newly created normative framework of lesbian or gay parents without recognizing the growing population of transgender people having children in seemingly heterosexual relationships that go far beyond the commonly understood family construct.

Ideas about how families operate are infused throughout early childhood teacher training programs and, as a result, educational institutions can implicitly and explicitly foster foundational knowledge that promotes a hegemonic or dominant perspective. Apple (1975) states that it is the hidden curriculum or what is not discussed that maintains the status quo. In deconstructing the influence of a positivist approach to early childhood studies, I choose to use the term "queer," especially in the education context. As Sears (1999) so aptly describes in *Queering Elementary Education*, "Queering education happens when we look at schooling upside down and view childhood from the inside out. Teaching queerly demands we explore taken-for-granted assumptions about diversity, identities, childhood and prejudice" (p. 4). I am not interested in an antagonistic approach but I believe that queer theory offers a new framework for understanding and analyzing traditional approaches in early childhood education. My research interests are driven by a desire to raise the salience of perspectives outside the normative approaches to child development. The work of Judith Butler creates a space to challenge, shift, create discomfort, and make noise about the gendering of children in early childhood programs. In "Critically Queer," Butler (1993b) suggests the following:

> To what extent, then, has the performative "queer" operated along side, as a deformation of, the "I pronounce you . . ." of the marriage ceremony? If the performative operates as the sanction that performs the heterosexualization of the social bond, perhaps it also comes into play precisely as the shaming taboo which "queers" those who resist or oppose that social form as well as those who occupy it without hegemonic social sanction. (p. 17)

Reimagining early childhood teacher training also includes developing a stronger understanding of how limited a heteronormative construct of family is in the Canadian context. According to Statistics Canada (2006), same-sex couples represented 0.6% of all couples in Canada and about 9.0% of individuals in same-sex relationships had children. This provides a statistical glimpse of queer parents with children, since the federal government does not collect census data on individuals or couples that may identify as bisexual, queer, or transgender and because it is recognized that not all queer parents may choose to self-identify in the census. However, the demographic information that Statistics Canada collects is relevant and provides the impetus to, at the very least, explore that parents beyond the typical heteronormative identity are having children in all kinds of combinations. In my study, I use the term "queer" to describe families that identify as lesbian, gay, bisexual, transgender, transsexual, and queer but I also use queer paradigms to describe how I question, and have a desire to shift early childhood training and research toward more reflective practice.

Although there is a significant interest in the connections between parent engagement and early learning, research related to the relatively new group of queer parents has been absent. Queer rights are represented by instances in which same-sex couples have the right to marry and adopt children. Yet the existing literature on the inclusion of queer families with preschool-aged children is limited in the Canadian context as is the discourse on the legal rights surrounding the complicated conception and birth arrangements permitted in Canada. Early childhood education is a young profession that has gained the increased attention of governments and the public in the past two decades, moving it from a marginal to a regulated and more mainstream sector (Friendly & Prentice, 2009). With this comes the responsibility to ensure that professional training and practice have currency and embed a critical view of what works and what needs to change in early childhood practice.

From Social Welfare to Public Policy: Moving Queer from Private to Public

The changing political landscape of early childhood education has brought with it recognition that early childhood care and education are entitlements for modern-day families. The emergence of a social policy framework in Canada must embed within it not only universal access to early childhood education and care, but also an understanding of the real needs of diverse Canadian children and their families in early childhood education settings. The visibility of queer children and families in early childhood training is critical to understanding gender and sexual identity and engaging diverse families toward establishing responsive early childhood practices that address their unique experiences.

Canada has a long history grounded in a social welfare approach that supports the idea that if children cannot be taken care of by their own parents, the public has some responsibility to ensure that the care of children is reasonable and meets minimal standards of care to enable parents to work (Standing Senate

Committee on Social Affairs, 2009). In spite of decades of early childhood programming, and investment from the public tax base to support early childhood programs, the bulk of the cost is still borne by parents, which ensures that, in fact, child care remains a market-driven commodity rather than a publicly funded program like public education and health care. As a result, only 20% of children have access to licensed child-care programs—the remaining 80% of children utilize a combination of informal care, self-care, and sibling care, ensuring at best minimal quality care and at worst danger to children (Beach, Friendly, Ferns, Prabhu, & Forer, 2009; Friendly, 2011). On occasion, when parents can, they juggle shift work to provide care for their child while one parent works and few families utilize extended family supports. The advances in women entering the workforce have done little to improve access to child care for young children, despite the fact that 73% of women in the workforce have children (Statistics Canada, 2010).

There is a standstill or perhaps a level of political denial about who is caring for the children while women are working. Certainly it is not the extended family, since they too are in the workforce. As a nation, the government contradicts a desire for an active workforce with a desire for a very traditional, albeit unrealistic social policy agenda in which women will refrain from joining the workforce to care for the children (Delacourt, 2011). As a result, early childhood programs vary by provincial jurisdiction, are inconsistent in quality and availability, and depend on the ability of parents to make private arrangements to pay for programs. In Ontario, licensed home child care and centre-based care are monitored by the provincial government in its legislative framework in the Day Nurseries Act (1990) that says nothing about diversity, equity, and inclusion, let alone queer identity.

At the same time, early childhood education in Ontario is undergoing a significant change with the introduction of full-day early learning programs offered by school boards across the province. The new legislation enables the implementation of full-day early learning programs in schools and also creates a new tier of early childhood educators who are employed by the public and by Catholic school boards governed by the Ministry of Education. Under an amended Education Act (2010), kindergarten teachers and early childhood educators are jointly responsible for implementing early learning programs. Unlike the licensed child-care sector, school boards are obliged to meet the requirements of the Education Ministry's Equity Strategy, which does make reference to the need to address student issues such as racism, homophobia, and gender-based violence (Ontario Ministry of Education, 2009). The recently released report *With Our Best Future in Mind: Implementing Early Learning in Ontario* (Pascal, 2009) establishes a policy framework that integrates early learning programs and recommends the consolidation of early learning services into a comprehensive approach to serve more families with young children. It recognizes that parent involvement is critical to optimal child development, and that the experiences of parents should include measures of inclusion, respect, and recognition for the knowledge they have of their own children. Pascal (2009) asks:

> If the goal is to increase parent engagement, we need to be thoughtful about who is included in the process. Are we truly involving parents if some educators and school leaders avoid the Muslim mother because she wears a hijab or are confused about how to approach same-sex families or the many configurations of blended families? (p. 31)

If there is a real desire to go beyond the rhetoric of diversity, equity, inclusion, and multicultural practice, the dominance of heteronormativity needs to be deconstructed in course texts to investigate how queer identity is silenced; how gender identity in children is placed in a male/female binary; and how the potential exclusion of queer families may have an impact on optimal early childhood experiences for children and their parents.

The further shift in child care toward an integrated model that includes family support services and a stronger emphasis on the value of professional training in early childhood gives early childhood more prominence in public policy. In addition, the newly established College of Early Childhood Educators in Ontario, a regulatory body for early childhood educators with a current membership of over 35,000 individuals, places new professional responsibility on the educators. In regulated early childhood programs including licensed child care and school board–operated early learning programs, provincial legislation requires that early childhood educators have a minimum of a two-year ECE diploma from one of the twenty-four publicly operated colleges in Ontario. As a result of these changes, the policy and jurisdictional shifts in early childhood education provide an opportunity to explore the currency of early childhood training and its links to the broader demographic changes in the province of Ontario.

My specific research interests are clearly tied to my professional role as a faculty member in an early childhood training program. It is also closely linked to my desire to reimagine early childhood teacher training and knowledge with a stronger infusion of criticality and engagement with respect to knowledge production. The research foci on the experiences of queer families utilizing licensed early childhood programs is due to my interest in the knowledge of early childhood educators who are professionally trained and in my own experiences as a queer educator. My research interests are grounded in a polemical process that questions existing knowledge but also posits possible solutions that shift knowledge from a dominant framework to one that is more reflexive and engaging.

Exploring Queer Identity in Early Childhood Training

Early childhood educators in Ontario are required to complete a minimum two-year diploma program offered at publicly funded community colleges. The program consists of foundational courses in early childhood development with a focus on program skills and practices that are considered to be developmentally appropriate. This notion of developmentally appropriate was initially established by the North American Association for the Education of Young Children (2009) and later taken up by Gestwicki (2011) making its way into the College of Early Childhood Educators in Ontario's Standards of Practice and Code of Ethics. The current early childhood training program in Ontario offers a pedagogical framework that is dominated by Anglo-American approaches to plurality and inclusion of all children and families. The seminal text often used in early childhood in training is *Developmentally Appropriate Practice (2011)*, and now extensively embedded in curriculum material, field placement expectations, and course readings. In my research, I am concerned with how this text and its implicit heteronormative values and approaches are entangled so extensively in early childhood studies, professional learning, and practice. I intend to rupture the dominant discourse of heteronormativity, and the propensity to silence the existence of queer families in early childhood settings, by moving "queer" from a position of other to one that is more apparent in early childhood, affecting both parents and children.

As Jagose (1996) suggests, queer theory enables us to understand "how gender operates as a regulatory construct of heterosexuality" (p. 83). By extension, Robinson (2005) describes queer pedagogy as enabling educators to "critically examine the natural order of things" (p. 7). Challenging notions of universality is imperative because, as Battiste (2005) has argued, "universality underpins cultural and cognitive imperialism, which establishes a dominant group's knowledge, experience, culture and language as the dominant form" (p. 224). With a growing diversity of family composition, it is now more critical than ever that early childhood training programs move away from a "single way of knowing and make room for multiple perspectives, which in turn influence innovative kinds of teaching decisions and practices" (Blaise, 2005, p. 184). In the process of taking apart the normative discourse of developmentally appropriate practice, and the propensity of educators to embed heteronormative perspectives in the schooling of early childhood educators, I took direction from Mac Naughton (1998), who suggests that "discourse analysis is critically reflecting on our social beliefs and practices and the contributions of social institutions to beliefs, practices and emotions" (p. 158). To explore why there is an absence of queer identity in early childhood training and practice in Ontario, I grounded my work in this methodology as I completed a textual analysis of core early childhood textbooks, course outlines, and readings to make connections between *developmentally appropriate practice* in early childhood training and its significance in teachers' capacity to encounter, deconstruct, and challenge the normative approach to early childhood teacher training. I am arguing that the term "developmentally appropriate practice" plays a significant role in relationships between early childhood educators and parents and by extension establishes a discourse that is dominated by heteronormativity in early learning and care programs. Viruru (2005) demonstrates that despite the existence of important scholarly work on the limitations and colonial assumptions underlying developmentally appropriate practice, dominant discourse of childhood continues to dominate and pervade not only Euro-Western practice but also early childhood development in the majority of the world.

Heteronormativity is reified and "embedded in things," as Warner observed—in ordinary, everyday activities (as cited in Adams, 2004, p. 16) and played out in the daily interactions and activities in early childhood settings. Examples include lining children up by gender; ignoring boys engaged in aggressive behaviour, suggesting instead that the boys are just being boys; and selecting children's books that depict only the heterosexual family makeup. The application of a queer and poststructural analysis in early childhood studies and a critical reading of developmentally appropriate practice problematizes a hegemonic perspective but also considers the potential movement of perspectives that are radically different from a universalizing discourse.

The infusion of a pluralistic approach to diversity, equity, and inclusion has become even more apparent in the very recent parameters established by Ontario's College of Early Childhood Educators. The college was established in 2007 to protect public interest and focus on the standards of practice in early childhood also governs early childhood educators. At the core of the college's mandate is a commitment to ensure that early childhood educators will deliver "inclusive play-based learning and care programs for both pre-school and school aged children" (College of Early Childhood Educators, 2011). This mandate takes a limited view of inclusion, which is often used to describe the inclusion of children with different abilities and sometimes used to describe the inclusion of different cultural practices. The use of language is a powerful tool in communicating core beliefs and the use of a term such as "inclusive" does not resonate with a desire for a more reflective discourse that struggles with injustice, oppression, and exclusion.

The College of Early Childhood Educators' new (2011) *Code of Ethics and Standards of Practice* is designed to define the professional knowledge required for an early childhood educator to function effectively. Although they seem well intentioned, the standards also limit educators interested in critical and reflective practice. Instead, they provide a framework that keeps educators accountable for their practice and, some would argue, regulates and controls early childhood practice. Responsibilities of early childhood educators as defined by the college include respecting the uniqueness of the child and the family. In fact, it names the need to "recognize and respect the diversity of families" (College of Early Childhood Educators, 2011, p. 11). The Code of Ethics embeds notions of diversity, equity, and inclusion, but does not specify what that means with respect to families. It may have been a useful exercise to embed language from the Human Rights

Act (1990) that more explicitly defines different identities and ensures that "every person has a right to equal treatment with respect to services, goods and facilities, without discrimination because of race, ancestry, place of origin, colour, ethnic origin, citizenship, creed, sex, sexual orientation, age, marital status, family status or disability." Although the Human Rights Act applies to all educators, the Early Childhood Educators Act (2007) is more salient with early childhood educators since membership to the College of Early Childhood Educators is mandatory and seems to carry more weight within the profession of early childhood education. It may have proved useful to utilize the regulations to ensure a clearer direction toward more reflective practice. Rather, the Early Childhood Educators Act (2007) defines the practice of early childhood education as the planning and delivery of inclusive play-based learning and care programs for children in order to promote the well-being and holistic development of children. It mandates communicating with the parents or persons with legal custody of the children in the programs in order to improve the development of the children. The new Standards of Practice for registered early childhood educators provide specific direction on how practice will be defined, demarcating the boundaries that educators must operate within. They include the following:

- Caring and Nurturing Relationships That Support Learning

- Developmentally Appropriate Care and Education

- Safe, Healthy and Supportive Learning Environments

- Professional Knowledge and Competence

- Professional Boundaries, Dual Relationships and Conflicts of Interest

- Confidentiality and Consent to the Release of Information Regarding Children and their Families (College of Early Childhood Educators, p. 9)

The new regulations standardize professional practice and are in fact used to determine and adjudicate issues of professional conduct. With such a clear and delineated list of professional conduct, how can early childhood educators be prepared to move outside these boundaries? One could argue that the professional education that early childhood educators receive enables them to design programs for children and engage parents in meaningful and thoughtful relationships. However, like the Standards of Practice, there remains a heavy emphasis in early childhood training on developmentally appropriate practice based on ideas that were first introduced by the Washington, D.C.–based National Association for the Education of Young Children and that now permeate professional education, standards of practice, curriculum frameworks, and professional learning. Challenging the discourse of developmentally appropriate practice within a pluralistic noncritical methodology brings with it a constant need to swim against the tide.

What is it about the dominant framework in early childhood education that has been so challenging to undo? Foucault (1974) argued that "for those who speak it, a discourse is a given" (p. 49). When spoken on a regular basis and with the authority of an educational institution or a dominant developmental framework, the discourse becomes the "truth" and socially sanctioned. Anything outside the normative discourse becomes questionable (Robinson & Jones Díaz, 2007)—too complex to comprehend and institute. Take, for example, the discourse of sexuality as it relates to children. In his famous *The History of Sexuality* (1978), Foucault argued that although children's sexuality was not discussed overtly, its presence permeated the halls of schools, the organization of health activities, and the division of sexual education. However, nothing so obvious happens in early childhood settings—we commonly practice the division of children based on gender in using the washroom, lining up to go outside, and preparing for transitions. One could argue this is to ensure simplicity in how children get organized. But in fact, is there an underlying heteronormative concern that when girls and boys intermingle, it makes more apparent the sexual and gendered nature of children—and this sometimes raises discomfort amongst educators. Although early childhood educators do not overtly sexualize children, there is a common desire to interject sexuality through the language used, the division of children by gender, the comments on boy/girl relations—consistently demonstrating a heteronormative discourse.

Reflective teaching practice that embeds criticality is complicated but recognizes that children are physical beings who engage in social and emotional relations but also play with gender identity and sexuality. The very idea that children in early childhood are completely innocent of any sexuality contradicts a common practice that assumes heterosexuality ("Oh look, your boyfriend is here") until proved otherwise (Cahill & Theilheimer, 1999). The innocence of children is often guarded through the avoidance of sexuality and queer relationships because it is thought that they are too young to understand. Sedwick (2008) suggests that "the essentialist understanding of sexual identity accrues a certain gravity" (p. 42). This is certainly true when educators become concerned with children's sexuality that orients toward queer.

In my professional role in a somewhat public position as a queer educator, my advice is sought on a regular basis on how to deal with children who exhibit attributes of the opposite gender. My response is consistently the same—children's exploration of their gender and sexuality is normative and like educators' ability to support physical and cognitive development, we have a responsibility to enable gender development and sexuality. I believe that teachers of early childhood educators need to improve their ability to embed these questions and discussions in early childhood professional education. Similar limitations arise when educators build their teaching practice based on a hegemonic notion that teaching signifies the transfer of information and knowledge to children through concepts like literacy and numeracy skills, which assumes a normative goal toward child development. In fact, teaching in early childhood is significantly more complex and relational. Moss (2010) argues for a different pedagogy that engages with children as active knowledge creators to create a space to challenge the way we teach. Children are very much attuned to how they relate to others, and their exploration of gender roles. Many of them are being raised in families that are very much part of a growing demographic and a social justice pedagogy that introduces topics such as prejudice, homophobic bullying, and resistance to differences that can create a climate of safety and protection, not harm for the children and their families.

Early childhood educators are well known for their expertise in child development and their knowledge about how to plan a program for young children. They are also to a certain extent known for their ability to support parents with young children. My interest in exploring the professional training that early childhood educators are engaged in with respect to parent engagement led to one consistent finding: a profound absence of knowledge about the needs of queer families primarily because of an absence of discussion of content related to queer families and their children. One educator who completed her studies in a large urban college said, "We never discussed queer families but we were always encouraged to use inclusive language and to be respectful of diversity. Some professors talked about inclusion but never talked about anything related to same-sex couples" (personal Communication, M.M., June 2010).

Although there is a desire to establish a framework of inclusion that engages parents in their children's development, there is little awareness of how the parent demographic has changed and the necessity to adapt the early childhood professional preparation program accordingly. Parent engagement is central to early childhood practice and unlike teacher education there is a provincial requirement for a separate course in the professional preparation program on how to involve parents. The principles of parent involvement are grounded in a long history and tradition that active parent involvement in a child's educational experience harnesses improved child outcomes and establishes a pattern of mutual reciprocity between parents and educators (Corter & Pelletier, 2005). However, the nature of parent involvement is often exemplified by invitations to participate in program activities, volunteer in the classroom, assist on field trips, and, to a certain extent, given the right kind of skills, participate in the governance of a program. I argue for a connection to parents and their children that is more meaningful and attuned to the interests of individual families.

In the early childhood context, existing research is unclear if queer parents' involvement includes commonly known practices such as enhanced and purposeful communication, and invitations to participate in program activities and governance structures including advisory committees as proposed by Epstein and Sheldon (2006). Existing research on the relationships between queer parents and educators has been limited to school settings with findings that demonstrate how queer identification challenges the normative policies and practice in educational settings. Baker (2002) found that the perception of school experiences is predominantly negative because children are outside the protection of their parents for extended periods of time, a situation that generally results in a propensity for bullying. According to Fryand and Capper (2003) and Silin (1993), schools are generally hostile environments for lesbian, gay, and queer parents. One Australian study of experiences of lesbian mothers in preschool settings in an urban community indicates a sense of vulnerability and fear for their children's safety especially if they choose to disclose their sexuality (Scattlebol & Ferfolia, 2007). The findings from these studies demonstrate that before early childhood educators are able to establish meaningful partnerships with queer parents, attitudinal changes are necessary. Early childhood teacher training that is focused on parent engagement within a framework of developmentally appropriate practice does have implications for the experiences of queer parents with young children. The question to explore further is, how do these contextual issues make a difference to queer parents?

Parent engagement builds a trusting relationship between parent and educator, in turn creating a safe and trustworthy environment for children. In addition, research confirms that parent engagement is important to child development but that it needs to extend to parents who may be situated outside the dominant framework of what is typically known as a parent. With queer parents in particular, the combinations of family structures go beyond most people's imagination and are more complex than they were even a decade ago. Pushor (2007) suggests that despite a historical pattern in which educators held authority through their professional knowledge, it is possible to move toward a shared terrain where parent engagement enables exploration of a relationship that is based on shared knowledge and respect that both parents and educators bring to the table. Paying attention to these attributes is critical to moving toward a connectedness between child, parent, and educator. There is a growing scholarship on the engagement of parents from diverse backgrounds that challenges the presumptions behind why some "minority" parents do not get involved in early childhood programs (Bernhard, Lefebvre, Kilbride, Chud, & Fahlman 1998). However, unlike parents who are new to Canada or who may be English language learners, the interests of queer parents are not embedded in early childhood training. This absence heightens the silence but also does not adequately prepare educators for a new reality of parent engagement in early childhood programs.

How families are defined has been transformed from a private entity to one in which the state has both direct and indirect involvement. The patriarchal and private historical narrative of the family has shifted to one where "the family comes to appear not as a special zone isolated from the rest of society, but as an integral part of it, and possibly a microcosm of its inequities and injustices" (Minot, 2000, p. 24). The state in some shape or form defines marriage and divorce laws, adoption rights, custody arrangements, financial obligations of parents, and, obviously connected to this research, what counts as "family" within an education and rights framework.

Canadians have a long history of challenging the government for additional rights using the legal systems in place, particularly the Canadian Charter of Rights and Freedoms, to ensure a fair and just society for all. The debate on the right to marriage between individuals of the same sex, the right of access to spousal benefits, the right to partake in health-care decisions, and the right to parent children within relationships outside the heteronormative construct of family has involved using existing laws to challenge discriminatory practices. The past decade has seen us continue to grapple with gay marriage as a socially and politically contentious issue. According to Statistics Canada (2006), between 2001 and 2006 there has been a surge in the number of same-sex couples with children in Canada. As reported above, about 9% of same-sex couples had children living with them despite the backlash they often experience. Same-sex families are becoming more socially acceptable, with a majority of Canadians supporting gay marriage (Angus Reid Public Opinion, 2010).

The development of new medical and scientific reproductive technologies has ruptured the dominant biological process and eroded the familiar social arrangements that relied on the traditional biological order. Although "jurisprudence and legislation regulating the family status of gay and lesbian people, and their children is a relatively new phenomenon in Canada" (Cameron, 2008, p. 103), increasing numbers of lesbian mothers are choosing to give birth and co-parent with their same-sex partners with the assistance of known or unknown sperm donors. Gay fathers are entering into surrogacy agreements with women in order to have and raise children in same-sex relationships. Transgender men are pregnant and calmly providing a family, in seemingly unsurprising ways given the advance of science and its large-scale modifications of what we once felt were immutable elements of biology (Crosbie, 2008). Sex and procreation have become uncoupled and making babies has increasingly occurred outside the heterosexual marriage norm (Cossman & Ryder, 2001).

However, in early childhood studies, notions of developmentally appropriate practice have become completely entangled and familiar in research and policy, as well as in practice. The term is almost intrinsic to early childhood programs but significantly problematic to the complexity of diversity and difference and how queer identity is silenced. In addition to the more commonly understood identities, children with queer parents may be adopted or may have been created with a known or unknown donor. Children may be born through surrogacy or may be part of a previous heterosexual relationship. These queer variations on conventional notions of "family" demand consideration by early childhood educators, again challenging the discourse of normative human development. The silence of queering identities invokes a pathologization, as Butler (1993a) has suggested.

I question, and have a desire to shift early childhood training and research to move toward more reflective practice. If educators have a desire to be responsive to all families, then reconceptualizing early childhood teacher training is necessary. Queer families and their children are increasingly a growing part of the Canadian landscape and although early childhood educators do not need to become family law experts, they do need to be attuned to the myriad of legal challenges that redefine family and parental rights. Just as they need to understand the issues that some immigrant families face, educators should also be aware of challenges that some queer families experience. As part of professional practice, maintaining knowledge of new research and information that affect early childhood programs is significant, particularly since parent engagement is such a critical component of establishing high-quality early childhood professional practice. In addition, being cognizant of the evolution of family law and human rights in Canada influences the policies that are developed in early learning programs, removing potential barriers that queer parents may experience.

References

Adams, S. (2004). Heteronormativity and teaching at Syracuse University in *Interrupting Heteronormativity*. Syracuse, NY: The Graduate School of Syracuse University. Retrieved from http://www.syr.edu/gradschool/pdf/resourcebooksvideos/Heteronormativity.pdf

Apple, M. (1975). The hidden curriculum and the nature of conflict. In W. Pinar (Ed.), *Curriculum theorizing: The reconceptualists*. Berkeley, CA: McCutchan.

Angus Reid Public Opinion. (2010). *Canadians and Britons are more open on same-sex relations than Americans*. Retrieved from http://www.angus-reid.com/polls/43149/canadians-and-britons-are-more-open-on-same-sex-relations-than-americans/

Baker, J. (2002). *How homophobia hurts children: Nurturing diversity at home, in the school and in the community*. Binghampton, NY: Haworth Press.

Battiste, M. (2005). Post-colonial remedies for protecting indigenous knowledge and heritage. In P. Tripp & L. Muzzin (Eds.), *Teaching as activism: Equity meets environmentalism* (pp. 224–232). Montreal, QC: McGill-Queen's University Press.

Beach, J., Friendly, M., Ferns, C., Prabhu, N., & Forer, B. (2009). *Early childhood education and care in Canada 2008*. Toronto, ON: Child Care Resource and Research Unit.

Bernhard, J., Lefebvre, M. L., Kilbride, K. M., Chud, G., & Fahlman, R. (1998). Troubled relationships in early childhood education: Interactions in ethnoculturally diverse child care settings. *Journal of Early Education and Development, 9*(1), 5–28.

Blaise, M. (2005). *Playing it straight: Uncovering gender discourses in the early childhood classroom.* New York, NY: Routledge.
Butler, J. (1993a). *Bodies that matter: On the discursive limits of "sex."* New York, NY: Routledge.
Butler, J. (1993b). Critically queer. *GLQ: A Journal of Lesbian and Gay Studies, 1*(1), 17.
Cahill, B. J., & Theilheimer, R. (1999). Stonewall in the housekeeping area: Gay and lesbian issues in the early childhood classroom. In W. J. Letts & J. T. Sears (Eds.), *Queering elementary education* (pp. 39–49). Lanham, MD: Rowman & Littlefield.
Cameron, A. (2008). Regulating the queer family: The Assisted Human Reproduction Act. *Canadian Journal of Family Law, 101,* 100–121.
College of Early Childhood Educators. (2011). *Code of ethics and standards of practice.* Toronto, ON: Author. Retrieved from http://collegeofece.on.ca/main.php?page_id=3
Corter, C., & Pelletier, J. (2005). Parent and community involvement in schools: Policy panacea or pandemic? In N. Bascia, A. Cumming, A. Datnow, K. Leithwood, & D. Livingstone (Eds.), *International handbook of educational policy* (pp. 295–327). Dordrecht, the Netherlands: Springer.
Cossman, B., & Ryder, B. (2001). What is marriage-like like? The irrelevance of conjugality. *Canadian Journal of Family Law, 269,* 269–238.
Crosbie, L. (2008, April 8). Could his reception mean a relaxing about gender? *The Globe and Mail.* Retrieved from http://www.theglobeandmail.com/subscribe.jsp?art=677192
Day Nurseries Act, R.S.O., ch. D.2. (1990). Retrieved from http://www.e-laws.gov.on.ca/html/statutes/english/elaws_statutes_90d02_e.htm
Delacourt, S. (2011, February 4). Minister Finley defends child care remarks. *The Toronto Star.* Retrieved from http://www.thestar.com/news/canada/article/933540--minister-finley-defends-child-care-remarks
Early Childhood Educators Act, S.O., Ch. 7, s. 8. (2007). Retrieved from http://www.e-laws.gov.on.ca/html/statutes/english/elaws_statutes_07e07_e.htm
An Act to Amend the Education Act, S.O. Ch. 10 (2010) Retrieved from http://www.e-laws.gov.on.ca/html/source/statutes/english/2010/elaws_src_s10010_e.htm
Epstein, J. L., & Sheldon, S. B. (2006). Moving forward ideas for research on school, family and community partnership. In C. F. Conrad & R. Serlin (Eds.), *Sage handbook for research in education: Engaging ideas for enriching inquiry.* Thousand Oaks, CA: Sage.
Foucault, M. (1974). *The archeology of knowledge.* London, England: Tavistock.
Foucault, M. (1978). *The history of sexuality.* New York, NY: Vintage Books.
Freiler, C., Rothman, L., & Barata, P. (2004). *Pathways to progress: Structural ways to address child poverty.* Toronto, ON: Campaign 2000.
Friendly, M. (2011, January 11). Death by indifference. *The Toronto Star.* Retrieved from http://action.web.ca/home/crru/rsrcs_crru_full.shtml?x=130663
Friendly, M., & Prentice, S. (2009). *About Canada: Child care.* Winnipeg, MB: Fernwood Publishing.
Fryand, D., & Capper, C. A. (2003). Do you have any idea who you just hired? *Journal of School Leadership, 13*(1), 86–124.
Gestwicki, C. (2011). *Developmentally appropriate practice: curriculum and development in early education* (4th ed.). Belmont, CA: Wadsworth Gengage.
Human Rights Act, R.S.O., ch. H.19. (1990). Retrieved from http://www.e-laws.gov.on.ca/html/statutes/english/elaws_statutes_90h19_e.htm#BK0
Jagose, A. (1996). *Queer theory: An introduction.* New York, NY: New York University Press.
Janus, M., & Duku, E. (2007). The school entry gap: Socioeconomic, family, and health factors associated with children's schoolreadiness to learn. *Early Education & Development, 18*(3), 375–403.
Mac Naughton, G. (1998). Improving our gender equity tools. In N. Yelland (Ed.), *Gender in early childhood* (pp. 149–174). London, England: Routledge.
Minot, L. A. (2000). Conceiving parenthood: Parenting and the rights of lesbian, gay, bisexual and transgender people and their children. In S. Long (Ed.), *A report of the International Gay*

and Lesbian Human Rights Commission (pp. 1–44). San Francisco, CA: International Gay and Lesbian Human Rights Commission.

Moss, P. (2010). *What is your image of the child? UNESCO policy brief on early childhood.* Paris, France: United Nations Education, Scientific and Cultural Organization.

National Association for the Education of Young Children. (2009). *Position statement on developmentally appropriate practice in early childhood programs serving children from birth through age 8* (3rd ed.). Washington, DC: Author.

Ontario Ministry of Education. (2009) *Realizing the promise of diversity: Ontario's equity and diversity strategy.* Toronto, ON: The Government of Ontario.

Ontario Ministry of Training, Colleges and Universities. (2000). *Early childhood education program standard.* Toronto, ON: The Government of Ontario. Retrieved from http://www.tcu.gov.on.ca/pepg/audiences/colleges/progstan/humserv/eerchedu.pdf

Pascal, C. (2009). *With our best future in mind: Implementing early learning in Ontario.* Toronto, ON: Queen's Printer of Ontario.

Pushor, D. (2007). *Welcoming parents: Educators as guest hosts on school landscapes.* Toronto, ON: Education Canada.

Robinson, K. (2005). "Queerying" gender: Heteronormativity in early childhood education. *Australian Journal of Early Childhood, 30*(2), 19–28.

Robinson, K., & Jones Díaz, C. (2007). *Diversity and difference in early childhood education: Issues for theory and practice.* Maidenhead, England: Open University Press.

Sadoway, G. (2002, February). Introduction: Children at risk. *Refuge, 20*(2) 2–3.

Scattlebol, J., & Ferfolja, T. (2007). Voices from an enclave: Lesbian mothers' experiences of child care. *Australian Journal of Early Childhood, 32*(1), 9–20.

Sears, J. T. (1999). Teaching queerly: Some elementary propositions. In W. J. Letts & J. T. Sears (Eds.), *Queering elementary education* (pp. 3–14). Lanham, MD: Rowman & Littlefield.

Sedwick, E. K. (2008). *The epistemology of the closet.* Berkeley, CA: University of California Press.

Silin, J. (1995). *Sex, death, and the education of children: Our passion for ignorance in the age of AIDS.* New York, NY: Teachers College Press.

Standing Senate Committee on Social Affairs. (2009). *Early childhood education and care: Next steps.* Ottawa, ON: The Senate of Canada.

Statistics Canada. (2006). *2006 Census: Family portrait: Continuity and change in Canadian families and households in 2006. National portrait: Census families.* Ottawa, ON: Author. Retrieved from http://www12.statcan.ca/census-recensement/2006/as-sa/97-553/p4-eng.cfm#note1

Statistics Canada. (2010). Women in Canada: Paid work. *The Daily.* Retrieved from http://www.statcan.gc.ca/daily-quotidien/101209/dq101209a-eng.htm

Tyyska, V. 2001. *Long and winding road: Adolescents and youth in Canada today.* Toronto, ON: Canadian Scholar's Press.

Viruru, R. (2005). The impact of post-colonial theory on early childhood education. *The Journal of Education, 35,* 7–29.

Chapter Seven

Immigrant Parents Taking Part in Their Children's Education

A Practical Experiment

Judith K. Bernhard

There is increasing recognition of the role of power in all social and authoritative discourses, especially those connected with family values and the rearing of children. Mainstream texts and articles, as well as definitive manuals such as DSM-IV, are entirely permeated with assumptions that are taken for granted and never identified, explained, or defended. Postmodern and poststructural theories have brought these assumptions forward for analysis and critique. Several themes have emerged about the underlying processes of child rearing and children's education. For example, Bourdieu (1986) has stressed the symbolic and real violence involved in conceptions of social and cultural capital. The assimilation and adaptation of immigrants have been subjects of debate for several decades.

Recently, however, several issues related to power and social conformity have come to the fore. For example, a Tennessee town debates whether to allow the construction of a mosque. A law providing fines for wearing head covering has been implemented in France and the first Muslim women challengers to the law have stepped forward. Another theatre of resistance has been opened. New and resurrected proposals for English-only instruction and official government documents have been in the news (e.g., in Arizona, Florida, and California) recently. The dismal economic and employment situation has led to social eruptions in certain areas. The summer riots of 2011 in London persisted for several days and have given rise to calls to investigate their underlying causes. There are basic facts about the situation of newcomers, some of them quite disturbing, that call for new approaches including the following: Particular immigrant groups, especially those of Latino or African background, have done rather poorly overall, as specifically evident in children's performance in the North American educational system. The dropout rate is a crude but well-known indicator of both disadvantage and fundamental disengagement.

Beginning in the 1960s, mainstream institutions undertook to address the problems of immigrants and the so-called urban underclass. Most were extremely limited in their success, and the best results were achieved only by structuring the entire day and place of residence of the students.

However, there has been an explosion of theoretical developments connected with continuing injustice found in prosperous and otherwise "advanced" societies. These have focused on the power relations of the social groups involved and have brought to light a number of crucial assumptions and questionable propositions about immigrant parents and students as they fare in the educational system (e.g., "You can expect the kids to fail because the parents simply don't care").

Our research team over the past decade has been addressing these problems and published the following reports among others. Bernhard et al. (2006); Bernhard, Freire, Pacini-Ketchabaw, and Villanueva (1998); Bernhard, Winsler, Bleiker, Ginieniewicz, and Madigan (2008); Garcia (2008); Pacini-Ketchabaw, Bernhard, and Freire (2001); and Pinkus (2008). The intention of this chapter is to summarize the data collected by these research teams and specifically to relate them to our developing theories and revisions of practice. I begin with a summary of background information on Canadian immigration and immigrant students in the educational system. Then follows a theoretical review. The following and major portion of the chapter looks in detail at a series of three interventions with parent groups. These illustrate the process of dialectic refinement of theory and practice. I briefly indicate at the end of each section where the practice worked, where it needed to be improved, and what refinements of theoretical ideas were desirable. The concluding section provides thoughts about moving forward.

These experiences and data are presented in the hope of stimulating further dialogue. Much remains to be clarified and accomplished in the field. Our research teams over the years have been challenged to deal in concrete ways with the realities of power as discussed in the literature; we have learned how to listen better and to talk to immigrant parents in specific ways that will assist them in resisting subordination.

Background Information: Canadian Immigration and Students in the Canadian Educational System

Immigration is transforming urban centers worldwide. More than 191 million people live outside their home countries according to recent figures (United Nations, 2007). As world economies continue to undergo changes, migration levels are likely to increase further. Internationally known for its multiculturalism policy and humanitarianism, Canada accepts over 260,000 newcomers every year. Depending on the neighborhood, in any major city in Canada "new Canadians" may constitute 80% to 95% of the pupils, with new students arriving every day. Academic performance in Toronto specifically, where almost 50% of residents were born abroad, provides a stark example of the outcomes of current arrangements. There is compelling evidence that children from some immigrant groups including Latino, African, and Portuguese continue to have lower academic achievement and higher dropout rates. At 39%, the dropout rate for Spanish-speaking Toronto high school students is almost double the average for English-speaking students. Only 10% of Latin Americans in Toronto graduate from university (Anisef, Brown, Phythian, Sweet, & Walters, 2008; Bernhard, 2009). Although more than 36% of these come from economically disadvantaged families, the Canadian situation appears to be consistent with an international pattern. The 2006 PISA(Programme for International Student Assessment) study of educational performance in 57 countries reported the widespread achievement gap of immigrant children (Organisation for Economic Co-operation and Development [OECD], 2006; Statistics Canada, 2007b).

Several factors have left Canadian teachers largely ill equipped to interact effectively with immigrants. Whereas earlier immigration waves to Canada were characterized by people from Europe and Commonwealth countries with closer cultural and racial matches between teachers and immigrants, recent shifts in Canadian immigration policies have meant that newcomers are now more likely to come from Asia, Africa, and Latin America. Although one of every six children under age fourteen in Canada is a member of a visible minority group (Statistics Canada, 2007a), Canadian teachers, predominantly white Francophones in Quebec and Anglophones outside the province of Quebec, are often unaware of the extent to which cultural differences affect students and their families. Despite the best intentions of school boards, teachers, and school administrators to account for the disparity between combined teacher–parent objectives and the large numbers of immigrant children meeting with academic failure, one needs to pay attention to social structures and perceived groupings, and their power or lack of it. The challenges faced by newcomers to Canada have been the focus of a number of studies (Bernhard, Landolt, & Goldring, 2009; George & Michalski, 1996; Goldring, Berinstein, & Bernhard, 2009; Lo et al., 2000; Murdie & Teixeira, 2000; Ng, 1993; Ng & Ramirez, 1981; Siemiatycki, 1998). Although immigrants feel angry and shocked at the unexpected, chilly reception they receive, hundreds of thousands continue to make their children's future their priority.

Work with immigrant parents of preschool and elementary children has brought to light multitudes of examples of encounters with institutional obstacles, cumbersome procedures, and teachers' ignorance or assumptions about the supposed superiority of advanced Western cultural norms and capital. To give the simplest of examples, the communications from school to parents including report cards are often incomprehensible despite any translations that might be provided. As well, they tend to disempower the recipient utterly (e.g., "We consider it in the best interest of your child to enroll him in a special needs program"). The parents may see a prize when in fact it is a sentence to academic failure.

There is much literature that I do not review here about preconceptions that are applied to immigrant children ranging from "spoiled and clinging" to "disruptive" and "like a wild animal" (Bernhard, 2004; Bernhard & Freire, 1996). Below I turn to a discussion of the theories on which our interventions were based.

Theoretical Frameworks and Other Interventions

Critical Pedagogy

A main underlying theory for our work is the work of radical educator Freire (1999), who strove to empower communities in Brazil, a clearly postcolonial situation. Freire believed that the oppressed should not be marginalized, nor should they live outside society. His solution was not to integrate them, but rather to transform the entire structure of society. He suggested that an educational program would be successful only when it began at the grassroots level and used a collaborative problem-solving model rather than a "banking" (Friere, 1999, p. 66) model wherein information is deposited in students. Freire (1999) held that the interaction between teacher and student did not occur in a vacuum, but rather in an elaborate social context in which the pupils did not passively reproduce the information presented to them. By empowering students and using cultural references, he tapped into sources of strength and ideals. For example, when Freire worked with peasants to teach them to read, he found that in order to be effective, the learning opportunity needed to be experiential and emotionally engaging. Freire's insight was to start with the position of the people themselves and their understanding of that position. Further, Friere (1999) emphasized the importance of their coming to see that legitimate structures were not set in stone, but could be challenged and altered:

> The point of departure of the movement lies in the people themselves. But since people do not exist apart from the world, apart from reality, the movement must begin with the human-world relationship. Accordingly, the point of departure must always be with men and women in the "here and now. . ." To do this authentically they must perceive their state not as fated and unalterable, but merely as limiting and therefore challenging. Whereas the banking method directly or indirectly reinforces men's fatalistic perception of their situation, the problem-posing method presents this very situation to them as a problem. (p. 66)

In summary, learners are learning to take charge of their own lives and acquiring a sense of agency. In this manner, they gain power in their situation and the ability to alter their circumstances.

The change process that learners both undergo and take charge of shows particular features to which I draw attention. In particular, Freire (1999) stressed the regaining of one's humanity through redressing violations that have occurred in the social processes:

> Resignation gives way to the drive for transformation and inquiry, over which men feel themselves to be in control. If people, as historical beings necessarily engaged with other people in a movement of inquiry, did not control that movement, it would be (and is) a violation of their humanity. (p. 66)

His teaching method strongly relied on discussion and dialogue rather than repetition and memorization. Such dialogue allows for the development of joint responsibility:

> Through dialogue, the teacher-of-the-students and the students-of-the-teacher cease to exist and a new term emerges: teacher-student with students-teachers. The teacher is no longer merely the-one-who-teaches, but one who is himself taught in dialogue with the students, who in turn while being taught also teach. They become jointly responsible for a process in which all grow. (p. 61)

The format and the content were both important. For example, Freire began one lesson with the letter *O* to allow the peasants to discuss the word "oppression" and how this term explained what had initially seemed like individual experiences of poverty. The specific, well-thought-out topics with which he began his lessons mattered deeply to the students and gave them the motivation to learn to read in order to understand how their individual problems were in fact part of systemic issues that led to their marginalization. The process of becoming conscious of their place in the system was labeled "conscientization," or *conscientização* (Portuguese). Freire's methods are outlined in *Pedagogy of Hope* (1994), a book that has inspired educators worldwide to encourage their students to read the world through the word.

Cultural Capital

The second theory on which we have relied to develop our work was that of post-Marxist, social theorist Bourdieu (1986). He has deepened our understanding of power and its mode of operation. He saw power as diffused in institutions and everyday practices of society (Cannella, 2002; Corson, 1998; Looker, 1994). Without being aware of it, the individual is highly constrained by these practices and has lost any vision of alternatives available to him or her. Based on Bourdieu (Lareau, 1989), we have employed the concept of "cultural capital," which is defined as those dispositions (habitus) and capabilities that establish a person of a particular background and social stratum in a set of social relations through which relationships he or she produces and reproduces his or her own socially constructed position.

An example given by Bauder (2008) is as follows: A person's passport can function as a form of cultural capital. It is a signifier, a mechanism that gives those who have it the capability to tap into employment opportunities, professional recognition, and so on. Those who are not given such citizenship tend to be vulnerable or exploitable. Bauder goes on to explain the subtle ways that members of the elite group show their status:

> Bourdieu suggests that the members of an elite social group may signify their status through embodied cultural capital in the form of subtle "gestures or the apparently most insignificant techniques of the body-ways of walking or blowing one's nose, ways of eating or talking." In this case, those who do not possess the code to read or enact these cultural performances lack access to important symbols of power. Another process of distinction exists in the form of institutionalized cultural capital represented by educational diplomas, certificates or other types of institutional acknowledgment. (p. 318)

In accordance with Bourdieu and Bauder, we see ethnicity not as an inherent group characteristic but primarily as an ongoing ascription and construction by those constituting themselves as the dominant group(s). In other words, "immigrant" can be viewed as a construction of official discourse, and his or her deficits follow as a matter of course. The same arguments generally applied to "race" categories (Darder, Torres, & Gutierrez, 1997; Dei, 2001) as well as those of class and nation of origin. These are key concepts that we have used from postfoundational theories.

Many educators have said that they are frustrated at the lack of response on the part of newcomer families. They say, with some justification, that the parents are not involved; they do not come to meetings and do not seem to be motivated or interested enough to participate in their children's schooling. What teachers call immigrant parents' lack of motivation and interest can be said to be an expression of the dynamic of their devaluation. Thus the teachers' ability to facilitate their students' success is undermined by their lack of understanding and valuing of the cultural capital that immigrant parents bring.

An important and related concept is that of funds of knowledge developed by Moll (González, Moll, & Amanti, 2005) to identify bodies of knowledge and know-how that are "historically accumulated" and circulated in marginalized communities and come to act as resources that are "essential for household or individual functioning and well-being."

The devaluing of immigrant parents' cultural capital is further exacerbated by educators' pre-service training in the age-stage theories prevalent in the field of child development that portray childhood as a fairly narrow range of ages and stages without accounting for discrepancy of background. Although it is now increasingly recognized that milestones of childhood and definitions of "optimal development" are diverse and culturally dependent (Bernhard, 2003; Bernhard, Friere, et al., 1998; Garcia-Coll, 1990; Hedegaard, 2009; Lerner, 1988, 1991; O'Loughlin, 2009; Onchwari, Onchwari, & Keengwe, 2008; Rogoff, 1990), immigrant children growing up with a different set of priorities than that of the educational system are often construed as behind and needing to catch up with their age-mates. Teachers, therefore, miss the many other ways that these children demonstrate strength and competence. Teachers, rather than turning to parents for information about their child-rearing goals in order to assess correctly their students' development, often devalue or are blind to newcomer families' cultural capital and unique "funds of knowledge" (González et al., 2005).

Identity, Engagement, and Community
The third theory on which we have drawn in our work is that of Cummins (1989, 2001, 2002), a critical theorist with a focus on bilingualism and biculturalism (see also Ada, 2003; Corson, 1998; New London Group, 1996). This focus has been on connections between developing a positive identity and increased academic achievement. Nurturing a student's identity involves not only recognizing the forms of prior knowledge (including home languages) that he or she brings to the class, but also incorporating them into classroom learning (Taylor, Bernhard, Garg, & Cummins, 2008). Insight into students' home environments and cultural contexts provides ways of understanding how children make sense of their world (Taylor, Bernhard, Garg, & Cummins, 2008; Westby & Atencio, 2002). When educators direct their efforts toward learning and understanding how children experience the world, and when they strive to become familiar with the complex context (including culture and language) in which students, educators, and families live and learn, they are better equipped to respond to students' needs and concerns (Artiles & Klingner, 2006; Klingner & Artiles, 2003). By cultivating an optimal learning environment—instructing a child in his or her first language, using a child's prior knowledge and personal experiences—educators and school personnel can provide greater opportunities for immigrant students to achieve academic success.

Language is one of the strongest elements in one's self-definition as an individual and a social being. Attending to and valuing a child's home language in the school context is an important way to show respect for the child and his or her family, community, and culture. All children have the right to retain, develop, and enrich their heritage language while learning a national language. Retaining one's own language offers many more opportunities for human growth and certainly creates greater opportunities to work on behalf of humanity (Cummins & Sayers, 1995; Fishman, 1989; Krashen, 1999).

The focus on language involves promoting not just explicit knowledge of how the linguistic code operates, but also critical awareness of how language operates deep within society.

Cummins's (2002) theories recognize that students' position in relation to the teacher, to other students, and to the learning community is the basis of *identity* investment and overall *engagement*, in particular cognitive. Learning is optimized when these interactions maximize both cognitive engagement and identity investment. Teacher–student interactions and other interactions in the learning community (including the classroom, the school, the family, and broader community, and virtual communities enabled through electronic communication) create an interpersonal space where knowledge is generated, identities are negotiated, and agency is developed.

To draw these threads together, the theories of Freire, Bourdieu, Cummins, and others have proposed a number of key concepts, among them empowerment and agency, identity, injustice in mainstream institutions, marginalization, cultural capital, and linguistic dominance as resisted by disadvantaged groups. All have proposed ways of challenging the structures that are in place and considered to be authoritative. In a broader sense, the theories challenge the foundations of the normative theories of child development and immigrant adaptation.

Using these theories, besides aiming for critical development of knowledge, our research projects were also meant to help empower immigrant groups. Specifically, we have focused on efforts to identify, analyze, and help overcome school difficulties by forming a special parents' group based on similar ethnic background and facilitated by native speakers of the parents' home language. We saw the parents' experiences as reflecting inequitable social structures, but also as a basis for action to change problematic situations. The following section provides an account of our interventions.

The Eight-Month Parent Group Intervention

A 1995 grant from the Canadian federal government allowed us to work with a group of twelve Latin American parents, primarily mothers, over an eight-month period (Bernhard, Freire, et al., 1998). Monthly discussions about aspects of their children's experience with Canadian schools took place at a Toronto community center. Participants had been recruited through word of mouth, television, and newspaper features. The solicitation did not require or presume that the children were experiencing academic difficulty.

One way that the researchers established their credibility with the Latin American parent group was their shared Latino background. One of the leaders for the parents' group had completed her medical studies in Chile and moved to Canada where she completed postgraduate training in psychiatry. She was at the time a school board chief psychiatrist. The other group leader had lived in Chile until sixteen years of age and had moved to Puerto Rico and then to Canada. On receiving her doctorate, she became a professor in education. Because the two researchers leading this group were seasoned professionals who had extensive knowledge of the Canadian educational system, they were easily able to answer all the parents' questions.

Our facilitators' opening invitation to parents was in line with Freire's views as a humanist, revolutionary educator. The parents were enlisted as partners who assumed their full role as empowered human beings.

The role of the facilitator was not as a dispenser of banked knowledge. Rather, she invited an alternate dynamic by initiating discussions with neutral, open-ended questions, giving parents a clear message that the topics of focus would be close to their reality and that the discussions would be meaningful rather than static and alien to their experience.

On a rotating basis, group members acted as co-facilitators and assumed responsibility for ensuring that the discussions were orderly, also reflecting Freire's problem-posing theoretical framework in which the roles of teachers and students are fluid and their relations dialogic. This process illustrates the joint responsibility to which Freire referred, quoted in my review above. One participant described her experiences of these novel arrangements:

> In the first place, the dynamism, the mutual trust, that I was given, I felt very sure of myself, I felt that this is my place. . . . I had a lot of freedom to express so many things. . . . So that is what I liked and really caught my attention. . . . I did not want to miss even one meeting and even with my work, I made every effort to come and I didn't want to miss even one moment of the class.

With the goal of empowerment, facilitators encouraged participants to comment on interpretations of their previous statements by summarizing the topics discussed in previous sessions and asking the participants whether they wanted to elaborate on those topics or discuss other issues. In this way, participants were helping to take charge of their own process. Further, this approach allowed facilitators to reevaluate their reflections and plans.

Families began to gain one another's trust and identify barriers to their involvement in the educational system, some including issues of sex, race, and class. The parents engaged in dialogue, posing problems they were encountering, and with the help of the facilitators and the other parents they developed a deepened consciousness of their situation including potentially transformative actions such as how to take action to transform their initial feelings of not being welcome when they entered the schools. This dialogic method was also intended to resonate with Freire's writings on the movement away from banking education.

In analyzing the results of this first phase, we realized that the parents now knew that there were policies encouraging parental participation, that they could challenge the labels of deficiency that they were being assigned, and could even act in resistance to the institutional procedures of mainstream schooling. We had successes in several important areas as mentioned above, for example, increased occasions during which the parents attended parent meetings at the school and knew that they were expected to take an active role in the children's education.

We discovered that because of the frequent marginalization of newcomer parents, it was important to show them that they had little to fear and much to gain by being actively involved.

In a number of cases, the parents did not agree with the decisions of the school and felt frustrated at not being able to shape decisions about their children. The consequences of these missteps were readily evident in the Latino parents whom we interviewed, who noted that the Canadian teachers speaking as experts left them feeling unable to make their views known. Parents also noted that the jargon and specialized terms that educators used during meetings such as "withdrawal," "special education," "below grade level functioning in English," and "reading clinic" were not understood even when translators were employed.

Our theoretical basis helped us to understand the objective features of marginalization, to see that the parents were unlikely to effect genuine and long-term changes without understanding and knowing how to contest the power structures involved. In the next intervention, we explicitly addressed the acquisition of such knowledge and how to exercise it. Our objective was to show parents that advocating on behalf of their children or expressing their legitimate complaints was their right, and that rather than producing ill feeling or retaliation on the part of the teachers, it would have a chance of being effective. This was seen as a means to our goal of empowerment.

We realized that despite the goodwill of all involved, the parents would not be able to bring about changes unless structures were altered to include recognition of their cultural capital, including, for example, two-way interactions wherein both sides listened and spoke. Parents needed some power to ensure that their ideas were given serious consideration and if possible acted on. Parents needed to learn how the system worked and what the codes of power were, and then act.

The Parenting Workshops Intervention: Learning the Codes of Power

In order to respond to the lessons learned in the first phase of the research, our research team worked to develop and pilot a ten-week project that was the basis of the parent groups that later came to be known as the Canadian Parenting Workshops (Bernhard, Freire, & Mulligan, 2004). The intent of this intervention was to see if in addition to the parents being able to tap into their networks and know that their voices would be heard, they would also learn to see schools as sites for the reproduction of the social order: in Bourdieu's (1986) terms, to acquire the "habitus" that signifies they are part of the code of power.

The primary changes involved bringing forward dialogue on information about the important role of attachment across cultures and biases in the definition of terms such as "developmentally appropriate" or "school-readiness." Also included in this second phase was information about school report cards, how to contact school superintendents and members of parliament, school committee structures, and the workings of the designation of children for the special education system.

In order to field-test and evaluate the intervention, it was implemented in four community-based settings in Vancouver, Montreal, and Toronto in fall 2002 and spring 2003; all were Latin American parents of children ages four to eight. A total of fifty-five mothers registered for the program. Forty-eight completed the program and final surveys. Most of the mothers were in their mid-twenties to late thirties, as might be expected for mothers of children age eight and under. Family size was generally one to three children. All the mothers and almost all the fathers were born in Latin American countries. Most had come to Canada recently: a large majority had been in Canada fewer than five years and half for fewer than three years.

In addition to being newcomers to Canada with young children, the mothers in the parenting groups were further isolated from the mainstream. Only one-fifth spoke the languages of their children's schools. Nine out of ten had an income below the Canadian Low Income Cut-Off. These parents had limited support for parenting—in addition to having left behind extended family members, a quarter were single parents, nearly half reported having no help with caring for their children, and one in ten had no help or advice about parenting.

As the groups progressed, parents indeed began to interact with the school personnel, assert themselves, and know that their views would be heard. One mother, Mrs. Blanco, said,

> My daughter was enthusiastic about taking a trip for three days, so I paid for the ticket. But then she told me she did not want to go because she was going to feel alone and she had never been away from home. The principal told me that my daughter still had to go because I had already paid. So I said to him: "Excuse me, but I cannot do that. If my daughter does not feel good about going, I will not send her." I was firm and they gave me the money back. The group gives one more assurance to do what we think is right with our children.

Thanks to her experience with the group, this mother now knew that her views had validity. In Bourdieu's (1986) terms, this mother had become aware of her subordination in the institution and the role that her language played in it. Further, she had developed additional cultural capital and had learned how to tap into the codes of power and behave in ways that the school staff recognized as legitimate and valid. In this way, her frustration gave way to transformation. This mother's experience with the problem-posing methods derived from Freire (1994, 1999) enabled her to understand her marginalization and how the system worked if not challenged. She learned what actions she needed to undertake to affect the system and the outcome for her child.

Our analysis indicated that the group experience helped the parents to comprehend better what was expected of them in the support of their children's schooling while retaining their own cultural assets. Parents learned not only to collaborate with teachers and express their concerns, but also to affirm their ethnocultural differences. This came up several times in the area of discipline, with parents reacting to how the children's behavior was dealt with by the schools in Canada. Mrs. Garcia's sister-in-law provided us with an example illustrating how a newcomer parent retained her cultural assets in an interaction with the school. Mrs. Rojas told us about her fourteen-year-old son Alfredo, who had misbehaved but later recognized his mistake and apologized to the school:

> Alfredo was suspended from school. We went to talk to the vice-principal and told him that he [Alfredo] recognizes he acted badly, but not to suspend him because he was going to lose the school year. We asked if the child could do some volunteer work as a penalty. The vice-principal was totally against it and said that in this school there is no volunteer work. I am not justifying Alfredo, but how can they be so rigid?

Alfredo eventually had to repeat the semester, but was also sent to work with his father for two weeks—twelve-hour days, six days a week. The parents implemented their own volunteer work program.

Participants' satisfaction was evident in focus-group responses and in their attendance. An average of 85% of registered mothers attended each session, with over half of all participants attending 90% or more of the sessions. Through their written and oral feedback, the mothers in parent groups affirmed the benefits of the intervention and its effect on their knowledge and behavior.

For example, one mother's comments shows how she had increased her use of informal and formal supports. She found the following way to overcome the barriers and penetrate the school walls.

> I decided I am going to start to get in the school and to bother teachers so much that they are going to listen to me. Now, I am there. And with all the parents

there are, and if we all start to get into the school and make them listen to us, they will let us in. The other day, the teacher asked me to go to school to help children with their reading.

Mothers reported learning and using certain Canadian ways such as offering children more choices, taking time to explain consequences of various choices, and reading frequently while also consciously retaining their own cultural capital including values such as the emphasis on respect for elders, a focus on good manners, and a sense of the interdependence of family members.

By the end of this second phase, mothers also understood better how to communicate with teachers and principals, and more mothers agreed that it is important to share information about their culture with their children's teachers; they told stories about teachers' positive responses.

Yet parents often picked up on teachers' implicit and not so implicit cues about speaking Spanish in the home and began to speak to their children in English or French instead of their native language. As one Colombian mother recounted,

> One day I told the teacher that I like speaking in Spanish with my daughter because I wanted her to learn both languages. The teacher answered me that I should speak in English and not in Spanish. She told me that she thought that I should speak to my daughter in English.

This mother understood that the school did not attach any particular value to her home language. The message that she received was that her knowledge and cultural capital were marginal to what was being taught at school.

Overall, the intervention enjoyed success according to several indicators. The parents developed an awareness of their social position, learned what cultural capital was, and came to understand the basis of their children's imminent marginalization. They learned what needed to be done in order to generate the desired responses from the teachers and the educational institutions generally.

However, the project brought to light problems in a number of areas. We had found that families' intentions and desires to maintain their mother tongue became overwhelmingly difficult to attain as they received little encouragement from dominant institutions. Practitioners' influence on parents' decisions and actions regarding their children's learning was shown to be enormous. For some of the mothers participating in our studies, feelings of insecurity and sometimes guilt led them to abandon the use of their mother tongue with their children.

We found the language issues to be especially clarified by the theoretical approaches described above. Language issues were a crucial structural constituent of the gulf between parents and children, as language heritage, as a rich emotional resource and carrier of an ideology associated with a particular view of the world, was being lost.

For all these reasons, proactively working with parents to recognize and build on their own cultural capital, including their home language, became a priority for further interventions. We found it was crucial to have a clear focus on helping newcomer parents affirm their linguistic and cultural identity. In this way, rather than lose cultural capital, newcomer families would develop their own capital, tapping into their own knowledge resources and experiences as expressed in their own language to help their children succeed in school.

The Parenting Circles Intervention

The opportunity to revise the intervention further to include a focus on linguistic and cultural identity came in 2007, when with a grant from the Ontario Ministry of Education, a research team worked with a group of eleven parents in a six-week program that combined the Freirian dialogue and content of the program with a focus on identity formation and affirmation of cultural capital that involved parents in writing books for and about their children.

In addition to the earlier goals of providing newcomer parents with relevant information about the local school system and how to access resources and networks of support in the community, we incorporated a creative book-authoring element to encourage Spanish-language maintenance and the acquisition of a strong sense of self-worth and pride in cultural identity.

The Authors in the Classroom Program (ACP) was developed to improve the possibility of more equitable outcomes for all children. Originated by Ada and Campoy (2003), it was implemented at the early education level under the name Early Authors Program (EAP) (Bernhard et al., 2006; Bernhard et al., 2008). The ACP/EAP incorporated a transformative literacy model in which parents and children self-authored books or "identity texts" about themselves, their families, and their goals. Scanned photographs and word processing were used to create the books, which allowed parents to communicate and share their personal experiences.

The process of involving immigrant parents in self-authoring books was aimed not only at enrichment of their children's school readiness (in particular, print motivation and increased vocabulary), but also at strengthening links between and among children and their families. The process was geared toward the acquisition of a strong sense of self-worth and pride in cultural identity. The focus of the texts written by the parents was on affirming the linguistic and cultural identity of their offspring and covered such themes as *This Is Who I Am*, *The Story of My Name*, *A Special Person in My Life*, and *Hopes and Dreams for My Child*.

The mothers came to recognize that the act of expressing their thoughts, feelings, and knowledge in writing had far-reaching benefits that they could not anticipate for their children and went beyond the immediate reaction they may have had. As the parents witnessed the positive feedback from their children, they began to fully comprehend how this was a new tool for positive communication and deeper expressions of love. Marta eloquently concluded,

> Another thing that I really liked was learning to make the books as a medium for family communication. It was a wonderful experience, and I will never forget it. My son saw the books and was stimulated, motivated and happy about the things that I communicated to him. . . . It is exactly the way to communicate with photos, designs, creativity, with written text, for our children, this type of written communication is what was really new for me.

Marta had been a French teacher in Ecuador, and she embraced this new form of communication with fervor, as did the other parents. Her identity investment was reflected in the books she wrote and shared with her children.

Before the start of the Parenting Circles intervention, the parents were asked to rate their goals and desires for their children for the next five years. Fluency in English, adaptation to the new environment, and academic success were the top three goals identified among the group, with adaptation and academic success seen as dependent on English fluency. By the end of the intervention, there was a heightened assertion and appreciation of the group's cultural heritage and recognition of the value of transmitting that heritage to their children. The factors of cognitive engagement and identity investment, central to Cummins's theory, were especially prominent. These successes are qualified by our knowledge of the resistance of all systems to fundamental changes. The efforts over a period of weeks or months have to be part of a long and intensive process involving several years or decades in order to have a significant effect on the system.

Carrying on the Work: Looking to the Future

The significance of our work has been in providing parents with the tools to reach out to educators. Parents gained the confidence and skills to engage with their children's academic development and enrich their lives. The appeal of the project is that it can be implemented at no great cost and without the need for external support or extensive facilitator training. Any institution can implement a process of Freirian dialogue groups given the willingness to listen with sensitivity to parental concerns and basic training in the principles covered here.

All these processes were informed by our theoretical commitments. The theories I mention were crucial in highlighting how the interventions could be improved, especially with regard to social agency, identity, and development of cultural capital.

When used again, the program could never be replicated exactly, nor should it be. Exact replication of the techniques and content of the program is not required, although fidelity to its principles certainly is. As we see it, the "package" is defined according to its basic principles; it does not depend on fine details of procedure or content. Even if particular procedures were outlined in detail, it would be inappropriate to transfer those specifications directly into another environment. An important point I make is about the value of research and evaluation in the development of the program. During each phase of our work, we have been guided by feedback obtained from both facilitators and participants. The consistent use of pre- and postinformation collection from participants allows the revisions of theory and practice that we undertook.

Our contribution has been to provide support to newcomer parents to find their voice and make meaningful contributions to their children's academic success. Although the parents may not speak the language of the school, or may not have high literacy levels, they have much to contribute. Our drawing from several theories, especially postfoundational and critical ones as developed by Freire, Bourdieu, and Cummins, guided and structured the process and pointed us to specific areas that needed to be addressed.

Yet the relevance of the work of the parenting interventions reaches beyond individual communities and their plights. We are living in turbulent times that discourage immigrants from challenging dominant institutions like schools. Social and educational institutions are subject to increased stresses. Crisis periods sometimes provide opportunities to address old issues, such as the high dropout rate, in new ways. As the theories on which we drew provided the tools that we needed then, they may in future inform continued efforts by these subordinated groups to achieve just outcomes in their new society.

References

Ada, A. F. (2003). *A magical encounter: Latino children's literature in the classroom.* Boston, MA: Allyn & Bacon

Ada, A. F., & Campoy, I. F. (2003). *Authors in the classroom: A transformative education process.* Boston, MA: Allyn & Bacon.

Anisef, P., Brown, R. S., Phythian, K., Sweet, D., & Walters, D. (2008). *Early school leaving among immigrants in Toronto secondary schools.* Toronto, ON: CERIS Working Paper Series. Retrieved from http://ceris.metropolis.net/Virtual%20Library/WKPP%20List/WKPP2008/CWP67.pdf

Artiles, A., & Klingner, J. K. (2006). Forging a knowledge base on English language learners with special needs: Theoretical, population, and technical issues. *Teachers College Record, 108*(11), 2187–2194.

Bauder, H. (2008). Citizenship as capital: The distinction of migrant labor. *Alternatives, 33,* 315–333.

Bernhard, J. K. (2003). Toward a 21st century developmental theory: Principles to account for diversity in children's lives. *Race, Gender, and Class, 9*(4), 45–60.

Bernhard, J. K. (2004). The school "misbehavior" of Latino children in a time of zero tolerance: Parents' views. *Early Years Journal, 24*(1), 41–62.

Bernhard, J. K. (2009). Latin American students in the Toronto District School Board: Research findings and recommendations. In D. Mantilla, D. Schugurensky, & J. F. Serrano (Eds.), *Four in ten: Spanish speaking youth and school drop out in Toronto*. Toronto, ON: Transformative Learning Centre, OISE/University of Toronto. [Also published in Spanish as *Cuatro en diez*; available at http://fcis.oise.utoronto.ca/~lared/]

Bernhard, J. K., Cummins, J., Campoy, I., Ada, A., Winsler, A., & Bleiker, C. (2006). Identity texts and literacy development among preschool English language learners: Enhancing learning opportunities for children at risk of learning disabilities. *Teachers College Record, 108*(11), 2380–2405.

Bernhard, J. K., & Freire, M. (1996). Latino refugee children in childcare: A study of parents and caregivers. *Canadian Journal of Research in Early Childhood Education, 5*(1), 59–71.

Bernhard, J. K., Freire, M., & Mulligan, V. (2004). *Canadian Parenting Workshops*. Toronto, ON: Chestnut.

Bernhard, J. K., Freire, M., Pacini-Ketchabaw, V., & Villanueva, V. (1998). A Latin American parents' group participates in their children's schooling: Parent involvement reconsidered. *Canadian Ethnic Studies Journal, 30*(3), 77–98.

Bernhard, J. K., Gonzalez-Mena, J., Chang, H. N., O'Loughlin, M., Eggers-Pierola, C., Roberts Fiati, G., et al. (1998). Recognizing the centrality of cultural diversity and racial equity: Beginning a discussion and critical reflection on "developmentally appropriate practice." *Canadian Journal of Research in Early Childhood Education, 7*(1), 81–90.

Bernhard, J. K., Landolt, P., & Goldring, L. (2009). The institutional production and social reproduction of transnational families: The case of Latin American immigrants in Toronto. *International Migration, 46*(2), 3–31.

Bernhard, J. K., Winsler, A., Bleiker, C., Ginieniewicz, J., & Madigan, A. (2008). Read my story: Promoting early literacy among diverse, urban, preschool children in poverty with the Early Authors Program. *Journal of Education for Students Placed at Risk, 13*(1), 76–105.

Bourdieu, P. (1986). The forms of capital. In J. C. Richardson (Ed.), *Handbook of theory and research in the sociology of education* (pp. 241–257). New York, NY: Greenwood.

Cannella, G. S. (2002). *Deconstructing early childhood education: Social justice and revolution*. New York, NY: Peter Lang.

Corson, D. (1998). *Changing education for diversity*. Philadelphia, PA: Open University Press.

Cummins, J. (1989). *Empowering minority students*. Los Angeles, CA: National Association for Bilingual Education.

Cummins, J. (2000). *Language, power and pedagogy: Bilingual children in the crossfire*. Clevedon, England: Multilingual Matters.

Cummins, J. (2001). *Negotiating identities: Education for empowerment in a diverse society*. Ontario, CA: California Association for Bilingual Education.

Cummins, J. (2002). Language and the human spirit. *TESOL Matters*. Retrieved from http://www.iteachilearn.com/cummins/langhuman02.htm

Cummins, J., & Sayers, D. (1995). *Brave new schools: Challenging cultural illiteracy through global learning networks*. New York, NY: St. Martin's Press.

Darder, A., Torres, R., & Gutierrez, H. (1997). *Latinos and education: A critical reader*. New York, NY: Routledge.

Dei, G. (2001). Rescuing theory: Anti-racism and inclusive education. *Race, Gender and Class, 8*(1), 139–161.

Fishman, J. A. (1989). *Language and ethnicity in minority sociolinguistic perspective*. Clevedon, England: Multilingual Matters.

Freire, P. (1994). *Pedagogy of hope: Reliving pedagogy of the oppressed*. New York, NY: Continuum.

Freire, P. (1999). *Pedagogy of the oppressed*. New York, NY: Continuum.

Garcia, C. (2008). *Parenting Circles Project: The key conditions for the meaningful engagement of Spanish-speaking parents to support their children's school success.* Unpublished manuscript, Ryerson University, Toronto, ON.

Garcia-Coll, C. T. (1990). Developmental outcome of minority infants: A process-oriented look into our beginnings. *Child Development, 61*(2), 270–289.

George, U., & Michalski, J. H. (1996). *A snapshot of service delivery in organizations serving immigrants, final report.* Toronto, ON: University of Toronto, Centre for Applied Social Research.

Goldring, L., Berinstein, C., & Bernhard, J. K. (2009). Institutionalizing precarious migratory status in Canada. *Citizenship Studies, 13*(3), 237–263.

González, N., Moll, L. C., & Amanti, C. (Eds.). (2005). *Funds of knowledge: Theorizing practice in households, communities, and classrooms.* Mahwah, NJ: Erlbaum.

Hedegaard, M. (2009). Children's development from a cultural-historical approach: Children's activity in everyday local settings as foundation for their development. *Mind, Culture, and Activity, 16*(1), 64–82.

Klingner, J. K., & Artiles, A. J. (2003). When should bilingual students be in special education? *Educational Leadership, 61*(2), 66–71.

Krashen, S. (1999). *Condemned without a trial: Bogus arguments against bilingual education.* Portsmouth, NH: Heinemann.

Lareau, A. (1989). *Home advantage: Social class and parental intervention in elementary education.* New York, NY: Falmer Press.

Lerner, R. M. (1988). Personality development: A life-span perspective. In E. M. Hetherington, R. M. Lerner, & M. Perlmutter (Eds.), *Child development in life-span perspective* (pp. 21–46). Hillsdale, NJ: Erlbaum.

Lerner, R. M. (1991). Changing organism-context relations as the basic process of development: A developmental contextual perspective. *Developmental Psychology, 27,* 27–32.

Lo, L., Preston, V., Wang, S., Reil, K., Harvey, E., & Siu, B. (2000). *Immigrants' economic status in Toronto: Rethinking settlement and integration strategies* (Working Paper No. 15). Toronto, ON: Centre of Excellence for Research on Immigration and Settlement.

Looker, D. E. (1994). Active capital: The impact of parents on youths' educational performance and plans. In L. Erwin & D. MacLennan (Eds.), *Sociology of education in Canada* (pp. 164–187). Toronto, ON: Copp Clark Longman.

Murdie, R. A., & Teixeira, C. (2000). *Towards a comfortable neighbourhood and appropriate housing: Immigrant experience in Toronto.* Toronto, ON: CERIS Working Paper Series.

New London Group. (1996). A pedagogy of multiliteracies: Designing social futures. *Harvard Educational Review, 66,* 60–86.

Ng, R. (1993). Racism, sexism, and nation building in Canada. In C. McCarthy & W. Crichlow (Eds.), *Race, identity and representation in education* (pp. 50–59). New York, NY: Routledge.

Ng, R., & Ramirez, J. (1981). *Immigrant housewives in Canada.* Toronto, ON: Immigrant Women's Centre.

O'Loughlin, M. (2009). *The subject of childhood.* New York, NY: Peter Lang.

Onchwari, G., Onchwari, J., & Keengwe, J. (2008). Teaching the immigrant child: Application of child development theories. *Early Childhood Education Journal, 36*(3), 267–273.

Organisation for Economic Co-operation and Development (OECD). (2006). *Where immigrant students succeed—a comparative review of performance and engagement in PISA 2003.* Paris, France: Author. Retrieved from http://www.oecd.org/dataoecd/2/38/36664934.pdf

Pacini-Ketchabaw, V., Bernhard, J. K., & Freire, M. (2001). Struggling to preserve home language: The experiences of Latino students and families in the Canadian school system. *Bilingual Research Journal, 25*(1 & 2), 115–145.

Pinkus, S. (2008). *The effect of the Parenting Circles Program on home language retention and parental engagement: The case of a Spanish-speaking parent group in Toronto.* Unpublished research paper, Ryerson University, Toronto, ON.

Rogoff, B. (1990). *Apprenticeship in thinking: Cognitive development in social context.* New York, NY: Oxford University Press.

Siemiatycki, M. (1998). *Immigration and urban politics in Toronto*. Paper presented at the third international Metropolis Conference, Israel.

Statistics Canada. (2007a). *Canada's national statistical agency: 2001 and 2006 census*. Ottawa, ON: Author. Retrieved from http://www.statcan.ca/menu-en.htm

Statistics Canada. (2007b). *Measuring up: Canadian results of the OECD PISA study*. Ottawa, ON: Author. Retrieved from http://www.pisa.gc.ca/81-590-E.pdf

Taylor, L., Bernhard, J. K., Garg, S., & Cummins, J. (2008). Affirming plural belonging: Building on students' family-based plural and linguistic capital through a multiliteracies curriculum. *Journal of Early Childhood Literacy, 8*(3), 269–295.

United Nations. (2007). *Global migration database*. Retrieved from http://www.un.org/english/

Westby, C., & Atencio, D. J. (2002). Computers, culture and learning. *Topics in Language Disorders, 22*(4), 70–87.

Chapter Eight

Making Developmental Knowledge Stutter and Stumble

Continuing Pedagogical Explorations with Collective Biography

Kathleen Kummen, Veronica Pacini-Ketchabaw, & Deborah Thompson

Drawing on data gathered through collective biography in a child development graduate course in a child and youth care program, this chapter proposes the notion of a developmental worker as mutually constituted in and emerging through an intra-action with the discursive and the material. We base our arguments on the premise that, in addition to deconstructing how developmental knowledge as discourse works, it is important to unmask how matter (bodies, materials, the physical world) comes to matter in the enactment of developmental knowledge, highlighting the complex materiality of the social. The chapter uses the metaphor of making developmental knowledge stutter and stumble as we revisit our work in an attempt to make visible how we might engage in pedagogical practices that not only cause us to stutter in the discursive but also to stumble into matter as developmental theory is enacted. We borrow from the work of theorists Karen Barad and Annemarie Mol, among others.

As educators, practitioners, researchers, and mothers who teach/apply/think-with/do/breathe developmental knowledge, we are interested in how we can make developmental theories stutter and stumble. Developmental conceptions of how childhood functions and what it means to be an educator who uses developmental knowledge are present in our language and our bodies (Burman, 2008a, 2008b; Morss, 1996; Rose, 1990). We have written elsewhere about how these processes take place—how developmental knowledge as a dominant discourse acts on us and how we act on it. Specifically, in an empirical investigation using a child development graduate course in a child and youth care program, we wrote about the subjectification processes by which practitioners simultaneously master and become mastered by developmental theory (Pacini-Ketchabaw, Kummen, & Thompson, 2010).

In this chapter we extend our work on making developmental knowledge stutter in our practices, our teaching, and our research (Pacini-Ketchabaw, 2008, 2011; Pacini-Ketchabaw et al., 2010). By making developmental knowledge stutter we mean that we have worked on challenging the presence and the hold that developmental discourses have in applied fields.[1] Like others (Blaise & Eldsden-Clifton, 2007; Cannella, 1997; Lenz Taguchi, 2008; Ryan & Grieshaber, 2005; Skott-Mhyre, 2008; Sumsion, 2005; Viruru, 2005), we have demonstrated the limitations of developmental knowledge for the complex work of practicing with children in the twenty-first century. Along with these reconceptualist scholars working in early childhood education and child and youth care, we have contested and offered critical analyses of the hegemonic narratives of developmental theory.

Now we wish to extend the *stuttering* of developmental knowledge by making it *stumble* as we introduce "new materialisms" (Coole & Frost, 2010; van der Tuin, 2011) to our reading of how developmental knowledge comes to matter in applied fields. Namely, we propose that we pay attention not only to how developmental knowledge as discourse works, but also how matter (bodies, materials, the physical world) comes to matter in developmental knowledge, highlighting the complex materiality of the social. In this chapter we revisit our previous work in an attempt to make visible how we might engage in pedagogical practices that not only cause us to stutter in the discursive but to stumble into a material understanding of developmental theory.

Through our stuttering and stumbling of developmental knowledge, we argue that developmental practitioners *emerge* in a complex intra-action with a multitude of elements that come together to create realities of developmental practice. Using examples from our work with collective biography in a graduate course, we propose that developmental knowledge emerges and is enacted as multiple, always in relationality with discursive-material components that are present in practice.

We begin the chapter by recounting some of our previous work on the stuttering of developmental knowledge within the context of our teaching in a graduate course in a child and youth care program. In this section, we provide methodological details of the data we work with later on in the chapter. We then move to expand our arguments by first outlining selected ideas that we have found productive in relation to our work in the new materialisms literature and, second, using these ideas as tools for rereading the analysis recounted in the previous section. We end with our current thoughts on how developmental knowledge works and brief reflections on our own teaching practices of child development.

---

1   The contexts of this chapter are early childhood education and child and youth care. For further information on how we conceptualize these applied disciplines, refer to Pacini-Ketchabaw, Kummen, & Thompson (2010).

Making Developmental Knowledge Stutter

In the article "Becoming Intimate with Development Knowledge: Pedagogical Explorations with Collective Biography" (Pacini-Ketchabaw et al., 2010), we worked theoretically with poststructural perspectives on knowledge/power (drawing on the work of French philosopher Michel Foucault and his contemporaries), with feminist poststructural ideas on processes of subject formation (as outlined by scholars such as Bronwyn Davies and Judith Butler), and with feminist Deleuzian-informed perspectives on embodiment (such as those described by Elizabeth Grosz and Allison Hayes-Conroy) to move beyond the humanist version of a bounded self that forms the basis of developmental discourses.

As described in the article (Pacini-Ketchabaw et al., 2010), in the graduate-level child and youth care course Child and Adolescent Development in Context, we used collective biography (Davies & Gannon, 2006) as a pedagogical tool to investigate the workings of developmental psychology in our practices as early childhood educators and child and youth care workers. As a form of critical narrative research, positioned within a poststructural paradigm, collective biography involves the writing, telling, and rewriting of memories (Davies & Gannon, 2006). Memories, in collective biography, are not acknowledged as objective truths:

> We take the talk around our memories, the listening to the detail of each other's memories, as a technology for enabling us to produce, through attention to the embodied sense of being in the remembered moment, a truth in relation to what cannot actually be recovered—the moment as it was lived. This is not a naive, naturalistic truth, but a truth that is worked on through a technology of telling, listening and writing. In a sense it is the very *unreliability* of memory that enables this close discursive work. (Davies & Gannon, 2006, p. 3)

The writing assignment instructions for the collective biography work in the course included relating a memory (a two- or three-minute event/experience/short narrative) and describing one's bodily and emotionally felt sensations during that event, avoiding clichés and explanations (Davies & Gannon, 2006). Students and instructors wrote memories and read their narratives to their group. Group members listened carefully to each story and asked questions when they did not understand or could not imagine being in the situation described. In this way, the group assisted individual writers in rewriting aspects of their memories that appeared opaque to their classmates (Davies & Gannon, 2006; Lenz Taguchi, 2005, 2007). Each member of the class then rewrote his or her narrative, incorporating group feedback to make visible the corporeal aspects of the memory. Following the rewriting of memories, class members collectively read (that is, worked deconstructively with) their own narratives using feminist poststructuralist practices (Lenz Taguchi, 2005, 2007). Through this process, the course offered tools for questioning developmental discourses and their implications in the reproduction of existing inequalities and for the continuous creation of spaces for social justice (Pacini-Ketchabaw et al., 2010). During the twelve-week course we wrote memories of mastering and being mastered by theories of child/adolescent development, learning to be appropriate gendered developmental workers, becoming and being made social beings, realizing and resisting being gendered, and becoming and being made school subjects.

We read and analyzed the memories within the anti-humanistic framework found in the work of thinkers such as Butler (1997), Davies (2000), and Walkerdine (1998). In our analysis we did not seek to discover an "originary" agency within the practitioner that assumes an essence universal within all practitioners (Zipin, 1998). Rather, we teased out those moments in which the subject was constituted to make visible the processes of subjectivity. Our analysis was also framed in Foucault's (1977, 1978) notion of power, and we attended to those moments in which the subject resisted discourses. In this way, we scrutinized the memories for moments of ambivalence, tension, and unease within the subject (Pacini-Ketchabaw et al., 2010).

Our interest has been in how the memories reflected the idea of submission and mastery in relation to the dominant discourse of developmental psychology. We argued that, in taking up and mastering developmental knowledge in practice, the developmental practitioner maintains and strengthens the dominance of developmental theory and, in turn, fully submits to its dominance. In other words, at the same moment in which the subject becomes recognized through dominant discourses of developmental psychology, the subject submits to them. In this way, the developmental worker is constructed through her or his use of developmental theory, validating its continued existence as the dominant knowledge of understanding children. Having developmental knowledge provided mastery in practice. Yet, in taking up the role of developmental worker, the subject must submit to its power in order to master its discursive practices. Butler (1997) says, "Subjection consists precisely in this fundamental dependency on a discourse we never chose but that, paradoxically, initiates and sustains our agency" (p. 2).

In our analysis of the memories, we also noted that developmental psychology is not only a discourse, but is *bodied* and therefore always uncertain and unfamiliar (Pacini-Ketchabaw et al., 2010). One of the most common themes reflected in the memories was the visceral reactions associated with being a good/bad developmental worker. Mastering child development knowledge created bodily pleasure and relief; not knowing created discomfort and anxiety. In these memories, bodies mattered at the very instance of power production. The memories showed that bodies and cognition do not work separately but are intimately intertwined. The memories somehow revealed the chaotic and unpredictable ways in which minded-bodies "are constantly developing, moving, shifting and working" and, simultaneously, "aligning with a movement's socio-political aims and (re)creating them" (Hayes-Conroy & Martin, 2010, p. 278).

In the next section, we expand on our previous work by arguing that our analysis, while attending to developmental psychology as not only discourse but also as bodied, maintained a humancentric perspective. That is, we examined how discourses acted on the body, thereby privileging discourse as the agentic force in how development theory is brought to life through practice. What was missing from our analysis was a consideration of how entities, both human and nonhuman, intra-act with discourse and the subject to bring to life particular practices—in this case, the practices of developmental theory. As we mentioned in the introduction, new materialisms have helped us to make developmental knowledge stumble. Before introducing our renewed analysis, we provide an overview of how we understand new materialisms.

Thinking with New Materialisms

As we delve into new materialisms, we need to consider the relationship between social constructionism and materiality with regard to the understanding of subjectivity, agency, knowledge, and practice. Poststructural writers such as Butler (1997), St. Pierre (2000), and Davies (2000) assert that hegemonic discourses make space for subjects to engage in particular practices while denying the possibility of other practices. Language, from this perspective, is understood as agentic in that it constitutes the practice of humans and their understanding of reality. Referred to as "the linguistic turn" by the American philosopher Richard Rorty (1967), this position has been challenged by writers across various disciplines (see, e.g., Barad, 2007; Hacking, 1999; Hekman, 2010; Heron & Reason, 1997) for silencing the existence of a material reality. Law (2004) asserts that the dualism of an active human/culture and a passive object/nature is hegemonic Euro-American thinking and "there is much fuss, perhaps especially in the social sciences, if the distinction is ignored" (p. 132). Hekman (2010) also argues that privileging discourse as the constituting agent creates a dualism of nature and culture. Lenz Taguchi (2010), writing in early childhood education, states that when materials are seen as equally agentic as discourse, thinking is not restrained by an either/or debate. She writes that we can think "in terms of the discursive being immanent to the material and the material being immanent to the discursive. This means that they depend upon each other and are mutually constitutive" (p. 29). Barad (2007) uses the term "posthumanist" to "signal the crucial recognition that nonhumans play an important role in natural cultural practices, including everyday social practices, scientific practices, and practices that do not include humans" (p. 32). Further, she writes, this term "is a refusal to take the distinction between 'human' and 'non-human' for granted, and to found analysis on this presumably fixed and inherent set of categories" (p. 32).

Barad (2007) asserts that the material exists as a performative agent. She writes that agency should not be understood as limited to the discursive, and calls for "a robust account of the materialization of *all* bodies—'human' and 'non-human'—including the agential contributions of all material forces (both the 'social' and the 'natural')" (p. 66, emphasis in the original). The concept of the material being agentic is illustrated by Lenz Taguchi (2009) in a scenario in which children are presented with buttons of different shape, colour, and size and are asked by a teacher to divide them into equal amounts. Instead of dividing the buttons as requested by the teacher, the children begin to sort and classify the buttons. The colour, shape, and size of the buttons exert an agentic force, asking the children to sort and classify, that is stronger than the teacher's request to divide the buttons. Lenz Taguchi writes that it would seem that the buttons "practically scream out: 'sort me!'; 'put me into piles!'" (p. 9). Law writes, "Everywhere there is agency ... the universe is filled with agency" (2004, p. 134) and, according to Hekman (2010), "dogmatic adherence to linguistic constitution cannot account for the reality and agency of that world" (p. 2).

Therefore, from a posthumanist perspective, discourse and reality are understood to intra-act so that neither precedes the other. Barad (2007) writes, "The relationship between the material and the discursive is one of mutual entailment. Neither discursive practices nor material phenomena are ontologically or epistemologically prior" (p. 152). Realities are "not explained by practices and beliefs but instead produced in them" (Law, 2004, p. 59). As Olsson (2009) explains, "before there is thought there is life, and life can never be totally organized or systemized. Thought here is a producer, not a discoverer or organizer. Thought happens through encounters. It is an effect of life, not a cause" (p. 94).

We find a study by Jackson (2001) helpful for thinking about material-discursive perspectives. In it Jackson describes the "wrenching, uneven experience" of one student teacher, Annie, who took on completely different personas and teaching practices as she moved between two classrooms (p. 388). Deconstructing Annie's experience within a feminist poststructural perspective, Jackson (2001) asserts that Annie constructed multiple identities as a teacher as she took up competing discourses of teaching presented by her two cooperating teachers. When reading the excerpts of Annie's interview, we see that Annie herself identified that the classroom's physical reality *required her to teach* in very particular ways, even in the absence of any verbal direction from the collaborating teachers. For example, Annie states that in one of the classrooms, worksheets requiring the right answers were used for instruction. The worksheets, for Annie, *spoke* to the students and to her as a student teacher, *telling* a story of pedagogy requiring students to "copy, memorize, and reproduce materials for a test" (Jackson, 2001, p. 390). Annie described an organized room in which everything "was colour coded, from her teaching files to her grade book" (p. 391), *a room that organized* everything and everyone into its/her/his correct place. In her discussion, Jackson (2001) focuses on the agency of the discursive on the student, yet her narrative is littered with the material. The objects, the temporal and spatial nature of the room were not passive; they called to Annie, telling her how to teach in the same way that her sponsor teacher provided verbal instructions on teaching. Law (2004) further illustrates the concept that agency is located within objects:

> A painted design or sculpted form may . . . be considered not merely a human being's depiction of ancestral Crocodile (or Kangaroo Woman), but an instance of that Dreaming's manifestation in the world. This is why pictures and carved figures can make people sick, give them strength, or cause accidents to happen—or so many Aboriginal people believed. (Sutton, 1989, as cited in Law, 2004, p. 134)

Another useful example comes from a memory we wrote in our graduate course on mastering and being mastered by theories of child/adolescent development. Linda recounts her experience in childbirth, describing her sense of panic and anxiety when her ability to be a good mother—as understood within the discourse of attachment theory—was impeded by an unexpected C-section. She describes the physical reality of the moment:

> The epidural wore off. Cramping pain flooding her body, beginning in her lower back moving to front, briefly fading, Immediately beginning again, a minute on, seconds of relief, a minute on, seconds of relief, and on and on, the baby wouldn't come. Where were the doctors going? They're back. Her doctor explained that she thought it was time for a C-section. Pain. No. She can't think. It's bad. It will ruin her attachment with her baby. Giving up. Can't concentrate on controlling the pain. Breathing in out, like they told her. Pain flooding, disappointment flooding, control evaporating. Panic. Where is Bruce? There he is, in a gown and mask. Wheeled out of the lowly lit birthing room, that has a bedroom feel to it, into the brightly lit operating room. Being drugged. Her arms tied down. She can't feel her body. No pain. No feeling. Panic. What if she is paralyzed forever? Panic. No feeling. Her eyes can move. Control it. She can talk. Her breathing is regular. She jokes with the anesthesiologist. So scared. Holding breathe. Breathe. Everything she has ever learned about birth in all her early childhood and prenatal classes tells her that this is an inferior way to give birth. Already she is a failure as a mother. Her throat is closing. She remembers what she has learned about the importance of the first moments after birth to mother–child attachment and of the critical importance of that attachment to a baby's emotional well-being. Her baby is born. They show her baby to her. She bursts into tears. *[Memory from Collective Biography]*

The possibility for being a labouring mother changed as Linda was moved from a birthing room to an operating room. In the birthing room, with her hands unrestrained, she would have reached out and held her newborn child. In the operating room, with her hands restrained and her body paralyzed, she was shown her newborn child. Hekman (2010) argues that if we rely on discursive knowledge to understand this event and then to employ this understanding to constitute reality, we are missing something. That something, Hekman argues, is not precisely a linguistic event.

In Linda's memory, a mother had an epidural, a baby was born, the mother's hands were tied down, and she could not touch her newborn. For Hekman (2010), when events such as giving birth occur, "matter manifests itself" (p. 2). Prout (2005) asserts that when we privilege the discursive reality, we silence the material elements of the discussion. While we may understand the world linguistically, there exists neither a material reality nor a construction of language. For Linda, her embodied response occurred in encountering both a discursive reality of what it meant to be a good mother and a physical reality of childbirth by C-section. In short, the materiality of the world matters (Hekman, 2010).

This understanding of reality is illustrated in Mol's (2002) research into what is commonly understood to be a singular disease, atherosclerosis. In her research, she encountered multiple enactments of atherosclerosis within one medical setting. For the patient, atherosclerosis is experienced as pain when walking; in a clinic, a physician understands this disease as being demonstrated by signifiers such as skin temperature and pulsations; to the radiologist, atherosclerosis is a condition recognized by arterial lesions and occlusions. Each of these understandings of atherosclerosis brings forth different practices. For example, the degree of pain may lead a patient to perceive that she or he is extremely ill and to seek medical treatment. Yet, on viewing a scan, the radiologist may feel that the condition is minor and does not require intrusive medical intervention. In this way atherosclerosis exists for the patient as being significant due to pain levels, and as insignificant to the radiologist due to the level of occlusion observed on the scan. Thus the disease of atherosclerosis is multiple, existing as significant and insignificant at the same time.

Mol (2002) also demonstrates how the existence of a particular apparatus[2] makes possible the existence of atherosclerosis, while other apparatuses deny the existence of atherosclerosis. For example, a patient may deny the existence of atherosclerosis because she or he does not have symptoms to signify or measure the presence of pathology. Yet, the use of a blood pressure cuff allows for a drop in blood pressure to be made visible and for the existence of atherosclerosis to be acknowledged. Using this analogy when looking at particular apparatuses, a "developing child" comes into existence/is made possible through our developmental

---

2 An apparatus can be understood as a technology or a method that makes a thing or an idea visible.

apparatuses. For example, a developmental test, such as the Peabody Picture Vocabulary Test, makes it possible for a child to be seen as language delayed, yet in the child's home, through the use of gestures and sounds, the child is able to communicate effectively. Mol's (2002) work illustrates how the body and subjectivity are not singular but multiple.

Returning to Linda's childbirth memory, it would seem that childbirth is not constructed purely by discursive knowledge. Within the hospital setting, childbirth is enacted and understood in one way in a birthing room and in another way in an operating room. Becoming a mother in childbirth occurs as an effect of the discourses and materials encountered in each of the childbirth settings. In the birthing room, the new mother encounters medications and materials that allow her body to move and to hold, touch, and even nurse her infant. In the operating room, the new mother encounters physical restraints and medications that restrict, if not paralyze, her body, and there she is only able to gaze at her newborn.

In another example, Lenz Taguchi (2009) describes a scenario in which a young girl encounters a climbing frame. In encountering the climbing frame, the child becomes a competent climber, yet the identity of confident climber occurred only as a result of the encounter with the climbing frame: "Different kinds of matter make her competent in different ways (Lenz Taguchi, 2009, p. 3). In a related study, Hultman and Lenz Taguchi (2010) note that although the authors were inspired by poststructuralist and feminist poststructural education research to view the child as "situational, contextual and discursively inscribed," they found that their "gazes were nevertheless persistently drawn back to the individual child" as the centre of their analysis (p. 525). They explain their dilemma in the following statement:

> Regardless of how theoretically informed we were of poststructural thinking about children as contextual and situational, our *perceptual style* and our *habits of seeing* still seemed to be guided by the same liberal humanistic notions of the child that we so long had sought to escape. (p. 525, emphasis in the original)

Drawing on the work of such scholars as Colebrook, Grosz, Deleuze, Guattari, Haraway, and Barad, Hultman and Lenz Taguchi (2010) challenged what they termed the anthropocentric (human-centered) and logocentric (language-centered) tradition of analysis in educational research. They began by decentering the child, so that their gaze was open to viewing material reality as being as agentic and the child emerged in their view in relation with the environment.

To engage in this process of thinking and seeing differently, Hultman and Lenz Taguchi (2010) evoke the ideas of *diffractive seeing* and *nomadic thinking*. Diffractive seeing is taken from the notion of diffraction in physics and is illustrated in the writings of Haraway (1997) and Barad (2007). Barad (2007) explains the concept of diffraction using an analogy of waves in the ocean: "Diffraction has to do with the way waves combine when they overlap and the apparent bending and spreading out of waves when they encounter an obstruction" (p. 28). This continuous process of transformation occurs as the overlapping waves change themselves in intra-action[3] with the obstruction, yet, in changing, each new wave contains parts of the original wave. Hultman and Lenz Taguchi relate this process of continuous transformation with Deleuze's proposal that subjects can be understood as "assemblages[4] of encounter that differentiate with each new encounter (or interference) in their continuous process of transformation" (Hultman & Lenz Taguchi, 2010, p. 535). Returning to Linda's memory of childbirth, the restraints and the medications given to her in the operating room interfered with her body movements, causing her to change in the same manner as the waves that encountered an obstruction in the ocean. Linda *becomes* with the restraints, the medications, the socioeconomic structures of the hospital setting, medical discourses, and more as the medications, restraints, socioeconomic structures of the hospital setting, medical discourses, and more *become* with Linda. In this way Linda, the medications, restraints, socioeconomic structures of the hospital setting, medical discourses, and more become an assemblage of elements existing, shifting, and intra-acting together.

Nomadic thinking, Hultman and Lenz Taguchi (2010) assert, supports the researcher in the process of decentering the subject by engaging with the data "without a thinking that formulates itself from a hierarchical division between humans and nonhumans" (p. 538). Understood as an onto-epistemological way of thinking, nomadic thinking no longer positions the researcher as a knowing subject in a reality in which the subject is seen as dominant to an object. Instead, "it becomes impossible to isolate knowing from being and discourse from matter; they are mutually implicated" (Hultman & Lenz Taguchi, 2010, p. 539). Barad (2007) asserts that "we don't obtain knowledge by standing outside the world. We know because we are of the world. We are part of the world in its differential becoming" (p. 185). In this way, practice is no longer seen as only a reflection of human knowing, but as having material consequences that evoke new possibilities and opportunities.

These examples of how different classroom organizations make it possible for teachers to act differently, how the physical reality of childbirth makes possible different realities of motherhood, and how different understandings of childhood emerge from physical structures such as a playground help us to begin to understand how developmental theory exists as both discursive and material knowledge.

---

3   "Intra-action" is a term used by Barad (2007) and Hekman (2010), among others, to refer to the relationships between any matter (human and nonhuman).

4   Within a material relational perspective, assemblages are the forces and flows that emerge during an encounter of social-material entities (Hultman & Lenz Taguchi, 2010; Lenz Taguchi, 2010, 2011; Sørenson, 2009).

In what follows, we argue that the developmental worker emerges in a similar manner as the child emerges in an assemblage such as child-climber-sand-and-more—in encounters with both the discursive and material. Different materials make the developmental worker competent or incompetent in different ways. Using insights from new materialisms (or, as Hultman and Lenz Taguchi [2010, p. 526] call it, a relational materialist approach), we reread the memories we had written in our course, this time decentering the human participants (whereby the human was not understood as the active agent handling passive materials of developmental theories). Following the work of Hultman and Lenz Taguchi (2010), Barad (2007), Coole and Frost (2010), Hekman (2010), and others, we analyzed the memories in which matter and humans were understood to be both intentional and agentic. In stumbling across matter, we took a material-discursive turn that caused us to see developmental theory and the practices it enacts as being both discursive and material knowledge.

Making Developmental Knowledge Stumble

In rereading the memories, we bumped and stumbled as we encountered material realities deeply entangled in the discursive aspects of the memories. We found materials such as paints, crayons, construction paper, chairs, walls, smells, pencils, written tests, written observation instruments, toys, books, and more scattered throughout the memories. For example, one student's memory contains a virtual shopping list of the things, sights, sounds, and smells associated with the enactment of developmental practice:

> The bright fluorescent lights of the group room glare brightly and piercingly down. The air is alive with the noise of excited and energized young voices. It is the first night of the children's group. He is sitting at a large plastic table. Six children and another facilitator are sitting with him. Pieces of cheese and crackers dot the hard plastic surface of the table. He can smell the processed cheese lingering in the air. The soft crunch of crackers punctuates the energetic chatter. He looks around as the children finish their snack. He feels poised—he is sitting up straight on his chair. His muscles feel relaxed, his hands clasped loosely in front of him on the warm surface of the table. His eyes feel open, taking in the information around him. He thinks about the instruction he is about to give the children. He is planning to ask them to write down their names and the things they are good at doing. He starts to hand out the pieces of construction paper. It feels thick and smooth between his fingers. He positions a box of markers in the middle of the table, next to the plate holding the remnants of cheese and crackers. He thinks about his developmental theory class, drawing upon the information about stages of cognitive development as he prepares to deliver his instruction. As he recalls the learned information, he feels a calming of his stomach and a loosening of his muscles. He is about to try out some of his learning.

He delivers his instruction. The children look at him as they pay attention to his voice. The children continue to look at him—time appears to freeze. The lights get brighter and more piercing. One child says quietly, "I don't understand." Another child says the same. Then another. His hands start to feel wet and clammy. The chair feels hard underneath him as his muscles tighten. He feels a flush of warmth down his face and neck. His stomach tightens and doesn't release. He feels the eyes of the other facilitator looking at him. He imagines a hole underneath his chair opening up and gradually encompassing his body. He thinks he doesn't belong here. He realizes it is he who doesn't understand. He got it wrong. *[Memory from Collective Biography]*

We will return to this memory to highlight its multiple aspects. For now, we want to briefly focus our attention on its materiality. If we draw on the concepts of diffractive seeing and nomadic thinking, the materials depicted in this memory call out to us, voicing their agentic force. Decentering the subject, these materials are seen as intra-acting with the participants, forming assemblages that create particular singularities, such as a developmental worker, a developing child, a specific developmental practice. We consider the significance of the presence of these materials as the materiality of developmental practice. Developmental practices are filled with matter that takes an agential part in the practitioners' enactment of developmentally appropriate practices, as well as, as we argue later, in the very enactment of the developmental practitioner. For example, developmentally appropriate materials, such as props for dramatic play, are thought to support children in play and creative activities, as seen in the memory above. Moving the material from the position of backdrop or stage, we begin to see how, through intra-action, the material products of developmental theory are entangled with the discourses of developmental theory. As Barad (2007) notes, "This is in contrast to the usual 'interaction', which assumes that there are separate individual agencies that precede their interaction" (p. 33). She explains that "the notion of intra-action recognizes that distinct agencies do not precede, but rather emerge through, their intra-action" (p. 33). Therefore, we can no longer speak of the developmental worker mastering and being mastered by developmental theory and all its instruments; rather, the developmental worker is mutually constituted in an intra-action with the discursive and the material.

To continue our relational materialist approach of analysis, let's consider the following memory written by a graduate student we have named Susan:

> She was sitting upright with a controlled gaze as she sat at a table observing a child in the early childhood program. She felt warm inside her body knowing that she had accomplished checking off items on the observation form. Her body felt tight, her arm extended and hand moving fast as she hurried to complete the form while scanning the environment. Her mind was racing with thoughts as she moved her head around from left to right watching the children. She was

alert and aware of her position and the position of the children in the room.
[Memory from Collective Biography]

In our previous analysis (Pacini-Ketchabaw et al., 2010), our attention was focused on the way in which the developmental worker used and created the technologies of developmental theory to know and understand children. Our use of the phrase "the developmental worker used and created" suggests that we thought of the developmental worker as the active agent and the checklist as the passive material that was used to measure. Our analysis was humancentric, so that the materials were represented as "the passive backdrop or stage of the active human subjects" (Lenz Taguchi, 2010, p. 37). By using a relational materialist analysis approach, we read the memory differently: the developmental worker is decentered and intentionality and agency are understood as existing between several performative agents (Barad, 2007; Hultman & Lenz Taguchi, 2010). The developmental worker acted on the checklist and the checklist acted on the developmental worker. The items on the checklist guided Susan's gaze toward particular images, allowing her then to check off a particular item, which also moved her gaze down to the next item. Susan emerges as a developmental worker as she becomes with the checklist and the checklist becomes with her. Like the child whose identity as a competent climber emerged from her interaction with the climbing frame, the developmental practitioner emerges as the checklist and the checklist emerges as agentic in becoming with the materiality of developmental practices.

In rereading the memories, we encountered many apparatuses (such as the developmental assessment checklist that Susan talked about in the previous memory) that were enmeshed in the emergence of developmental practice, forming assemblages with the practitioners and creating the possibility for practitioners to *become* developmental workers. The following memory recalls a student's embodied encounter with a different kind of apparatus that *measures* her knowledge as developmental worker.

> She enters the room shivering; her legs feel heavy as she walks into the musty smelling room and sits in the cold chair. Quickly the shivering changes into a rush of hot. The test is happening right now. She will have to demonstrate how much of developmental theory she knows. The instructor begins to hand out the test. She can only hear the echo of the instructors' steps which slowwwwly approach her chair. The room now seems deadly silent. She tries hard not to move her head, and fixes her eyes on the piece of paper the instructor just placed on her desk. The anticipation is devastating, her body constantly alternates between shivering and sweating, creating a sick feeling in her stomach and a sour taste in her mouth. Will she get the answers right? She thinks that she has been studying these ideas for a very long time. She knows the material. But she doubts that her knowledge will be sufficient. She thinks that, after all, she learned development psychology in another country and that foreign knowledge might not be good

enough. These doubts create more tension in her body—her heart is racing, beating fast. Then she hears instructions that she can begin. The words of the instructor resonate in her head as though they've come from far away. The room is totally silenced for one second. Suddenly she hears the sound of moving papers and pens coming from all sides of her desk. Moving her pen through the paper is difficult as her hand is not very steady. The printing on the paper becomes fuzzy for one split second. But she manages, as always. She goes through each question with intensity, thinking where exactly on the page she read this. She thinks that it doesn't matter whether the information will be in her head tomorrow when she faces her group of children at the centre. She knows that she can get this test right. Her cheeks are flushing red—will everyone know what she's thinking? Tension in her neck continues to accumulate as she has these thoughts. Her limbs are tense, her cheeks are hot and her hands are cold. The marks she makes on the paper somehow begin to smooth out the tension in her body. It feels as if the pen absorbs the tension and relieves her anxiety. She bites her pen while no marks are made on the paper. A sour taste continues to live in her mouth. Excitement briefly comes and goes as she moves from question one to question two to question three. In an instance of a second this excitement that she feels as her heart beats fast is transformed into tension in her whole body. She thinks that her body must overcome this intensity, this rushing of anxiety and excitement. She knows that it will go away. Her anticipation of letting her body relax after the test creates a further state of tension in her muscles. But she knows she will be able to survive. *[Memory from Collective Biography]*

When adopting a relational materialist approach, the test is seen as an apparatus that demonstrates a particular kind of developmental knowledge, allowing the student to become a developmental practitioner. Each question, existing as marks on the test, is an artifact produced by and producing knowledge of developmental theory. The student's singularity as a developmental worker emerges as she makes the marks on the paper—more specifically, as she makes particular marks that demonstrate appropriate knowledge of developmental theory. In this way, the test can be compared to the blood pressure cuff that acknowledges the existence of atherosclerosis by measuring a drop in blood pressure (Mol, 2002). The number score produced by the blood pressure cuff allows for a diagnosis of atherosclerosis; the number score produced by the test confirms the existence of developmental knowledge. Mol (2002) explains that "*ontologies* are brought into being, sustained, or allowed to wither away in common, day-to-day practices" (p. 6, emphasis in the original). The student's act of writing a test to assess her developmental knowledge brings into being her existence as a developmental worker; without the test to assess her knowledge, she cannot be identified as knowing developmental theory.

In continuing in the analysis of this memory from a relational materialist approach, the relationship between physical location and knowledge is illustrated. The student expresses concern that her developmental knowledge was acquired in another country and that foreign knowledge might not be good enough in her present location. Mol (2002), in her study of atherosclerosis, writes that atherosclerosis is understood as a single disease, yet it is enacted differently in multiple locations. In the clinic, the physician inquires into the pain a patient feels when walking to make a diagnosis of atherosclerosis, while in the pathology lab it is the thickening of blood vessels seen under a microscope by a pathologist that allows for atherosclerosis to be acknowledged. In this way, we come to see that developmental theory is not a single body of knowledge, but instead a multiple knowledge; the specificities of enacting developmental theory are dependent upon location. The units of knowledge, such as definitions of concepts pertaining to developmental theory, required in the test that the student is about to write are not necessarily the same as developmental knowledge acquired in a different country. Thus, while the title of developmental worker suggests a single identity, between locations the knowledge required to be identified as a developmental worker may be different, even contradictory or irrelevant.

We now return to the student's memory in which he recalls a moment in which children, adults, and materials come together to enact the practice of developmental theory in the form of a developmental activity (the first memory included in this section). At first glance, the humancentric tendency to see active children and adults in a passive classroom setting is overwhelming: the noise of excited young voices dims the bright fluorescent lights of the group room, which "glare brightly and piercingly down." Materials sit passively waiting to be intentionally acted upon by the human subjects. From a humancentric view, the directions given by the practitioner appear to result in the children's inability to act on the materials in the desired fashion. Within this perspective the practitioner—using developmental theory to construct an activity, select materials, and give directions—failed to elicit the correct response from the children. The children intentionally act on the instructions and demonstrate, in this case, their inability to comply with the instructions. However, when we analyze this memory from a relational materialist approach, materials such as the construction paper and the markers are no longer seen as passive objects waiting to be acted upon in a predetermined manner by humans, but as performative agents. A performative agent is human or nonhuman matter that is understood to result in an action or transformation (Barad, 2007). In explaining the notion of matter as performative agents, Lenz Taguchi (2010) uses the example of dots placed on a classroom floor to indicate where children should place their bodies. The dots are performative agents in that they direct the children to keep their bodies in a particular place, and their appearance tells the children that they have moved out of their designated place. In our original reading of the memory (where we paid attention only to discourse), the student's instructions to the children were read as the single performative agent in directing the children's actions. From a material relational perspective, our gaze shifts to objects such as the construction paper and the markers as *being with* the verbal directions in the memory as multiple performative agents. Agency and intentionality are distributed among several performative agents (Lenz Taguchi, 2011). Together, elements such as the physical traits of the construction paper and markers, the children's past experiences with these objects and other mark-making tools, the words of the students, the glaring lights, and the sound of other voices (amongst many other things) come together as performative agents offering the children possibilities for action. In this case, the material-discursive interconnections and intra-actions within this encounter create the possibility for children to act, specifically by speaking the words, "I don't understand."

When we use this material-discursive lens, we begin to move beyond the idea that the practitioner fails in his use of developmental theory, thereby *confusing* the children (and himself) so that *they* are not able to perform, to seeing a practitioner within an assemblage in which developmental discourses, children's physical presence, and materials come together in a productive manner. Within the forces and flows of this assemblage, the materials, children, and practitioner become entangled to produce a confused practitioner; a change in any one of the many elements would have transformed the encounter, bringing different possibilities of action into existence.

Through our analyses of the memories we have illustrated how developmental theory stumbles when humans are dethroned as the sole source of agency in development. New possibilities for understanding development and the developmental worker emerge when we view developmental theory/practice as taking place in the interconnections in-between children and different entities (human and nonhuman; Barad, 2007). The child and the practitioner are not separate entities but are understood, from a relational materialist approach, as a "consequence of the world in a state of mutual inter-dependence with everything else" (Lenz Taguchi, 2011, p. 40). The developmental worker is not viewed as a separate entity observing, assessing, and knowing developmental theory outside of relationships with other entities. Rather, the developmental worker is seen as emerging in a complex intra-action with a multitude of human and nonhuman elements.

We now understand that the developmental worker emerges in the force and flow of interconnections (in the in-betweens; Hultman & Lenz Taguchi, 2010). The competent developmental worker emerges only in an assemblage with matter (human and nonhuman entities) that makes it possible for the developmental worker to be competent. With different matter, the developmental worker may not be competent or even identifiable. In this way, the developmental worker does not exist as a single entity, but rather exists as multiple entities, produced and maintained within multiple material-discursive realities and enacted in practice.

Mol's (2002) work with atherosclerosis as a multiple disease that enacts multiple practices (as opposed to a single disease) is useful to help us understand how developmental theory emerges as multiple in specific practices and how developmental workers emerge in practices. In the memory, the student selected materials and constructed a script using cognitive developmental theory, in much the same manner in which a physician would select particular instruments and diagnostic questions to practice medicine. For example, a patient complaining that his/her feet are very cold to touch might go to a clinic to seek help from a physician. After confirming that the skin on the patient's feet is in fact cold to the touch, the physician may consider a possible diagnosis of atherosclerosis and would then inquire if the patient is experiencing any pain upon walking. It may happen that, in response to the questions, the patient indicates that there is no pain and therefore deny the existence of atherosclerosis as she or he has no symptoms to signify or measure the presence of pathology. In that moment, the physician and patient may remain confused, and a lack of intentional action may be indicative of that confusion. Yet, with the addition of the blood pressure machine into the assemblage of physician and patient, it is now possible for a drop in blood pressure to be made visible and for the existence of atherosclerosis to be acknowledged. The physician now emerges as competent in the diagnosis of atherosclerosis and the patient now understands that she or he has a pathology. Prior to the introduction of the blood pressure machine, the diagnosis of atherosclerosis was not possible; similarly, had the physician chosen another instrument the diagnosis may not have been possible.

If we apply this thinking to the memory, we see that the practitioner provided directions using a body of knowledge in the same way the physician asked questions using a body of knowledge. The materials that the practitioner selected were markers and construction paper, and the students were asked to perform/share what they were good at, using those materials. What if the instruments used to inquire what the children were good at were changed? What if the practitioner asked the children to select activities from photos, talk into a microphone, or use a camera to take photos of activities? Would a change in the materials have changed the outcome? Would the practitioner have felt that he was a competent developmental worker because the children performed the activity of sharing their name and the activities they were good at doing? When materials and humans become equal in a consideration of agency, new questions and possibilities for understanding events become apparent.

It is important not to assume that the above analysis is a polite nod to the material world, nor does it signify the removal of the discursive world. Instead, it is an acknowledgement of a world in which humans and nonhuman matter exist in an encounter in a nonhierarchical relationship. In our new analysis of the memories, influenced by the work of Barad (2007) and others, we "read the world around us from embodiedness and being a part of the world, and being an equal state among other organisms and matter" (Lenz Taguchi, 2011, p. 40). Returning to Barad's (2007) illustration of diffraction, where even the slightest change in the height or position of a rock in water results in the waves forming new patterns, so too will the removal of any one element of the encounter, such as markers or children, affect the other elements, resulting in different actions and responses. The materials that are part of developmental practice are not passive objects or technologies that we use or apply to enhance or measure development. We cannot simply ask, Can we use this object to achieve developmental goals? Instead we need to look at how objects, humans, and discourses intra-act with one another in an encounter and what occurs within that encounter (Sørenson, 2009). The questions we ask begin to change, allowing for new ways of understanding development and the developmental worker.

Developmental Knowledge as a Doing

In this chapter, we returned to the memories we had previously analyzed, but now we ask new questions: How does the physicality of our practices, such as a particular instrument or an object on a table, invoke us as developmental workers to act in particular ways? How does the intra-action of discursive-material elements play a role in the emergence of our ways of doing developmental practice? How do the materials (e.g., a piece of paper, a book) speak to and with us about how we engage in developmental practice? These questions allow us to see developmental knowledge and the developmental worker differently, but not necessarily from different perspectives. They allowed us to see how developmental knowledge is constantly enacted in practice, and that it is through these enactments that it comes into being—always as something different, always in relation to the actants (human and nonhuman) that participate in its enactment.

Through the memories, we encountered multiple enactments of developmental practices and multiple versions of developmental workers within similar settings. For the student, developmental knowledge is experienced as pain when writing a test, but also as accomplishment. In a classroom of young children, a developmental worker understands this developmental practice as being demonstrated by signifiers such as having children's attention and focus. To the developmental practitioner making an observation, developmental practice is something written in an observation protocol that can be checked off. Each of these forms of developmental knowledge brings forth different practices that are related to the particular understanding of those very practices. For example, a practitioner will use an observation checklist to examine a child's behaviour, while for another practitioner (such as the student) a child may not even be part of developmental practice, as she relies on the textbook used in the child development course. Thus, developmental knowledge and practice are multiple, existing as significant and insignificant at the same time and enacting different practice.

This approach challenges the idea of developmental knowledge as a static entity that is *used* by developmental workers. In the memories above, it is not only the developmental worker who does developmental psychology; developmental knowledge emerges as an event that is made to happen by individuals (e.g., workers, children, families) and materials that come in many, many shapes and sizes, including, for example, tables, smells mixing in the room, paperwork, classroom rules, buildings, chairs, walls, tests, and assessment tools. In each of the memories, all of these things and discourses together give shape to different realities of developmental knowledge. Developmental knowledge becomes an event, a practice. Furthermore, the developmental practitioner emerges in the very enactment of these practices, always differently, always in an assemblage that shapes and is shaped by its different components.

Our own teaching practices begin to shift. We try to teach developmental knowledge "never isolated from the practices in which they are, what one may call, *enacted*" (Mol, 2002, p. 33, emphasis in the original). We read ideas written in a textbook about the facts of developmental knowledge, but we never stop there. We are interested in how developmental knowledge and developmental practitioners are situated within historical, political, social, economic, and cultural circumstances. We are interested in what the words on the page of the textbook do, how they function when we are reading them with others, individually, in the classroom, in relation to our own experiences with children. We are interested in how the developmental assessment tool we bring to the classroom functions when students use it in a classroom with children during their practicum. We are interested in what happens when a student sits down with a family and the practicum supervisor in a conference room to check off items on a developmental assessment checklist and discuss a child's progress. In other words, we are interested in practices that make developmental knowledge "visible, audible, tangible, and knowable" in different places at different times (Mol, 2002, p. 33)—practices that always exclude each other. Our interest is in seeing developmental knowledge as multiple and the developmental practitioner as emerging in the process of doing developmental practice.

We see this approach, with Barad (2007), as a way of becoming "responsible for the world within which we live, not because it is an arbitrary construction of our choosing, but because it is sedimented out of our particular practices that we have a role in shaping" (p. 203). With this quote, we leave the reader with a question: What other localized versions of developmental knowledge and developmental practitioners can be generated?

References

Barad, K. (2007). *Meeting the universe halfway: Quantum physics and the entanglement of matter and meaning*. Durham, NC: Duke University Press.

Blaise, M., & Elsden-Clifton, J. (2007). Intervening or ignoring: Learning about teaching in new times. *Asia-Pacific Journal of Teacher Education, 35*(4), 387–407.

Burman, E. (2008a). *Deconstructing developmental psychology* (2nd ed.). London, England: Routledge.

Burman, E. (2008b). *Developments: Child, image nation*. London, England: Routledge.

Butler, J. (1997). *The psychic life of power: Theories of subjection*. Palo Alto, CA: Stanford University Press.

Cannella, G. (1997). *Deconstructing early childhood education: Social justice and revolution*. New York, NY: Peter Lang.

Coole, D., & Frost, S. (2010). *New materialisms: Ontology, agency, and politics*. Durham, NC: Duke University Press.

Davies, B. (2000). *A body of writing: 1990–1999*. New York, NY: AltaMira Press.

Davies, B., & Gannon, S. (Eds.). (2006). *Doing collective biography*. Maidenhead, England: Open University Press.

Foucault, M. (1977). *Discipline and punish: The birth of the prison*. New York, NY: Vintage Books.

Foucault, M. (1978). *The history of sexuality*. New York, NY: Pantheon Books.

Hacking, I. (1999). *The social construction of what?* Cambridge, MA: Harvard University Press.

Haraway, D. (1997). *Modest_witness@_second_millennium. FemaleMan©_meets_OncoMouse: Feminism and technoscience*. New York, NY: Routledge.

Hayes-Conroy, A., & Hayes-Conroy, J. (2008). Taking back taste: Feminism, food and visceral politics. *Gender, Place and Culture: A Journal of Feminist Geography, 15*(5), 461–473.

Hayes-Conroy, A., & Martin, D. G. (2010). Mobilising bodies: Visceral identification in the Slow Food movement. *Transactions of the Institute of British Geographers, 35*(2), 269–281.

Hekman, S. (2010). *The material of knowledge: Feminist disclosures*. Bloomington: Indiana University Press.

Heron, J., & Reason, P. (1997). A participatory inquiry paradigm. *Qualitative Inquiry, 3*(3), 274–294.

Hultman, K., & Lenz Taguchi, H. (2010). Challenging anthropocentric analysis of visual data: A relational materialist methodological approach to educational research. *International Journal of Qualitative Studies in Education, 23*(5), 525–542.

Jackson, A. Y. (2001). Mulitple Annies: Feminist poststructural theory and the making of a teacher. *Journal of Teacher Education, 52*(5), 386–397.

Law, J. (2004). *After method: Mess in social science research*. New York, NY: Routledge.

Lenz Taguchi, H. (2005). Getting personal: How early childhood education troubles students' and teacher educators' identities regarding subjectivity and feminism. *Contemporary Issues in Early Childhood Education, 6*(3), 244–255.

Lenz Taguchi, H. (2007). Deconstructing and transgressing the theory-practice dichotomy in early childhood education. *Educational Philosophy and Theory, 39*(3), 275–290.

Lenz Taguchi, H. (Ed.). (2008). *Deconstructing and transgressing the theory-practice dichotomy in early childhood education*. Oxford, England: Blackwell.

Lenz Taguchi, H. (2009, November). *Investigating learning, participation and becoming in early childhood practices with a relational materialist approach*. Keynote presentation at the ninth annual conference for the Centre for Equity and Innovation in Early Childhood, Melbourne, Australia.

Lenz Taguchi, H. (2010). *Going beyond the theory/practice divide in early childhood education: Introducing an intra-active pedagogy*. New York, NY: Routledge.

Lenz Taguchi, H. (2011). Investigating learning, participation and becoming in early childhood practices with a relational materialist approach. *Global Studies of Childhood, 1*(1), 36–50.

Mol, A. (2002). *The body multiple: Ontology in medical practice.* Durham, NC: Duke University Press.

Morss, J. (1996). *Growing critical: Alternatives to developmental psychology.* London, England: Routledge.

Olsson, L. (2009). *Movement and experimentation in young children's learning: Deleuze and Guattari in early childhood education.* New York, NY: Routledge.

Pacini-Ketchabaw, V. (2008). Perspectives on child and adolescent development: Challenges and possibilities for teaching. *Relational Child and Youth Care Practice, 21*(3), 39–42.

Pacini-Ketchabaw, V. (2011). Developmental theories and child and youth care. In A. Pence & J. White (Eds.), *New perspectives in child and youth care* (pp. 19–32). Vancouver: University of British Columbia Press.

Pacini-Ketchabaw, V., Kummen, K., & Thompson, D. (2010). Becoming intimate with developmental knowledge: Pedagogical explorations with collective biography. *The Alberta Journal of Educational Research, 57*(3), 335–354.

Prout, A. (2005). *The future of childhood.* London, England: RoutledgeFalmer.

Rorty, R. (1967). *The linguistic turn: Methods in philosophical method.* Chicago, IL: Unversity of Chicago Press.

Rose, N. (1990). *Governing the soul: The shaping of the private self.* London, England: Routledge.

Ryan, S., & Grieshaber, S. (2005). Shifting from developmental to postmodern practices in early childhood teacher education. *Journal of Teacher Education, 56*(1), 34–45.

Skott-Myhre, H. (2008). *Youth and subculture as creative force: Creating new spaces for radical youth.* Toronto, ON: University of Toronto Press.

Sørensen E. (2009). *The materiality of learning: Technology and knowledge in educational practice.* New York: Cambridge University Press.

St. Pierre, E. (2000). Poststructural feminism in education: An overview. *Qualitative Studies in Education, 13*(5), 477–515.

Sumsion, J. (2005). Putting postmodern theories into practice in early childhood teacher education. In S. Ryan & S. Grieshaber (Eds.), *Practical transformations and transformational practices: Globalization, postmodernism, and early childhood education* (pp. 193–215). Amsterdam, the Netherlands: Elsevier JAI.

van der Tuin, I. (2011). New feminist materialisms. *Women's Studies International Forum, 34,* 271–277.

Viruru, R. (2005). Postcolonial theory and the practices of teacher education. In S. Ryan & S. Grieshaber (Eds.), *Practical transformations and transformational practices: Globalization, postmodernism, and early childhood education* (pp. 139–159). Amsterdam, the Netherlands: Elsevier JAI.

Walkerdine, V. (1998). Developmental psychology and the child-centred pedagogy. In J. Henriques, W. Hollway, C. Urwin, C. Venn, & V. Walkerdine (Eds.), *Changing the subject: Psychology, social regulation and subjectivity* (2nd ed., pp. 153–202). New York, NY: Routledge.

Zipin, L. (1998). Looking for sentient life in discursive practices: The question of human agency in critical theories and school research. In T. Popkewitz & M. Brennan (Eds.), *Foucault's challenge: Discourses, knowledge, and power in education* (pp. 316–347). New York, NY: Teachers College Press.

Chapter Nine

Children's Representations of Cultural Scripts in Play

Facilitating Transition from Home to Preschool in an Intercultural Early Learning Program for Refugee Children

Anna Kirova

The focus of this chapter is the role of play as a cultural activity in refugee children's transition from home to preschool. The study challenged the "culture-free" view of play as a means for development of a "universal" child. It provided an alternative view of play as cultural leading activity in the development of a culturally situated child based on the work of Vygotsky (1978) and Leont'ev (1981). These theorists frame a community-initiated project that aimed at providing learning opportunities in both children's home languages and English so that linguistic and cultural continuity as well as smooth transition from home to school cultures was provided for the children. The children and the first-language facilitators spoke four languages in the classroom (i.e., Kurdish, Somali, Sudanese Arabic, and English). The pilot study, using participatory action and learning methodology, demonstrated that the intercultural approach to education could open possibilities for new directions in early childhood practice in which a hybrid space is open for children and adults who share it to bring together their knowledges and ways of being in the world. In this space, play is a vehicle for preserving cultural group identities while creating a common culture.

Background and Purpose

Immigrant and refugee populations in Canada are growing fast. Between 2001 and 2006, those populations grew by 13.6%, four times faster than the Canadian-born population (Statistics Canada, 2006). Research on immigrant and refugee families suggests they encounter a number of sources of stress in their lives, including parental underemployment or unemployment (Harvey & Houle, 2006), language difficulties, separation from extended family and familiar social networks, loneliness, discrimination, family conflict, and perceived cultural incompatibilities. Newcomers and the children of newcomer parents may experience conflict due to changed family dynamics as they are adapting to the host culture at differing rates and making the transition from home to the community at large with varying degrees of perceived success (Adams & Kirova, 2007; Guarnaccia & Lopez, 1998).

In 2008, 12.5% of all newcomers to Canada were refugees ("Citizenship and Immigration Canada," 2008). Refugees are a special population. According to the Convention Relating to the Status of Refugees (UN General Assembly, 1951), refugees are persons in need of protection due to fear of persecution or are persons at risk of torture or cruel and unusual treatment or punishment (Article 1A[2]). Thus, unlike most other immigrants who had given the decision to live in another country due consideration and who had had time to physically and emotionally prepare themselves for the resettlement process, refugees had not intended to leave their country of origin. For refugees or asylum seekers, "the sudden and involuntary nature of the process generates tremendous tensions within the family" (Suarez-Orozco & Suarez-Orozco, 2001, p. 27). The authors further identified these tensions as being related to (1) parental feelings of guilt, failure, or grief for not having been able to provide for the basic safety and well-being of their children; (2) separation of family members and fear for the lives of the relatives left behind; (3) experiences associated with the terrors of war such as death and torture, which often result in post-traumatic stress disorder; and (4) lack of hope of returning to their country of origin due to war or complete destruction of the political system. Beyond these specific stresses, the resettlement process is influenced by "the physical and psychological availability of parents, the family's socioeconomic background, and the context in which the family resettles" (Suarez-Orozco & Suarez-Orozco, 2001, p. 28).

Newcomer families with young children experience additional challenges related to child care and early education opportunities (Bernhard, Lefebvre, Murphy Kilbride, Chud, & Lange, 1998; Bernhard, Pollard, Eggers-Pierola, & Morin, 2000; Guarnaccia & Lopez, 1998). In the urban context in which the study took place, the ethnocultural communities and the nongovernmental, not-for-profit organizations (NGOs) working with the families prior to the beginning of the study identified a number of difficulties and barriers that the refugee families encountered regarding culturally relevant early educational opportunities for their children. These barriers can be grouped in two major categories: accessibility and responsiveness.

Accessibility barriers include the following: (1) lack of space in early learning programs in the city for refugee children from families dealing with multiple social vulnerability factors; (2) transportation difficulties; (3) labeling the child as having a "mild to moderate" developmental delay in order to secure a place for him or her in an early learning program, which contributes to stigmatization and can have detrimental effects on the school life of the child; (4) rigid age cutoffs; (5) income criteria for working refugee families who, like other working poor, do not meet income criteria at first glance.

Responsiveness barriers include (1) lack of understanding of the special life circumstances of refugee families; (2) lack of flexibility with the current expectations or requirements for parental volunteering within the program; and (3) language and cultural limitations of parents that prevent them from fully engaging and being involved in their children's participation in available early learning programs.

It is worth noting that these difficulties are not unique to Canada. Rutter (1998) found that "refugee children in the UK do not have equal access to early years provision, even though their need may be greater than that of the population as a whole" (p. 23). Refugee families are among the least likely to receive the preschool support they need.

In addition to the barriers described above, both research and practice have suggested other more implicit or hidden factors, such as the fact that in the majority culture, early learning programs typically consider differences in culture as a deficit rather than an asset in schools (Bridging Refugee Youth, 2007). As Cannella (1997) pointed out, the "child's knowledge is not only disqualified, but its existence denied" (p. 19). She maintained that the National Association for the Education of Young Children's (NAEYC) position on developmentally appropriate practice, which was published a quarter century ago in Bredekamp (1987) and revised ten years later in Bredekamp and Copple (1997), has privileged child-centred, play-based instruction as the "universal human pedagogy that is appropriate for all human beings, the truth for everyone" (Cannella, 1997, p. 117). Similarly, Göncü (1999) stated, "In the effort to identify the universal features of children, the mainstream research adopted certain scientific values that promoted a decontextualized description of children" (p. 4). What this tradition left out, Göncü continued, "is what is important for children's development from the point of view of their cultures" (p. 8). Thus, child development theory serves to perpetuate regimes of power, with those categorized as "normal" dictating how and by whom deficiencies in the other are to be addressed (Cannella, 2001). Jipson (2001) too pointed out that early childhood curriculum, based on Western traditions of thought, reproduces "classed, raced, and gendered distortions in its representation of the world" (p. 5).

Even among the proponents of developmentally appropriate practice there was a view that although the 1997 revised version (Bredekamp & Copple, 1997) addressed the issue of cultural diversity by "including a more complex discussion of cultural relevance as a critical factor in teaching practices" (Morgan, as cited in Hatch et al., 2002, p. 446), the document fell short in that Western values were still presented as the standardized starting point from which to evaluate and modify practice. More recently, Bernhard (2002), Penn (2005), and Fleer, Tonyan, Mantilla, and Rivalland (2009) indicated that much of the research informing current early childhood practice in Western nations is based upon limited cultural and historical contexts.

Despite the critical concerns raised by a number of scholars within the early childhood community, developmental theory is still holding the power in early childhood education. Knowledge of child development is listed by the NAEYC as the first of the three areas of knowledge that an early childhood practitioner must consider in making both long- and short-term decisions. Knowledge of child development is defined as "knowledge of age-related characteristics that permit general predictions about what experiences are likely to best promote children's learning and development" (NAEYC, 2009, p. 9). The other two types are knowledge of the child as an individual (i.e., "individual variation," p. 9, of the age-related characteristic) and knowledge of the social and cultural contexts in which children live, including the values, expectations, and behavioural and linguistic conventions that shape children in their homes and communities.

However, by putting knowledge of child development first and knowledge of social and cultural context last on the NAEYC's list, its 2009 position statement does not help the field go beyond the notion of universal childhood. Instead, such a position perpetuates the deficit model describing children of color, children growing up in poverty, and English language learners as "most likely to begin school with lower levels of the foundational skills needed to succeed and most likely to fall behind with time" (NAEYC, 2009, p. 6).

Therefore, there is an urgent need for additional research on effective models that are built on the strengths young children from immigrant and refugee families bring to the early learning settings. This need exists even though the importance of valuing a child's home culture and home language, as well as infusing multiculturalism and diversity throughout early learning program content, increasingly is seen as important (e.g., Matthews & Jang, 2007).

The study described here addressed this need by documenting how the development of an intercultural early learning program initiated by three refugee communities in a large city in western Canada could provide insights into the place of culture in early childhood practice. For the purposes of this chapter, however, I will focus on only one aspect of the pilot program—classroom practice. Specifically, I will explore the role of play as a cultural activity in refugee children's transition from home to preschool culture.

Intercultural Early Learning Program for Refugee Children: A Participatory Learning and Action (PLA) Project

To address the above-mentioned challenges identified by the ethnocultural communities and the NGOs in the city where the study took place, in 2007 the board of trustees of the public schools realigned some district funding to enable the implementation of an innovative support model to better serve English language learners (ELLs), including refugee and immigrant children and youth. The model involved three clusters of schools serving ELL students and families within geographic proximity. The intent of the initiative was to provide access to culturally and linguistically diverse resource staff and ELL services at school sites and to increase collaboration with families and communities through community agencies and organizations. The ultimate goal was to have an early learning program serving preschool children from schools within each cluster.

As the principal researcher in the study, my role in this community-initiated and government-supported program was to provide guidance and research support to communities and community organizations, families, educators, policy makers, service providers, and administrators in developing and piloting an intercultural early learning program. The main research question of the pilot study was, What approaches to curriculum and pedagogy lead to a genuine inclusion of both refugee children's home languages and cultural traditions, and the English language and Canadian cultural traditions in early learning programs?

The pilot program involved one early learning program in one of the school clusters. The goals of the program included the following:

1. To be genuinely responsive to the unique early learning needs of refugee children growing up in a particularly complex social/economic and multicultural context.

2. To be focused on providing cultural and linguistic continuity for young refugee children.

3. To be supportive of children's first/home language while also facilitating English language learning.

4. To be attentive to the total life circumstances of refugee families as they affect parenting and early learning.

5. To be culturally sensitive and inclusive of the refugee families' perspectives.

6. To be based on the combined expertise and strengths of the public school board and the community partners as well as based on academic knowledge of early learning and thus be holistic, strength based, and equity based.

7. To be collaborative, interrelational, and interdependent so that mutual learning is fundamental to its success.

Intercultural Early Childhood Practices: A Theoretical Framework

Sociocultural-Historical Learning

In order for this intercultural early learning program to meet its goals, the researchers adopted a sociocultural-historical view of learning as an alternative to the developmentalism inherent in the current early childhood practices guided by the NAEYC's 1997 position statement on developmentally appropriate practice (DAP). From a sociocultural-historical point of view, child development is context sensitive and occurs within the meaning systems of cultural-historical circumstances (Vygotsky, 1978). Influenced by Vygotsky's work, Wertsch (1991) described the basic goal of a sociocultural approach to the human mind as creating "an account of human mental processes that recognizes the essential relationship between these processes and their cultural, historical, and institutional settings" (p. 6). More specifically, based on the work of Rogoff (2003), individual development was conceptualized as occurring through individuals' "changing participation in the sociocultural activities of their communities, which also change" (p. 368).

The idea of change was particularly important in the pilot program, especially in relation to the transition between cultures experienced by the refugee families and their children. For the purposes of this chapter, however, it is most important to distinguish the view of play used in the program from the view based on DAP philosophy that is promoted in most preschool programs.

The Value of Play Promoted by DAP: Development of the Universal Child

The history of play in the Western context has been well studied (Bruner, Jolly, & Sylva, 1976; Herron & Sutton-Smith, 1971; Lowenfeld, 1969), as has the role of play in the evolution of early childhood care and education (Bloch & Choi, 1990; Spodek & Saracho, 1991). In their cultural-historical analysis of play, Fleer et al. (2009) contended that play is a powerful discourse in the early childhood education community. The value of play in the development and education of young children in institutionalized settings has been emphasised since the establishment of Froebel's first kindergarten more than 150 years ago (Saracho & Spodek, 1998). Manipulation of Froebelian gifts and participation in making crafts under the strict supervision and direction of the teacher was seen as play that had a particular educational purpose. Although with a different purpose, Montessori too developed a set of play materials to be manipulated by young children with the specific goal of acquiring knowledge of the properties of the objects and skills related to these properties. It wasn't until the first quarter of the twentieth century when the nursery school movement, along with the reform of the kindergarten movement, brought the notion of the value of natural, organic play as a vehicle for young children's learning in its own right.

The publication of the NAEYC's *Developmentally Appropriate Practice* in the 1980s (Bredekamp, 1987) set the stage for the development and wide distribution of new print resources that were designed to support the implementation of the philosophy of learning through play (e.g., Jones & Reynolds, 1992; McKee & Association for Childhood Education International, 1986; Reynolds & Jones, 1997), and the publication of companion volumes (e.g., Gestwicki, 2007; Sluss, 2005). In general, play within the developmentally appropriate practice construction is considered an antidote to academics in the early years that prepared the child to enter formal schooling.

The most recent edition of the NAEYC's position statement on developmentally appropriate practice states, "Research shows the links between play and foundational capacities such as memory, self-regulation, and oral language abilities, social skills, and success in school" (NAEYC, 2009, p. 14). Thus, the view that play has benefits in different areas of development—intellectual, cognitive, physical, social, emotional, and academic—and should be part of the early childhood curriculum is still prevalent in both the theory and practice of early childhood education.

It is important to note, however, that in the field of early childhood education there has been a "'culture-free' approach to children's play" (Kushner, 2007, p. 62). This approach reflects the view of the universal child, implying that universal principles of child development apply to all children regardless of their backgrounds and experiences. In his critical review of the 101 articles on the topic of play published in 184 issues of the journal *Young Children* from 1973 to 2002 (the total number of articles published was 1,408), Kushner found that only one article directly addressed the issue of cultural differences and play. He noted that this article, authored by Boutte, Van Scoy, and Hendley in 1996, promoted the use of multicultural prop boxes for a children's sociodramatic play area in which props and artifacts from different cultures were placed to increase multicultural awareness and appreciation of diversity. Kushner also identified two articles (Griffing, 1983; Nourot & Van Hoorn, 1991) that emphasised the need for teachers to understand the differences children may exhibit in play that might in fact be cultural.

This alarming omission in *Young Children*, the most widely disseminated professional publication in the field of early childhood education, speaks clearly to the lack of recognition in the field of early childhood in general of the role of culture as one of the most important aspects of children's play context (King, 1992). While writings on play in other publications, including child development texts (Fromberg & Bergen, 2006; Frost, Wortham, & Reifel, 2005; Hughes, 1999) might bring the reader's attention to how play is influenced by gender, culture, and special needs and to how play is appropriate in some cases, attempts to understand play from contexts outside of developmental psychology are relatively recent.

The reasons for such delayed attempts are numerous. Perhaps the most important one is that developmental theorists—for example, Parten (1932), Piaget (1945), and Vygotsky (1978)—agreed on two points regarding play: First, the development of children's play follows similar patterns in terms of its origins, frequency, and types observable at different ages/stages of development. Second, play is an activity necessary for young children's optimal development with somewhat different emphases on areas of development most significantly influenced by play—language development, perspective thinking, and problem solving, for example (Göncü, Tuermer, Jain, & Johnson, 1999). Children whose play did not fit the developmental norms established by the dominant developmental theories were seen as in need of intervention. As a response to the interventionist view of play, play researchers such as Roopnarine and Johnson (2001), who were of the opinion that "existing play theories may be inadequate in guiding research on diverse groups of children because they appear insensitive to considerations of factors within the ecocultural system that may influence growth and development" (p. 301), were motivated to explore the role of culture and class in the development of children's play. Vygotsky's (1978) sociocultural theory of development provides a foundation for such explorations.

Play as a Cultural Activity: Development of the Culturally Situated Child
Roopnarine and Johnson (1994) stated that cultural-ecological models of behaviour and development reveal three interacting layers of environmental influence on play—(1) the physical and social aspects of children's immediate settings; (2) the historical influences that affect the way that individuals conceptualize play; and (3) the cultural and ideological beliefs relative to the meaning of play. Vygotsky's (1978) conceptualization of the role of play in the process of internalization or appropriation of skills that first exist on the interpsychological plane before they exist on the intrapsychological plane is central to the understanding of play as a cultural activity. Vygotsky (1977) believed that in pretend play, children recreate real-life events regardless of the fact that they take place in an imaginary situation. The imaginary situation in play allows children freedom from the con-

straints of the real world that surrounds them and stimulates them to try on social roles and skills they have not yet mastered.

> In play a child creates an imaginary situation. . . . Imagination is a new [newly formed] formation which is not present in the consciousness of the very young child . . . and represents a specifically human form of conscious activity. . . . Action in the imaginative sphere, in an imaginary situation, the creation of voluntary [not imposed] intentions and the formation of real-life plans . . . all appear in play and make it the highest level of pre-school development. (Vygotsky, 1977, p. 552)

Therefore, the freedom created by the imaginary situation in play allows children not only to play with play objects (e.g., toys) but more important to play with meanings they assign to these objects, and thus to use higher order mental processes based on signs and language as mental tools. Vygotsky (1978) stated that pretend "play creates a zone of proximal development of the child. In play a child always behaves beyond [his] average age, above [his] daily behaviour; in play it is as though he were a head taller than [himself]" (p. 102).

Building on Vygotsky's theory of development and the role of play in it, Leont'ev (1981) explained children's engagement in play as a desire to act like adults, which they cannot do in real life. Taking Vygotsky's theory further by suggesting that play is a leading activity in preschool, Leont'ev (1978) used the concept of leading activity to distinguish a particular type of interaction between the child and the environment that produces major development accomplishments, provides the basis for other activities, and induces the creation of new mental processes and the restructuring of old ones. For Leont'ev (1981), activities are "processes that are psychologically characterised by what the process as a whole is directed to (its object) always coinciding with the objective that stimulates the subject to this activity, i.e., the motive" (pp. 39–40). It is through the child's engagement in activities that he or she appropriates "historically formed human properties, capacities, and modes of behaviour" (p. 422). Play, he found, is a leading activity for preschool-aged children because it produces imagination, symbolic function, and the integration of thinking and emotions as the major developmental accomplishments for this age (Bodrova & Leong, 2007). These accomplishments are possible through children's participation in and appropriation from activities by using the tools of their culture.

Culture, therefore, is not an "add-on" to a universal play activity but rather the origin of what children do in play, the cultural tools they use in mastering social roles and skills, and the ways in which they appropriate a particular cultural activity with its developmental functions that may vary within as well as across cultures. As Göncü et al. (1999) stressed, "an adequate examination of children's play in a given community can be accomplished only by taking into account the unique cultural milieu in which play is embedded" (p. 152).

Research Question and Methodology

Studying play in its cultural context is absolutely essential to understanding it as a cultural activity in a particular community. However, the question explored in this chapter—Which cultural context do refugee children represent in their play?—brings the study of children's play in a multicultural context to a level of greater complexity. This chapter investigates through examples how the refugee children in an intercultural early learning classroom incorporate in their play actions and operations appropriated through their participation in activities specific to their home culture.

The methodology used in the study, participatory learning and action (PLA), allows for challenging prevailing biases and preconceptions about people's knowledge, and thus offers opportunities for mobilising local people for joint action toward life-enhancing changes. Because of these characteristics, participatory research methods are appropriate for working with populations, including children, young people, and adults, who might come from oral traditions in which sharing in groups is more comfortable than one-on-one interviews or written questionnaires and surveys. Like the other participatory approaches, PLA emphasises equal collaboration and results in an "emancipated researcher" (Creswell, 2005, p. 552).

Setting and Participants

A core component of the pilot program included children's home languages as a language of instruction, in addition to English, to ensure linguistic and cultural continuity as well as smooth transition from home to school cultures. The program was unique in that it involved four languages: Somali, Arabic (Sudanese dialect), Kurdish, and English. The pilot program, situated at an inner-city elementary/junior high school (pre-kindergarten to grade 9) with a dense immigrant student population, began in the fall of 2007. One-third of all children were coded as English language learners, and more than twenty languages and dialects were spoken among these children. The school also offered a bilingual Ukrainian/English program.

The intercultural early learning program was designed to include sixteen children, who were three and a half years old by September first, and their families. The communities these families were selected from were the Kurdish, Sudanese, and Somali living within the boundaries of that area of the city. The families, through a series of shared activities undertaken as part of a parenting group program provided by one of the partnering NGOs, had already begun to form intergroup relationships. Given the number of different languages and dialects spoken within the Sudanese community (close to one hundred), the program was designed to offer support of children's Sudanese Arabic, considered to be a common language of that community. However, due to transportation difficulties in the second year of the pilot program, fewer children actually attended the program on a consistent basis.

The mix of numbers of the participating children and their backgrounds are as follows: three children were from a Sudanese background; three children were from a Somali background; three were nonimmigrant, Canadian-born, English-speaking children; and one child was Kurdish speaking. Only one child, a Sudanese boy, had been born in a refugee camp. The other children from the three refugee communities were each the first child born in Canada after a family's arrival.

The early childhood educators in the classroom included a home-language facilitator for each of the children's three home languages. The educators were chosen by their communities because of their passion for their culture, ability to work with young children, and ability to tell stories and sing songs from their native culture. Also included was an English-speaking classroom teacher with over twenty years of experience working with diverse populations served by ABC Head Start (2011).

The program was offered four half days a week, with time for instruction and activities divided equally between English and the children's home languages. Research suggests that in partnership, parents and educational practitioners can and should work simultaneously toward developing language learning milestones in both languages through exploration of language and literacy patterns in the home and integration of culture and language into classroom learning (e.g., Coltrane, 2003; Wong Fillmore, 1991). To help parents understand the importance of using their mother tongue at home, bimonthly parent meetings were held. It was anticipated that the children would develop their home language so that they could maintain communication and relationship with their parents, extended families, and communities (Hepburn, 2004). It was also expected that developing English language proficiency would put the children in a more equitable position in school with peers who were native English speakers.

Data Collection and Procedures

As a qualitative design, PLA employs the following data collection methods: research conversations, focus groups, field notes, and focus observations.

Research conversations as a method in participatory inquiry (Herda, 1999) allowed for participants from diverse cultures in this program to work together and assess their actions. These were ongoing and initiated by both participants and researcher. The classroom team consisted of the classroom teacher, three first-language facilitators, the researcher, and the research assistant. The team met every Monday morning, when the children did not attend the program, to reflect on the previous week and to plan the week ahead. These conversations changed focus from one week to the next as the classroom routines became smoother and the planning of the activities for the whole group (English only) and the small groups (first language only) became more easily organized and carried out. It was during these conversations that the emerging curriculum was discussed. The team negotiated topics such as babies, siblings, friends, animals, animal and people houses "back home" and in Canada, fruits and vegetables, and the market, to list but a few, and they made decisions regarding materials and culturally specific activities.

Three focus groups (Bloor, Frankland, Thomas, & Robson, 2001) were conducted with the parents and ethnocultural community leaders to discuss their goals and aspirations for their children as well as their expectations regarding the success of the program. Once they had gathered parents' and community members' knowledge of culturally specific activities (e.g., making the orange-peel necklaces and carved apple faces typical of the rural impoverished areas in Kurdistan; playing shooting marbles on the floor and name games typical of the Somali and Sudanese communities), as well as stories, songs, and rituals, the team brought these ideas to the Monday morning meetings to consider them for inclusion in classroom activities.

Field notes from the team, in the form of jotted notes and direct observations (Neuman, 2009), documented the conversations, events, and behaviours that occurred in the classroom. The intent of these focused observations was to describe and record behaviours of a child or a group of children or particular aspect of a classroom practice. For example, during the first couple of months of the program, the major concern was how to include four languages in the classroom. Because the first-language facilitators were also fluent in English, and because English was the common language in the classroom as well as among the classroom team and the research team, special attention was given to the time and activities in which the children's first languages would be used in the most meaningful way. Classroom routines (e.g., snack, toilet, and circle time) and ways in which everyone became a member of a community were also aspects of the classroom life that the team observed and documented. Reflecting on the observations and setting new goals regarding the observed behaviours and practices were parts of the ongoing conversations among the members of the team. For the purposes of this chapter, however, only the observations that focused on the cultural aspects of play will be discussed.

The classroom observations were conducted two times a week for four months by a research assistant of East Indian heritage who was highly sensitive to cultural differences in children's day-to-day behaviours and learning. The role of researcher and research assistant was that of participant observer (Merriam, 1998), in which one "relies totally upon one's sensitivity, one's ability to grasp motives, beliefs, concerns, interests, unconscious behaviours, customs, and the like," and upon tacit as well as propositional knowledge (Guba & Lincoln, as cited in Merriam, 1998, p. 103).

Playing "Reality": Cultural Scripts in Children's Play

Play scholars such as Gaskins, Haight, and Lancy (2007) and Göncü, Jain, and Tuermer (2007) highlighted play as a cultural construction that must be contextualized. "Understanding children's play requires an examination of how children represent their worlds in play" (Göncü et al., 1999, p. 158). According to the authors, such an examination should also include "the kinds of roles adopted by children, the types of events represented in children's play, and the ways in which the physical environment is used in the service of children's play desire, as well as the communicative context in which play desire are developed" (Göncü et al., 1999, p. 158).

In the following section, examples of such an examination of two play episodes observed in the intercultural early learning classroom are presented. The names used in the descriptions are pseudonyms.

Playing Tea Serving

The following description of a play episode, which the team called "tea serving," is based on the research assistant's focused observations of play.

Figure 1

She noted that two of the children, Abuko (a Sudanese girl) and Laho (a Sudanese boy), followed Achi (the Sudanese Arabic home language facilitator) to the kitchen/hut centre. The children began to bring out cooking utensils and a baby doll. Laho dressed the baby while Achi told him to get the baby ready for the day. The children decided that Abuko would cook something first. Abuko took a small stool and converted it into a small stove (Figure 1).

> Research Assistant (RA): "What are you making?"
> Abuko: "I am cooking potatoes for you to eat. My mom makes potatoes for supper."
> RA: "This is very kind of you, Abuko, thank you."
> Abuko: "I will make you tea."
> RA: "Oh, this is wonderful, Abuko. I love tea. Thank you."
> RA (to Achi): "Is it a Sudanese tradition to offer tea after dinner?"
> Achi: "Back home everyone drank tea after supper."
> RA: "In the East Indian culture we call tea 'chai.'"
> Achi: "We call it 'shaah' in Sudanese Arabic."
> While the assistant was "drinking" tea, Hasan, one of the Somali children, came over to the group.
> Hasan: "Are you drinking tea? I want some too."

It seemed that drinking tea was a familiar event in his home life as well, so they conversed about when one drinks tea at home and how it is made. The other first-language facilitators and most of the other children came to the kitchen area and shared how tea is made in their homes. Questions such as "When do you drink tea at home?" "Do you drink it with snacks, and if so, what are these snacks?" "Is it common to drink it with sweets?" "Are certain spices used to make tea?" "How is tea served in your home?" and "How many times a day do they drink tea?" were asked in all four languages spoken by the children in the classroom and resulted in an animated discussion.

The following day, the first-language facilitators brought special teapots, teacups and saucers, spoons for stirring, and a steel and ceramic mortar and pestle for grinding

Figure 2

spices, which they had carried from their countries of origin. They also brought specialty tea, some of it in bags and some it loose; sugar (cubed and loose); and a variety of spices (cardamom, cloves, cinnamon) to make the "shaah."

As these artifacts and ingredients were taken out of the bags and put on a table for everyone to explore, Hasan picked up a mortar and pestle and simulated grinding up spices that were at the tea table (Figure 2).

As Hasan was pretending to grind special spices for the tea, he was explaining to Maryam (the Somali language facilitator) how tea is served in his home and how his father drinks tea after his dinner. Laho, a Sudanese boy, said that his mother grinds things in a spice grinder like the one in the classroom. He also picked up the grinder during his play and knew exactly how to use it (Figure 3).

Figure 3

Figure 4

The Kurdish girl, Hana, who loved to play at the kitchen centre pretending to be a mother, also showed interest in the tea sets and immediately began setting up the cups and saucers in a straight row on the floor and counted them. Tara, the Kurdish language facilitator, informed the research assistant that Hana was imitating perfectly her own mother's way of serving tea, as it is the Kurdish tradition to serve food and drinks on the floor (Figure 4). When Tara was demonstrating to all the children how the Kurdish people serve tea, Hana came up to help. Because the tea was too hot, Tara poured the tea in a saucer; Hana quickly came and blew on it to make it cool down, as is customary in the Kurdish tradition (Figure 5).

The play continued for a week. Every child had a chance to "make" tea in the play area following the four cultural traditions in the classroom: Kurdish, Somali, Sudanese, and Canadian. Learning one another's cultural traditions, some of the Sudanese children and the Canadian-born, English-speaking children started dipping their cookies in the teacup, just like Maryam (the Somali language facilitator) did. Putting a sugar cube in the mouth and then drinking tea from the cup, a Kurdish tradition, was joyfully adopted by almost all the children in the class. At the end of the week, a real tea party took place; the children from each culture, guided by their first-language facilitator, set up a table according to their cultural traditions and invited the other children for tea. Visiting one another's "homes" brought a lot of excitement and turned into a shared tea party celebration. The shared party stimulated children to observe, try, and discuss different ways of drinking tea. At the end, one of the Sudanese boys said, "My favorite part of school is having a tea party."

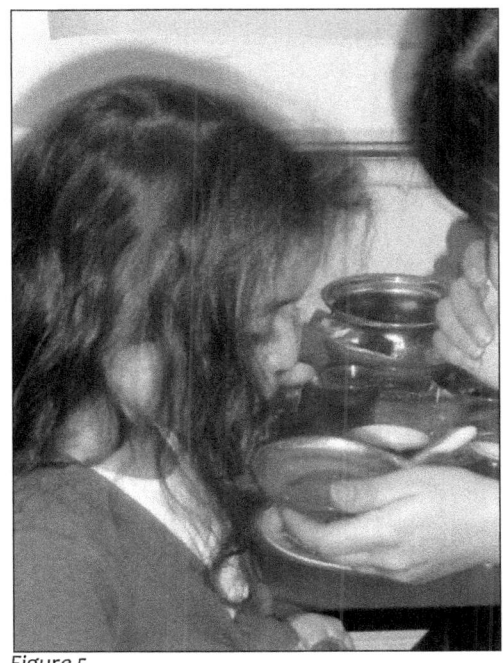

Figure 5

Playing Going to the Market

As a play theme, the marketplace developed as a natural extension of the children's exploration of tea-drinking rituals in their homes. Questions such as "Where does tea come from?" "Where does it grow?" and "What else can we grow?" led to rich conversations about growing fruits and vegetables and the kinds of produce children knew from their countries of origin. The first-language facilitators brought a variety of fruits and vegetables typical in their respective countries. Cultural artifacts such as hand-woven shopping baskets, banana leaf baskets, wooden fruit bowls, paper currency (Kurdish, Sudanese, and Somalian), and a seller's vest and hat were also brought into the classroom and made available for the children to explore. A colorful fabric to cover the market table finished the preparation for the opening of the market.

Figure 6

Roles were discussed among the children, teachers, and first-language facilitators. Children decided that they would be the buyers and the teachers would be the vendors. Currency, both from their countries of origin and from Canada, was divided equally among the children. After some discussion, the children decided that the teachers too had to have some money so they could make change if they needed to. The shopping baskets were also divided among the children according to their preferences.

The play began with one of the language facilitators shouting out the different fruits she had for sale (Figure 6). As she held up the different fruits, she shouted, "Fresh oranges and lemons for sale! Fresh mangos for sale!" The children held on to their money and began lining up, choosing different baskets to carry their purchases in.

In their play, the children carried the baskets in a variety of different ways, each specific to their culture. Some children swung the baskets over their shoulders; the Sudanese boy, who was the only child in this group born in a refugee camp, placed a basket on his head (Figure 7). One girl carried a heavy basket with both hands behind her back.

Since it was play and not a real market, the children did not pay for their purchases in an orderly way. Some of them pushed their way through to get their favorite fruits. They held out all of their money at once and pushed it into the seller's face (Figure 8). One of the first-language facilitators demonstrated how to bargain with the money when making purchases. She encouraged them to count it first to make sure they were paying the right amount, speaking to the children from

Figure 7

Children's Representations of Cultural Scripts in Play | 163

Figure 8

her ethnocultural community in their mother tongue. In applying the cultural way of shopping by bargaining, one of the children said, "How about three not four dollars?"

The children proceeded with their purchases to a fruit and lemonade stand, where they counted their fruits and practiced using a scale to weigh the different fruits. The first-language facilitator who was the seller counted the money she earned from the marketplace and told the children how rich she was. Some of the other children wanted to play the role of the seller as well. They took turns putting on the seller's vest in the market, while some of their peers bought fruits. While acting as seller, the children shouted out the various fruits that were for sale, imitating what they previously had seen their teachers doing. Some of the children shouted out what was for sale in their mother tongues.

The children who were the buyers kept running back to get more money from the language facilitators so that they could continue buying more fruits. When the children were done shopping, they wanted to "cook," so a language facilitator and a teacher helped them cut up their different fruits to make a fruit salad for a snack. Many of the children did not put all of the fruit they purchased in the class fruit salad. A few of the children took their baskets to the hut/kitchen centre and put the food into a pot to make soup. They played in the kitchen area and stirred the food around. The lemons were enjoyed by many of the children, especially the Sudanese and Somali children who were accustomed to eating sliced lemons with a bit of salt.

The market stand was so popular that one of the children proposed that an open/closed sign should be placed on the table so that the students would know when they could play in it. The language facilitators thought it was a good idea and made signs in English and in their native languages for the children to post. The children thoroughly enjoyed playing market with the language facilitators all week.

Examining Children's Worlds as Represented in Classroom Play

In understanding the significance of these play episodes in refugee children's transition from home to school cultures, one needs to take into account how play is viewed in these children's communities. Perhaps Rogoff's (1993) description of the cultural differences between play in nonindustrialized and industrialized/Western communities can be useful:

> Children [in nonindustrialized communities] most often emulate adult activities in play, whereas in middle-class communities children's play is less frequently modeled on adult activities (which such children have less opportunities to observe) and more frequently involves imaginary characters such as those on television. (pp. 25–26)

In considering this distinction, one can see how play in the pilot program was characteristic of play representative of the children's home cultures. Children playfully imitated and reconstructed at the different stages of the development of these particular play episodes important themes of adult life—serving tea and going to the market. From the point of view of the activity theory, an activity as "a unit of life that is historically determined and social in origin" (Göncü et al., 1999, p. 154) has a purpose driven by a need (e.g., grocery shopping to satisfy the need for food) and thus motivates an individual to engage in the activity. The particular actions involved in the "going to the market" play episode, such as selecting fruits and vegetables and paying for the purchased goods, require the use of cultural tools, including language and gesture, that are appropriated within the context of a particular historical and social meaning. Although the overall motives of the activity and its actions and goals occur at a conscious level, some automated actions, which depend on specific environmental circumstances, do not involve conscious attention. In the classroom, play provided context in which the children were able to demonstrate culturally specific operations (e.g., carrying a shopping basket or blowing on a saucer to cool down the tea poured into it) not typical for the culture of their host country but typical for their home culture.

Children's motivation to engage in a play activity is different from adults' engagement in real-life activity, however. Unlike adults, children do not aim at tangible end results of their play activity. Rather, their motive is to be like adults and thus to play their roles by performing the actions associated with adult roles. These actions, according to Leont'ev (1981), are real even though they are performed without the goal of achieving an end result and usually involve play materials or other objects, not the actual tools used in life. Therefore, imagination or an imaginary situation is the requirement for the child to be able to perform real, culturally formed actions and operations.

In the play episode of "serving tea," for example, children adopted adult roles in preparing, serving, and consuming tea and enjoyed visiting one another's tea party, just as adults do. Both the actions involved in the tea-serving activity and the roles that required these actions necessitated the use of cultural tools, which were predominantly demonstrated in children's gestures (e.g., grinding the tea spices and dipping cookies in the teacup).

However, one can also see that because of children's somewhat limited experiences and knowledge of the larger cultural context in which tea rituals and shopping at the local market take place in their countries of origin, they could enact only a small portion of these everyday activities on their own. Although the tea rituals were practiced in their homes on a daily basis and most children were able to talk about and demonstrate how tea was served and consumed in their homes, going to the market was an experience that had been initiated in the host country for all but one of the children, the one born in a refugee camp. The cultural scripts demonstrated in play were limited to carrying the shopping baskets and picking fruit from the stand, activities the children observed their parents doing in Canada. Thus, depending on their first-hand experiences, the children relied, to different degrees, on the first-language facilitators' involvement in developing "serving tea" and "going to the market" as sustained dramatic play themes. Adopting roles and participating as playmates in children's play were new experiences for both the first-language facilitators and the children, since it is not typical for adults in their cultures to play with children. Furthermore, children needed the cultural artifacts as scaffolds in enacting their cultural knowledge, which in their countries of origin would have been replaced by child-made or improvised play objects.

The use of play objects and cultural artifacts in the children's play episodes deserves special attention. From birth, children are surrounded by objects and artifacts of their culture, which they experience first by observing adults, next by imitating, and then by using them creatively to satisfy their own needs and desires; ultimately, they develop their own useful tools and objects. It is an expectation and an overall goal of each society for the young to learn to be proficient in the use of the older generation's tools and to "modernize" them to meet the needs of their own generation. Tudge and Odero-Wanga (2009) maintained that children do not merely reproduce cultural practices, but also re-create them. Children's manipulation of the objects available to them in different contexts and participation in activities requiring the use of these objects allows them to develop different competencies that are related to different practices and different knowledge systems—home and school. As these episodes illustrate, play allows space where the practice of these knowledge systems safely overlaps and where new, hybrid knowledge and practice associated with play can emerge.

The children in this particular program have already made, to some extent, a transition from their cultural way of playing at home, with less involvement of adults and use of fewer play objects, to playing at school, with more adult involvement and more provisions made for arranging a conducive, culturally appropriate play context. It seems that play was significant in these children's transition from home to school culture, since it served as affirmation of their cultural knowledge in a context outside of their home and allowed for sharing cultural knowledges in an attempt to create a new one that combined elements of all. Play then allowed children to create a new culture of childhood in their adopted homes.

Discussion and Implications for Practice

Referring to the work of Eiser (1988) on children's play in the Holocaust, King (1992) discussed the joy and satisfaction that adults in general and early childhood educators in particular received from providing play settings for children and taking part in this play. She brings several arguments in support of her main thesis that contrary to the common perception, children's play in any institutional/organizational setting is far from being "free." King stated, "In summary, classroom play is never, simply, the free expression of children" (p. 47). Along with the importance of adult-made choices of physical environment (i.e., the space designated in the classroom as a play area), the play materials made available to children, and the time allowed for play activities or "free play," the type of interactions between adults and children in play also shapes how children use materials and perform roles in play.

The play episodes described above can serve as examples of how the adults' thoughtful consideration of the cultural context of play created space for children's enactment of cultural scripts pertaining to important day-to-day practices in their home lives. These practices, in which knowledge of cultural traditions surface, are not individual and unique but rather sociocultural and historical. It is important here to emphasize the availability of cultural artifacts in the classroom defined as objects, "created as an embodiment of purpose and incorporated into life activity in a certain way" (Backhurst, 1990, p. 182). This definition is particularly useful in understanding the role of adults, and most important the role of the first-language facilitators who also served as cultural brokers in the classroom, in guiding children's use of these artifacts in culturally appropriate ways in their play. The definition is also useful in understanding culture as "not a random array of artifacts, but rather a heterogeneously, dynamically changing set of practices and resources that require constant active engagement for their continued existence" (Cole, as cited in Cole & Gajdamaschko, 2007, p. 208). In the Vygotskian tradition, this definition of artifacts helps us to see how a child enacts as well as acquires knowledge of culturally specific ways of being in the world by participating in activities that were initiated and scaffolded by the more competent members of their own cultural group—the first-language facilitators and cultural brokers. Thus, the examples provided above challenge the idea of using a "multicultural prop box" without the cultural mediation needed in scaffolding children's use of these props.

Summary and Conclusion

This chapter explored the role of play as a cultural activity in refugee children's transition from home to preschool culture, challenging the "culture-free" view of play as a means for development of a "universal" child and presenting an alternative view of play as a cultural leading activity. The works of Vygotsky and Leont'ev framed theoretically a community-initiated project that provided learning opportunities in the child's home language and English. The purpose of the initiative was to provide linguistic and cultural continuity to smooth children's transition from home to school. Although linguistic continuity was achieved through the consistent use of first languages in the classroom while the children were learning English, cultural continuity was provided through the cultural content and cultural activities relevant to each of the cultures present in the classroom. The availability of artifacts that children recognized as belonging to their culture allowed them to enact their narrative knowledge of everyday events in their home life. Thus, having cultural artifacts in children's dramatic play was not simply an act of recognition and appreciation of diversity. Rather, it was an essential element of the play environment that allowed children from diverse backgrounds to enact their cultural knowledge.

Children's enactment of cultural scripts in play in a preschool context in their host country demonstrated that "children take on important roles in mediating between their world of origin and the host society" (Knörr, 2005, p. 15) by bringing their cultural narrative knowledge to their new cultural context. Each child is a participant in a number of sociocultural contexts and, in the case of immigrant and refugee children, a member of different ethnocultural groups. Thus, he or she is both a product of these contexts and an agent of their change. Children's understanding and knowledge about the different sociocultural contexts in which they live are most freely represented in preschool-aged children's dramatic or pretend play.

Play provided a hybrid space in which young children and their mothers engaged in practices that merged different cultural forms into a "bricolage" (Hebdige, 1979, p. 102) in Dachyshyn and Kirova's (2008) work based on observations of

Sudanese mother/son dyads. Play in this study was also conceptualized as providing a liminal space for new identities to emerge through contestation. Dachyshyn and Kirova concluded, "If we allow room for alternate expressions of being to arise then early childhood institutions can become a hybrid space, a third space, for children and parents new to Canada in which to negotiate the hybrid identities that are essential to healthy integration into life in the host country" (p. 294).

The play episodes in which the children recreated their cultural knowledge were possible because the intercultural early learning program was designed to open a hybrid space for the children and adults who shared it to bring their knowledges and ways of being in the world. Such examples challenge the goal of the implementation of the federal multicultural policy within the educational system in Canada, which has resulted in "folklorisation" and construction of minority groups in static, essentialist, and exoticized terms while situating such groups outside the Canadian nation (e.g., Bannerji, 2000; Walcott, 1997). The elements of the piloted intercultural early learning program presented here suggest the possibility of a new direction of multicultural education practice that moves beyond the celebration of difference on special occasions/dates that are typically add-ons to the regular curriculum and integrates multiple perspectives into the explicit curriculum. By critically analysing the Eurocentric basis of early childhood practices and adopting sociocultural historical theory of learning and its foundational principles, this intercultural early learning program demonstrates that it is possible to preserve cultural group identity and practices while creating a common culture. Following children's lead in negotiating cultural scripts and realities, early childhood educators can learn to see the tension between preservation and interpenetration of cultures as creative possibilities.

The program also demonstrates that the intercultural approach to education cannot become a reality in schools without parallel changes in the wider social world—that is, provincial government initiatives to better meet the needs of young refugee and immigrant children. The program exemplifies how communities' and families' cultural needs as well as their high aspirations for the education of their children in Canada can be addressed in a sensitive and comprehensive manner though collaborative grassroots efforts.

References

ABC Head Start. (2011). Our history. Retrieved from http://www.abcheadstart.org/ourHistory

Adams, L., & Kirova, A. (Eds.). (2007). *Global migration and education: Schools, children, and families*. Mahwah, NJ: Erlbaum.

Backhurst, D. (1990). *Consciousness and revolution in Soviet philosophy: From the Bolsheviks to Evald Ilyenkov*. New York, NY: Cambridge University Press.

Bannerji, H. (2000). *The dark side of the nation: Essays on multiculturalism, nationalism, and gender*. Toronto, ON: Canadian Scholars Press.

Bernhard, J. K. (2002). Toward a 21st century developmental theory: Principles to account for diversity in children's lives. *Early Childhood Education Publications and Research* (Paper 21). Retrieved from http://digitalcommons.ryerson.ca/ece/21

Bernhard, J. K., Lefebvre, M. L., Murphy Kilbride, K., Chud, G., & Lange, R. (1998). Troubled relationships in early childhood education: Parent-teacher interactions in ethno-culturally diverse settings. *Early Education and Development, 9*(1), 5–28.

Bernhard, J. K., Pollard, J., Eggers-Pierola, C., & Morin, A. (2000). *Infants and toddlers in Canadian multi-age childcare centres: Age, ability and linguistic inclusion.* Ottawa, ON: Research Connections Canada. [Also published in French as *Les poupons et les jeunes enfants dans les garderies pour âges multiples.* Ottawa, ON: Research Connections Canada.]

Bloch, M., & Choi, S. (1990). Conceptions of play in the history of early childhood education. *Child & Youth Care Quarterly, 19*(1), 31–48.

Bloor, M., Frankland, J., Thomas, M., & Robson, K. (2001). *Focus groups in social research.* Thousand Oaks, CA: Sage.

Bodrova, E., & Leong, D. J. (2007). *Tools of the mind: The Vygotskian approach to early childhood education* (2nd ed.). Englewood Cliffs, NJ: Prentice-Hall.

Bredekamp, S. (Ed.). (1987). *Developmentally appropriate practice in early childhood programs serving children from birth through age 8.* Washington, DC: National Association for the Education of Young Children.

Bredekamp, S., & Copple, C. (Eds). (1997). *Developmentally appropriate practice in early childhood programs* (Rev. ed.). Washington, DC: National Association for the Education of Young Children.

Bridging Refugee Youth and Children's Services. (2007). *Spring 2007 spotlight: Involving refugee parents in their children's education.* Retrieved from http://www.brycs.org/brycs_spotspring2007.htm

Bruner, J. S., Jolly, A., & Sylva, K. (1976). *Play—its role in development and evolution.* New York, NY: Basic Books.

Cannella, G. S. (1997). *Deconstructing early childhood education: Social justice and revolution.* New York, NY: Peter Lang.

Cannella, G. S. (2001). Natural born curriculum: Popular culture and representation of childhood. In J. Jipson & R. Johnson (Eds.), *Resistance and representation: Rethinking childhood education* (pp. 15–23). New York, NY: Peter Lang.

Citizenship and Immigration Canada. (2008). *Immigration overview: Permanent and temporary residents.* Retrieved from http://www.cic.gc.ca/english/resources/statistics/facts2008/index.asp

Cole, M., & Gajdamaschko, N. (2007). Vygotsky and culture. In H. Daniels, M. Cole, & J. Wertsch (Eds.), *The Cambridge companion to Vygotsky* (pp. 193–211). New York, NY: Cambridge University Press.

Coltrane, B. (2003). *Working with young English language learners: Some considerations.* Washington, DC: U.S. Department of Education, National Library of Education, Office of Educational Research and Improvement. Retrieved from http://www.cal.org/resources/digest/0301coltrane.html

Creswell, J. W. (2005). *Educational research: Planning, conducting, and evaluating quantitative and qualitative research.* Upper Saddle River, NJ: Pearson Education.

Dachyshyn, D., & Kirova, A. (2008). Understanding childhoods in-between: Sudanese refugee and children's transition from home to preschool [Special issue on early childhood education and care]. *Research in Comparative and International Education, 3*(3), 281–294.

Eiser, G. (1988). *Children and play in the Holocaust: Games among the shadows.* Amherst: University of Massachusetts Press.

Fleer, M., Tonyan, H. A., Mantilla, Benitez, A. C., & Rivalland, C., M., P. (2009). A cultural-historical analysis of play as an activity setting in early childhood education: Views from research and from teachers. In M. Fleer, M. Hedegaard, & J. Tudge (Eds.), *Childhood studies and the impact of globalization: Policies and practices at global and local levels* (pp. 292–312). New York, NY: Routledge.

Fromberg, D. P., & Bergen, D. (2006). *Play from birth to twelve: Contexts, perspectives, and meanings* (2nd ed.). New York, NY: Routledge.
Frost, J. L., Wortham, S. C., & Reifel, R. S. (2005). *Play and child development* (2nd ed.). Upper Saddle River, NJ: Prentice-Hall.
Gaskins, S., Haight, W., & Lancy, D. F. (2007). The cultural construction of play. In A. Göncü & S. Gaskins (Eds.), *Play and development: Evolutionary, sociocultural, and functional perspectives* (pp. 179–202). Mahwah, NJ: Erlbaum.
Gestwicki, C. (2007). *Developmentally appropriate practice: Curriculum and development in early education* (3rd ed.). Clifton Park, NY: Thomson Delmar Learning.
Göncü, A. (1999). Children's and researchers' engagement in the world. In A. Göncü (Ed.), *Children's engagement in the world: Sociocultural perspectives* (pp. 3–25). Cambridge, England: Cambridge University Press.
Göncü, A., Jain, J., & Tuermer, U. (2007). Children's play as cultural interpretation. In A. Göncü & S. Gaskins (Eds.), *Play and development: Evolutionary, sociocultural, and functional perspectives* (pp. 155–178). Mahwah, NJ: Erlbaum.
Göncü, A., Tuermer, U., Jain, J., & Johnson, D. (1999). Children's play as cultural activity. In A. Göncü (Ed.), *Children's engagement in the world: Sociocultural perspectives* (pp. 148–170). Cambridge, England: Cambridge University Press.
Griffing, P. (1983). Encouraging dramatic play in early childhood. *Young Children, 38*(2), 13–22.
Guarnaccia, P. J., & Lopez, S. R. (1998). The mental health and adjustment of immigrant and refugee children. *Child and Adolescent Psychiatric Clinics of North America, 7*, 537–553.
Harvey, E. B., & Houle, R. (2006). *Demographic changes in Canada and their impact on public education*. Toronto, ON: The Learning Partnership.
Hatch, A., Bowman, B., Jor'dan, J. R., Morgan, C. L., Hart, C., Soto, L. D., et al. (2002). Developmentally appropriate practice: Continuing the dialogue. *Contemporary Issues in Early Childhood, 3*(3), 439–457.
Hebdige, D. (1979). *Subculture. The meaning of style*. London, England: Routledge.
Hepburn, K. S. (2004). *Building culturally and linguistically competent services to support young children and their families, and school readiness*. Baltimore, MD: The Annie E. Casey Foundation.
Herda, E. (1999). *Research conversations and narrative: A critical hermeneutic orientation in participatory inquiry*. Westport, CT: Praeger.
Herron, R. E., & Sutton-Smith, B. (1971). *Child's play*. New York, NY: Wiley.
Hughes, F. P. (1999). *Children, play, and development* (3rd ed.). Boston, MA: Allyn & Bacon.
Jipson, J. (2001). Introduction. In J. Jipson & R. Johnson (Eds.), *Resistance and representation: Rethinking childhood education* (pp. 1–15). New York, NY: Peter Lang.
Jones, E., & Reynolds, G. (1992). *The play's the thing: Teachers' roles in children's play*. New York, NY: Teachers College Press.
King, N. R. (1992). The impact of context on the play of young children. In S. Kessler & B. B. Swadener (Eds.), *Reconceptualizing early childhood curriculum: Beginning the dialogue* (pp. 43–61). Springfield, IL: Charles C. Thomas.
Knörr, J. (Ed.). (2005). *Childhood and migration: From experience to agency*. London, England: Transaction.
Kushner, D. (2007). Children's play in the journal, *Young Children*: An analysis of how it is portrayed and why it is valued. In D. J. Sluss & O. S. Jarrett (Eds.), *Play and Culture Studies: Vol. 7. Investigating play in the 21st century* (pp. 55–73). Lanham, MD: University Press of America.
Leont'ev, A. N. (1978). *Activity, consciousness, and personality*. Englewood Cliffs, NJ: Prentice-Hall.
Leont'ev, A. N. (1981). Activity, consciousness and personality. In J. V. Wertsch (Ed.), *The concept of activity in Soviet psychology* (pp. 37–71). Armonk, NY: M. E. Sharpe.
Lowenfeld, M. (1969). *Play in childhood*. Portway Bath, England: C. Chivers.
Matthews, H., & Jang, D. (2007). *The challenges of change: Learning from the child care and early education experiences of immigrant families*. Washington, DC: Center for Law and Social Policy (CLASP). Retrieved from http://www.clasp.org

McKee, J. S., & Association for Childhood Education International (Eds.). (1986). *Play, working partner of growth*. Wheaton, MD: Association for Childhood Education International.

Merriam, S. B. (1998). *Case study research in education: A qualitative approach*. San Francisco, CA: Jossey-Bass.

National Association for the Education of Young Children (NAEYC). (2009). *Position statement: Developmentally appropriate practice in early childhood programs serving children from birth through age 8*. Washington, DC: Author. Retrieved from http://www.naeyc.org

Neuman, W. L. (2009). *Understanding research*. Boston, MA: Pearson.

Nourot, P. M., & Van Hoorn, J. L. (1991). Research in review. Symbolic play in preschool and primary grades. *Young Children, 46*(6), 40–50.

Parten, M. B. (1932). Social participation among preschool children. *Journal of Abnormal Psychology, 27*, 243–269.

Penn, H. (2005). *Unequal childhoods: Young children's lives in poor countries*. New York, NY: Routledge.

Piaget, J. (1945). *Play, dreams and imitation in childhood*. London, England: Heinemann.

Reynolds, G., & Jones, E. (1997). *Master players: Learning from children at play*. New York, NY: Teachers College Press.

Rogoff, B. (1993). Commentary. *Human development, 36*, 24–26.

Rogoff, B. (2003). *The cultural nature of human development*. New York NY: Oxford University Press.

Roopnarine, J. L., & Johnson, J. E. (1994). The need to look at play in diverse cultural settings. In J. L. Roopnarine, J. E. Johnson, & F. H. Hooper (Eds.), *Children's play in diverse cultures* (pp. 1–8). Albany, NY: SUNY Press.

Roopnarine, J., & Johnson, J. E. (2001). Play and diverse cultures: Implications for early childhood education. In S. Reifel & M. H. Brown (Eds.), *Early education and care, and reconceptualising play* (pp. 295–319). New York, NY: JAI Press.

Rutter, J. (1998). Refugee children in the early years. *Multicultural Teaching, 17*(1), 23–26.

Saracho, O. N., & Spodek, B. (1998). A historical overview of theories of play. In O. N. Saracho & B. Spodek (Eds.), *Multiple perspectives on play in early childhood education* (pp. 1–10). Albany, NY: SUNY Press.

Sluss, D. J. (2005). *Supporting play: Birth through age eight*. Clifton Park, NY: Thomson Delmar Learning.

Spodek, B., & Saracho, O. N. (Eds.). (1991). *Issues in early childhood curriculum*. New York, NY: Teachers College Press.

Statistics Canada. (2006). *Immigrant status and place of birth*. Ottawa, ON: Author. Retrieved from http://www.12.statcan.ca/census-recensement/2006/dp-pd/index-eng.cfm

Suarez-Orozco, C., & Suarez-Orozco, M. (2001). *Children of immigration*. Cambridge, MA: Harvard University Press.

Tudge, J., & Odero-Wanga, D. (2009). A cultural-ecological perspective on early childhood among the Luo of Kisumu Kenya. In M. Fleer, M. Hedegaard, & J. Tudge (Eds.), *Childhood studies and the impact of globalization. Policies and practices at global and local levels* (pp. 142–160). New York, NY: Routledge.

UN General Assembly. (1951). *Convention relating to the status of refugees*. U.N.T.S. 189. Retrieved from (http://www.unhcr.org/refworld/docid/3be01b964.html)

Vygotsky, L. S. (1977). Play and its role in the mental development of the child. In J. S. Bruner, A. Jolly, & K. Sylva (Eds.), *Play: Its role in development and evolution* (pp. 537–554). New York, NY: Basic Books.

Vygotsky, L. S. (1978). *Mind and society: The development of higher mental processes*. Cambridge, MA: Harvard University Press.

Walcott, R. (1997). *Black like who? Writing Black Canada*. Toronto, ON: Insomniac.

Wertsch, J. V. (1991). *Voices of the mind: A sociocultural approach to mediated action*. Cambridge, MA: Harvard University Press.

Wong Fillmore, L. (1991). When learning a second language means losing the first. *Early Childhood Research Quarterly, 6*(3), 323–346.

Chapter Ten

Resituating Practice through Teachers' Storying of Children's Interests

Mary Caroline Rowan

I believe that stories engage the mind, warm the heart, and open us up to the possibility of resisting institutionalized normality. In the winter of 2011, I travelled to the Tasiurvik Child Care Centre in Inukjuak in Nunavik, Arctic northern Quebec, to research the potential of learning stories in that setting (Rowan, 2011). The overarching question for this study was, What kinds of knowledge(s), linguistic identities, cultural identities, and relationships can learning stories generate? I am interested in troubling the impacts of colonialism and the imposition of Euro-Western systems. This chapter is part of that larger study and examines how, through the adoption of an approach informed by Indigenous methodologies, learning stories might become a mechanism for transformation. I argue that learning stories can be a device for validating Inuttitut language usage; revealing Inuit knowledge(s); making visible and strengthening multiple layers of relationships with people, places, and things; and positioning educators to reflect on the cultural nature of the educational endeavour—and construct culturally meaningful programming.

I begin by presenting three vignettes, which I use to connect past, present, and future thinking about Inuit education. Following, I consider contextual information pertaining to the impacts of colonialism in Canada's Inuit communities. I then turn to a discussion of postcolonial and decolonizing theories, as well as Indigenous methodologies and action research. I also explain why I chose to use learning stories for the research project. Finally, I share two contrasting learning stories.

In Aotearoa/New Zealand, learning stories are narrative-style, structured observations designed to show children's actions associated with one or more of five learning dispositions: interested and curious; involved; persevering after failure; expressing opinion; and taking responsibility (Carr, 2010). Learning stories document children *as they are* in the process of showing interest, being involved in activities, expressing ideas and emotions, taking responsibility, and/or considering another's point of view (Carr, 2001). In Nunavik these stories serve as a method for validating, making visible, and creating spaces for Inuit knowledge(s) and the Inuttitut language in Inuit early childhood education.

The stories featured in this chapter were created by educators who work at the Tasiurvik Child Care Centre in Inukjuak, Nunavik. Inukjuak has a population of 1,600 (Statistics Canada, 2006a), and is located on Hudson Bay. It is one of 14 Inuit communities situated in Nunavik. The Nunavik region expands throughout the northern third of the province of Quebec and has a population of 11,000 (Duhaime, 2008). I have been actively involved in Inuit early childhood education (ECE) since 1988 when I co-founded the Iqaluit Child Care Association out of a desire to create a child-care program for my children in the Inuit language and culture of their Inuk father and his family.

Connecting the Past, Present, and Future

To begin, I present two quotes from Inuit scholars and one story from an educator in Nunavik. I do this to consider the construction of education in Inuit spaces across time. Starting in the late 1940s formal school was imposed on Inuit communities as part of a strategy of assimilation (Department of Indian Affairs and Northern Development, 1990). For instance, Arnaquq (2008) reflects on her personal schooling experiences during the 1960s, in Iqaluit on Baffin Island: "At school, the cultural tension was the strongest. As we conformed to the Qaallunaaq [white] teacher's directions, expectations and commands, unbeknownst to us it had been eroding our parents' way of life" (p. 63). In the late 1970s a shift was made away from unilingual English education, and school boards in Inuit communities began to teach the Inuttitut language and hire Inuit teachers. However, Annahatak (1994) lamented the absence of opportunities to integrate discussions concerning deep values that connect with culturally related purposes in Inuit education.

> More often than not Inuit values are left out of school. I have taught many lessons which I have come to term "floating lessons." These I find not to be connected to our cultural purposes and I see them more for surface learning, that is, to learn the physical aspects of our culture (food, clothing, tools, customs, etc.). They rarely touch upon students' choices, decisions and identity. (Annahatak, 1994, p. 17)

In June 2011 the National Committee on Inuit Education published a national strategy for Inuit education. Early childhood education was identified as one of the core areas for investment. Key priority areas for Inuit ECE include the rich Inuit language and culturally appropriate programming. This work has started in earnest in Nunavik, as evidenced in the following story:

Brushing Teeth

> Lizzie wears kamiik,[1] which she knows will keep her feet warm.
> She's brushing her teeth so that one day she can make her own kamiik.
> Her grandmother makes her kamiik. When she grows up she wants to make her own kamiik. That's why she's taking care of her teeth.

On speaking with the author and educator about this story, I learned that these girls wear kamiik to the child-care centre, and that the educator wanted to recognize the grandmother's work while at the same time positioning the girls to consider the possibilities of becoming kamik[2] makers when they grew up. Strong teeth are needed for kamik making because the sealskin from which they are made must be chewed as part of the process.

I find this a powerful story, which speaks directly to what learning stories are doing now, at the child-care centre, to position children with cultural identities grounded in Inuit knowledge(s). I am excited by this story because it represents how Inuit knowledge(s) with deep and valuable cultural meanings are being developed in educational spaces. Perhaps the work of the educators in Inukjuak can become understood as part of a process of cultural rejuvenation connected with early childhood education. These ideas will be further explored toward the end of this chapter.

Although the assimilationist purposes of education, which Arnaquq experienced in the 1960s, continues, steps have been taken to include cultural learnings in the curriculum, as described by Annahatak. Our project sought to recognize and celebrate community values in the curriculum, and to push deeper for meaningful identity-connected experiences as evidenced in the tooth-brushing story. In this chapter, I examine some of the theoretical underpinnings of educational practices in Nunavik and in Inuit lands, which have contributed to the disruption of Inuit systemic processes. At the same time, I make visible the approach I used for my research, which culminated in the creation of more than fifty wonderful, educator-made learning stories in the Inuttitut language.

Theoretical Background

Colonial Discourses in Inuit Communities

My theoretical approach is grounded in an understanding that locally based social and cultural knowledge(s) provide a foundation for meaning, understanding, and strength at the community level. Hugh Brody is a British anthropologist who first

---

1 Kamiik are two (a pair of) sealskin boots.
2 Kamik is one sealskin boot.

travelled to the Canadian Arctic on behalf of the Canadian government in the early 1970s. He has written extensively about Inuit and First Nations land claims and relationships with the government, and with the land (Brody, 1975, 1987, 2001). His work has significantly contributed to the approach I adopted for this research project. Brody (1987) wrote, "The voices of the people must be heard; their words breathe life into our understanding. We cannot know other cultures by looking at them; we must hear their accents, absorb their intonations, and enter their points of view" (p. xv). I strive not only to hear those points of view and incorporate these voices in my work, but also to develop partnerships with community stakeholders and to work collaboratively.

Inuit knowledge(s) have been severely compromised and undermined by colonial practices and policies (Igloliorte, 2009; Pauktuutit Inuit Women of Canada, 2006). Action must be taken to reposition the power balance in Inuit lands to restore Inuit control and redress the inequities; injustices; and social, cultural, and linguistic disruptions that have their roots in colonialism and that have been so destructive. Brody (2001) continued:

> Hunters and gatherers have experience and knowledge that must be recognized. Their genius is integral to human potential, their skills are appropriate to their lands, and their rights are no less because their numbers are small. Political inequality, hostile and racist stereotypes, and conflicts of interest over land have created incomprehension and suspicion of hunter-gatherers. The powerful find it difficult to listen. But listening is what must happen, somehow, on every frontier, for only if the powerful listen will the needs and rights of the vulnerable be respected. (p. 7)

Listening is not what has happened, and Inuit approaches to living have been systematically undermined in relationship with a southern society that "believed that it knew best how to use the north, how to develop its economic potential, and how to improve the moral, intellectual and material lives of its inhabitants" (Brody, 1975, p. 13). For example, pre-contact Inuit had equal access to the land and its resources, and their society was based on egalitarian principles of mutuality, not hierarchical systems. The system assured food for most people, most of the time (Brody, 2001). In contrast, in an analytical paper connected with the 2006 Aboriginal Peoples Survey, Heather Tait reported (2006) that 24% of Inuit children experience hunger every month. Today major problems exist with Inuit social/community/economic structures.

In 1975, when Brody first wrote about police being feared in the north, there were very few police in northern regions (Brody, 1975). Things have changed dramatically, to the extent that in 2009 the regional newspaper *Nunatsiaq News* reported that crime is on the rise in the Nunavik region and that the Kativik Regional Police Force (KRPF) had responded to 9,812 calls that year—more than double the 4,232 calls answered in 2007 (George, 2009). The total regional population is approximately 10,000. Why were there almost as many calls to the police as there are people in the territory?

Concerning health—as the impacts of colonization gained strength, the physical well-being of Inuit declined. Davis (2009), writing about Indigenous peoples of the Americas, notes that "90% of the Amerindian population died within a generation or two of contact" (p. 66). In January 2010, a Canadian Medical Association study reported an infant mortality rate amongst Inuit infants three times greater than the national average. Nunavik's infant death rate was the highest in Canada, with 18 deaths for every 1,000 births (Rogers, 2010). How is it that in Canada there are such inequities in the area of public health?

Concerning education—Brody exposed the depth of the problem with the colonial educational project in writing about the racism experienced by residential school children as they were taught that every aspect of their so-called primitive home life was wrong and their language, clothing, food, and spirituality were challenged and denigrated by the non-Inuit teachers. Brody (2001) wrote,

> The residential school was part of a process of ethnocide. . . . The intention was to stop people being who they were—to ensure that they could no longer live and think and occupy the land as hunter-gatherers. The new and modern nation-states make no room for hunter-gatherers. (p. 189)

In 2008 the prime minister apologized to the Aboriginal people of Canada for the wrongs inflicted in the residential school system. However, the education system continues to be dysfunctional. In 2006 Statistics Canada (2006b) reported that only 39.3% of Inuit students completed high school, a figure about half of the 76.9% completion rate for the non-Aboriginal population. Why is the gap in the graduation rates of Indigenous and non-Indigenous populations so substantial?

Recapitulation Theory

The nineteenth-century theory of recapitulation is one of several powerful ideas that have made possible the colonization of Inuit lands and peoples, that have silenced Inuit voices and quieted the Inuttitut language. This theory, popularized by Herbert Spencer and others (Egan, 2002), has " served colonist interests well" (Lesko, 1996, p. 460). Recapitulation theory suggests that each of us in our development repeats "all of the stages of development of our species, from a simple-celled creature, through gilled fishlike ancestors, and so on, to the present" (Egan, 2002, p. 27). According to this problematic and discounted theory, some children and races will develop further than others. People of white, Euro-Western origin are privileged in this theory, which was used by colonizers to justify imperialistic practices (Gould, 1977). An example of the enactment of this practice of white privilege is presented below.

In *The People's Land*, Brody (1975) told a story about a fisheries officer who came into an Inuit settlement and consulted with other whites but did not meet with any local Inuit. Brody wrote, "At no time did these experts on fish and fishing discuss with the local people their reason for visiting the settlement" (p. 7). How can Inuit voices be heard when those in power do not consult with them? How is it acceptable for white officials to come to town and not speak with people of that place, of that land, of that sea? This racist silencing of Inuit voices is inherent in connected theories of colonization that are intended to undermine Indigenous knowledge(s) and provide license to take over Indigenous lands.

Evolutionary Theory
Another idea, closely connected with the theory of recapitulation and equally problematic for the colonized, is based in evolutionary theory. Brody (2001) explained:

> In the Americas of the nineteenth and early twentieth centuries, both the practices of settlers and the application of legal theory to indigenous peoples' rights to land were based on ideas of human evolution, with the hunter-gatherers at the bottom of a developmental ladder and Europeans seated at its peak. (p. 122)

Davis (2009) laments the continued presence in the scholarly literature of academic reasoning grounded in evolutionary theories. He writes,

> Such a transparently simplistic and biased interpretation of human history, though long repudiated as an intellectual artifact of the nineteenth century as relevant today as the convictions of Victorian clergy who dated the earth at a mere 6,000 years, has nevertheless proved to be remarkably persistent, even among contemporary scholars. (p. 65)

Evolutionary theories, which categorized people by colour and ethnicity, have played and, I would argue, continue to play an important role in perpetuating white privilege in the north. This privilege has had a pivotal role in shaping human disequilibrium, to the extent that Brody (2001) wrote, "The Indigenous peoples of Canada have been forced to respond to a strong implication in modern legal theory that they do not qualify as fully human" (p. 282). An example of this is found in the Canadian Human Rights Act (CHRA) of 1982, which stated in Section 67 that the CHRA did not apply to the Indian Act. Section 67 was finally repealed in June 2011 (Assembly of First Nations, 2011). Another example is that the Canadian Multiculturalism Act "does not give any special recognition to First Nations, Métis, or Inuit languages as the founding languages of Canada, nor does any other federal law. Attempts to do so have all failed" (Tulloch, 2009, p. 48).

In recent years political steps have been taken to shift the balance. These include big steps such as the creation of the Nunavut territory in 1999 and, more recently, the release of the Inuit Education Strategy in June 2011. Can small steps of renaissance and resistance, taken within child-care spaces, work to unravel the bindings that persistent, invasive, racist, and unjust false thinking have tied? Margo Greenwood (2009) suggests that they can. She writes,

> The key findings of this research suggest that early childhood (and related educational considerations) is a critical site for cultural rejuvenation, for the (re)building of community, and for the establishment of healthy Aboriginal communities in the future. Fundamental to this (re)building is autonomy by Indigenous communities over language and culture, over the care and education of their children, over their lives and futures, and over the lives and futures of their children. (p. ii)

Can the power shift from a paternalistic externally driven system to one that is controlled by Inuit, from within Inuit communities and regions? Can functional frameworks be repositioned through early childhood projects? The work I share in this chapter was developed with the intention of contributing to Indigenous rebuilding, revitalization, and renaissance by introducing learning stories to ECE practice in Nunavik. In the next section, I examine two practices that contribute to the repositioning of colonialistic and racialized practices: decolonial theory and postcolonial discourses.

Decolonial Theory

Smith (1999) claimed, "Western culture constantly reaffirms the West's view of itself as the centre of legitimate knowledge" (p. 63). Decolonial perspectives recognize the imbalance of power relations and the destructive processes of colonialism and Eurocentrism. I once attended a lecture by Battiste (2010), during which she showed a cartoon featuring a pickle jar with the caption "Marinated in Eurocentrism." I believe she used this image to depict how colonizing practices, which undermine Indigenous knowledge(s) and pedestal Eurocentric superiority, have influenced us all. At a later point in her talk Battiste introduced the concept of cognitive imperialism, which she explained has left no conventional place where Indigenous knowledge has been allowed to thrive.

Decolonial theory sets out to make visible the domination of Eurocentrism and its goal of assimilation. De Lissovoy (2010) argues that "decolonial theory might be said to extend the anticolonial project into consideration of the domain of being and knowing; at the same time it draws from the complex account of cultural discontinuity and imposition offered by postcolonial studies" (p. 280). Decolonial theory suggests working globally toward co-existence and developing "sensitivity to difference" (p. 280).

Postcolonial Discourses

Postcolonial discourse is a way to first make visible systems, situations, and actions that are founded in colonialism and that erode Indigenous knowledges and frameworks; in a second step, it enables "actions and activities which have the potential to make accessible Inuit knowledges" (Rowan, 2010). Battiste (2010) speaks about a two-pronged project of deconstruction and reconstruction. Deconstruction involves addressing political, moral, and theoretical inadequacies and dismantling racism and colonialism. Reconstruction incorporates Indigenous perspectives, transforms the educational status quo, and supports the formation of human beings connected to Indigenous communities.

Indigenous Research

Indigenous scholars Battiste (2010), Martin (2008), and Wilson (2008) have provided us with insights into relational theory as a holistic way to approach research. In this section I touch on their epistemological and ontological views, which have informed my own study in Inuit communities.

Battiste (2008) describes Indigenous epistemology as incorporating ontology. She writes, "It is a knowledge that required constant vigor to observe carefully, to offer those in story and interactions, and to maintain appropriate relationships with all things and people in it" (p. 499). She goes on to explain how Indigenous knowledge is dynamic and always changing; it is relational and "collectively developed and constituted. There is no singular author of Indigenous knowledge and no singular method for understanding its totality" (p. 500). Indigenous knowledge must be learned in Indigenous ways and come to be known within the context of a community; it is gained through experiences on the land and with people.

Karen Martin (2008) is a Noonuccal/Quandamoopah researcher from Australia. In her book, *Please Knock Before You Enter: Aboriginal Regulation of Outsiders and the Implications for Researchers*, she presents an "Aboriginal epistemology within the framework of relatedness" (p. 7). Her relatedness theory includes three parts: Ways of Knowing, Ways of Being, and Ways of Doing. Martin (2008) positions ontology within the Indigenist research paradigm, explaining that all things and experiences exist in relatedness. Engagement is dialogic, expression is polyphonic, and ways are multiple. Epistemology is also relational. Wilson (2001, as cited in Martin, 2008) wrote,

> An Indigenous paradigm comes from the fundamental belief that knowledge is relational. Knowledge is shared with all the creation. . . . It is with the cosmos, it is with the animals, with the plants, with the earth that we share this knowledge. It goes beyond the idea of individual knowledge to the concept of relational knowledge. (p. 82)

Relatedness theory is founded in the integration of ontology and epistemology. I approach my work with an understanding of the construction of knowledge (epistemology) and ways of being or perceiving reality (ontology) that is rooted in this theory of relatedness.

Mashon (2010) defines an Indigenous research method as "a tool for decolonization"; an "enactment of self-determination"; as validating Indigenous knowledge; and as grounded in "research priorities of Indigenous people" (p. 40). She writes about building foundations for Indigenous early childhood education; in her work she "found that critical to community involvement is the development of equitable relationships between teachers/institutions and families" (p. 32). The research project featured in this chapter was constructed as a practice of Indigenous research methods and methodologies. It facilitated the development of a practice of making learning stories that I hoped would make Inuit knowledge(s), patterns, and meanings accessible and, in so doing, make spaces in ECE practice for Inuit ways of knowing and being.

Transformative Education

My approach is also embedded in the practice of transformative pedagogy, which recognizes the value of home and community knowledge. Ada and Campoy (2004) write, "Transformative education recognizes the importance of voice, the need for education to foster the critical consciousness that leads to speaking one's personal and social truth. Voice takes special force when words are not only spoken but also written" (p. 14).

For this project, which set out to support educators in documenting stories about children in their classrooms, Ada and Campoy's emphasis on transformative education is significant. As one example, their transformative education model "sees home and community knowledge as integral parts of students' lives and as valuable sources of knowledge" (Rowan, 2010, p. 162).

Action Research Approach

Mac Naughton and Hughes (2009) write about doing action research in early childhood settings. They describe theoretical foundations concerning action research for professional change, and explain how "praxis is knowledge for a purpose" (p. 46) and how "educational change is most effective when practitioners own and manage change" (p. 46). My research project set out to support educators in learning to use learning stories to "promote professional growth and learning in individuals and teams" (p. 47) and with a mind to developing an approach to early childhood education that could serve as a means of first recognizing and, second, deepening Inuit cultural and linguistic approaches to early childhood education.

Learning Stories in Nunavik

In documenting a learning story, teachers recognize a child's learning-related action and take pictures or notes, and/or save the child's artwork, and write about the activity (Carr, 2001). Teachers describe the learner's strengths and create a document that details learning and can be used for discussion of future learning. Learning stories accumulate over time and are collected in portfolios and binders; they can then be referred to by teachers, families, and children and may be employed to inform discussions about learning, assessments and self-assessments, and decisions about possible learning activities.

The work from Aotearoa/New Zealand informed this project and inspired us to assemble our own approach to constructing learning stories. The educators in the child-care centre started by looking for moments of children's engagement. Specifically, they photographed children who were demonstrating interest in relationship with people, places, and things. The photos were then assembled on single 8" x 10" pages and stories were written to describe the activity. Later the stories were shared with children, families, and colleagues. Discussions about the stories then led to further planning and activities. The project took place over a period of eight weeks in the winter of 2011.[3]

Two Stories

In this section, I share two stories: The first story is titled "Snow Illu" and is presented in Figure 1. The English language text is presented below.

Snow Illu

> Mary[4] and the children went to see the illu.
> They saw a qulliq.
> They left the illu through the broken hole.
> Then they visited the qummaq.
> Mary was surprised to find a rock on the floor.
> She picked up the rock and smelled it.
> They were so happy to visit the illu and the qummaq, on the hill.[5]

Reflection on the story

When I read "Snow Illu" I became aware of a story about an educator who takes a group of children to visit two traditional Inuit shelters. Inside the children find a stone stove—a qulliq—and stones on the ground. In the pictures the reader sees the exteriors of both structures and the children with them. Greenwood (2009)

---

3 For further insights into the methodology, please refer to Rowan (2011).

4 Names have been changed throughout to honour the confidentiality agreement.

5 Illu is a snow house; qulliq is a stone lamp; qummaq is a sod house.

ᐃᓝᓯᖅ ᐊᐳᑎᒃ

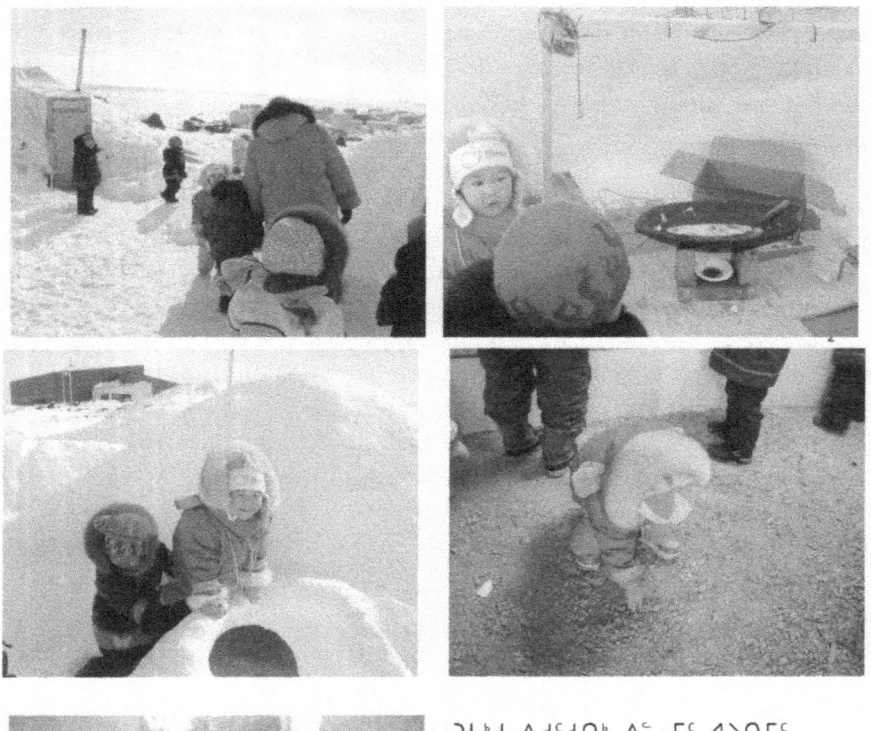

ᑐᕝᑯ ᐱᓯᕐᓯᑎᒃ ᐃᓝᒐᑦ ᐊᐳᑎᒐᑦ
ᑕᑯᐊᔾᔪᑐᐱᓇᒐᑦ.ᖁᑦᓯᓂᒐᓚ
ᑕᑯᕐᓯᑎᒃ,ᑐᕝᑯᑦ ᑭᔅᔭᑦ ᐊᓂᖃᓇᒐᑦ
ᑭᓝᓇᑐᐸᓪᐃᑦ ᑭᔅᔭᖅ. ᐊᒡᓗ ᖁᕐᓚᑦ
ᑕᑯᐊᔾᔪᐊᔾᑎᒃ, ᑐᖅ ᐊᕐᓚᐃᓝᔪᓂ
ᐅᖅᖃᓕᓇᓪᒐᑦ, ᐅᖅᖁᕐᑦ ᑎᒍᕐᔾᓇ
ᓇᐃᕐᔫᓇᖅ.ᑕᑯᐊᖄᒐᒃᑦ ᐊᓇᐊᓚᐅᔨᑦ

Figure 1

writes, "The importance of stories for children is critical—stories offer pathways to their Elders, their history, their knowledge(s), and ultimately to their identity as individuals and members of the collective" (p. 67). Later, when the educator shared the story with her colleagues, she explained that the little girl really wanted to see the qulliq lit. This eventually led to an important event that involved the lighting of the qulliq.

Discussion

What does this story demonstrate in terms of Inuit language identities, cultural identities, knowledge(s), and relationships? This story provides a pathway to Elders' history and knowledge (Greenwood, 2009). Through recording the children's presence at the illu and qummaq, positions grounded in cultural knowledge(s) become available to the children and all readers, and these positions are reinforced when the children return to review the story. This story acted as a springboard to setting up more activities based in Inuit knowledge(s) and culture. This happened when Sara, the educator, thought after reviewing the story that Mary, the girl we see smelling a rock, would like to see the qulliq lit. Further, the story acted to build and fortify relationships with Elders, for example, when strategies for involving Elders in the qulliq lighting at the child-care centre were proposed during the educator discussion group about the story. The story also provided a place where the educator could consider the child's point of view—as in the educators' consideration of the young girl wanting to see the qulliq lit. With reference to the Inuttitut language, "Snow Illu" provided a mechanism for uncovering new words. The educator had not known the name for a broken illu, which was revealed in discussions with the centre-based Elder. The activities around writing the story led to an expanded Inuttitut vocabulary. This in turn provided an opportunity to recognize and value Elders' knowledge. Finally, Sara confirmed with me that the story made available to the children "what they did not see at home anymore"(interview notes). I suggest that this story generated meanings rich with Inuit cultural and linguistic foundations and further served to build relationships, identities, and knowledge(s).

Going to the Playground

"Going to the Playground" depicts a trip to the municipal playground, which features a large plastic and metal construction with bars and a slide. In the first image we see the children attached to a harness on their way to the playground. The two middle images show the children playing with the equipment, and in the last we see the children on the return trip, back in the harness again. The story is presented in Figure 2.

The English translation of the Inuttitut language original text is as follows:

> *Today is a beautiful day. We children are in the Yellow Room.*[6]
> *Today we are going to the playground. First we tie ourselves together with the rope.*
> *After a long walk we finally get to the playground. We slide many times.*
> *One of the girls looks at the camera—she was so happy.*
> *On our walk back to the child-care centre we watch for anything and everything.*

---
6 The name has been changed to honour the confidentiality agreement.

ᐊᓂᖕᒍᐊᕕᓕᐊᖅᑐᑦ

ᐅᓪᓗᒥ ᓯᓈᖅᐊᖑᐱᒥ
ᐃᓄᓪᐊᑭᓯᖅ 2ᒥᐅᑦ
ᐊᓂᖕᒍᐊᕕᓕᐊᖕᒍᐊᓚᐅᖅᓯᑦ
ᐱᑐᕐᒪᓲᑎᖕ

ᑕᒪᓕ ᑎᑭᖕᒥᖕ
ᓯᑐᖃᖕᒍᐊᓚᐅᖅᓯᑦ
ᐊᒥᓴᓯᓲᑎᖕ
ᓯᑐᓚᐅᖅᓯᐃᑦ

ᐸᓂᐅᑦ ᐃᓚᖕᒃ ᓯᑐᓯᒥ
ᑕᑯᓯᖓᖅᑐᖅ
ᐊᓕᐊᑦᒪᓂᐅᑦᓱᓂ

ᐅᑎᓯᓚᐅᖅᓯᕐᖕᑦ
ᓯᓇᑐᐃᓐᓇᓕᓯᓂᑦ
ᑕᑯᖃᑦᑕᑎᖕ ᐅᑎᓘᑦ
ᐱᓯᑎᖕ

Figure 2

Reflection on the story

The story describes children outdoors on a beautiful winter's day. I am disturbed by the images of harnessed children. It is the being harnessed that bothers me. I think about Inuit dogs and the elaborate harnesses used to confine and control dogs. I look again and see children climbing the steps to the slide, confident and capable, and the smiling girl warms me. The story creates an opportunity to consider the place of imported equipment, an opportunity for comparison, and more in-depth reflection

In Figure 3 below, photos from the two stories were placed side by side to see what reaction would occur, what ideas would be provoked and what analysis could ensue.

Figure 3

Reflection on contrasting cultures

I wonder what happens when children's lives are filled with imported plastic playground equipment and materials like the children's harness. Then I wonder, How do the children see themselves when they are harnessed? What do the parents think? Where do ideas about harnessing children originate and how do they connect with Inuit child-rearing practices? I wonder how, inside and outside

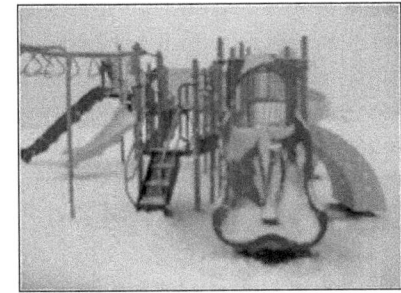

Figure 4

of the child-care centre, children's minds and beings absorb materials like the playground equipment and systems like the licensed, regulated child-care system and how this time spent immersed in this imported and imposed world might interfere with the absorption, in early childhood, of ways of knowing and being grounded in Inuit cultural and linguistic realities.

Discussion

"Snow Illu" creates a space for considering pedagogy from within an imagery, which includes recognizable and symbolic Inuit spaces. Weenie (2008) writes about curricular theorizing and cites Campbell and Gregor (2002) in the following quote: "We enact the world we inhabit and know about" (p. 550). When I think about this quote, I say, "Aha!" "Snow Illu" is important because, in rereading and reviewing this story, the children can see and feel themselves in a space that is recognizably Inuit and they can act on that. Greenwood (2009) explains:

> The early childhood setting becomes the context in which children are embedded and where they become sites of cultural transmission. With this in mind, one of the greatest challenges facing early childhood caregivers is to take principles of Indigenous knowledge and actualize them in current practice. (p. 75)

"Snow Illu" provides a record and presents a sequence of events involving the children that were rich with Inuit cultural knowledge. The story then creates opportunities to think about and comment on those moments and makes them accessible for future consideration. On fathoming the import of documentation, Rinaldi (2000) contributes the following:

> Documentation, or all the materials produced during observation, is also an important instrument for the children. Through procedures that are analogous to those of adults, children can see themselves in a new light, and revisit and reinterpret their own experiences of events in which they were the direct protagonists. This kind of process produces new cognitive dynamics, a new and different vision of oneself and one's actions in relation to others. (p. 130)

I purposefully placed "Snow Illu" beside "Going to the Playground" in an effort to make visible the contrast between local and imported materials and systems. In this section it has been my intent to show how the "Snow Illu" learning story, which was inclusive of the Inuttitut language and embedded in Inuit culture, provided a place through which identities grounded in Inuit knowledge(s) could be formed. "Snow Illu," I suggest, acts as a decolonizing device by making available Inuit ways of knowing and being.

Conclusion

The postcontact history of Inuit in Canada has led to dramatic changes in the structure of Inuit society. The relationship with the colonizer has been difficult and inequitable (Brody 1975, 1987, 2001; Davis, 2009; Igloliorte, 2009), profoundly affected by theoretical underpinnings rooted in racialized conceptions of human growth and development as evidenced in the discussion about evolution and recapitulation (Egan, 2002; Gould, 1977; Lesko, 1996). However, much effort has been made to shift the purposes and frameworks of education. Whereas

Arnaquq attended a school purposefully dedicated to assimilation, children in today's child-care centres are beginning to experience educational opportunities in which the Inuttitut language is valued and experiences consistent with Inuit ways of knowing and being are being developed.

The snippets of the research project featured in this chapter adopted an approach grounded in decolonizing theories and guided by Indigenous methodologies. At the Tasiurviq Child Care Centre in Inukjuak, we successfully used learning stories as a way to position the Inuttitut language as both a written and a spoken language. We also used learning stories as a way to make visible actions and activities connected to Inuit worldviews. In the "Snow Ilu" story Inuit language, knowledge(s), and culture were seen to occupy important space in children's lives. The analysis of "Going to the Playground" provided an opportunity to reflect on tensions inherent in the environment when imported and plastic materials take up space in children's lives. Inuit knowledge(s), language, and culture must be available, must be lived, and must be embodied to be known. It is this accessibility that makes possible the continued construction of Inuit knowledge(s), linguistic identities, cultural identities, and relationships.

References

Ada, A. F., & Campoy, F. I. (2004). *Authors in the classroom: A transformative education process.* Boston, MA: Pearson.

Annahatak, B. (1994). Quality education for Inuit today? Cultural strengths, new things and working out the unknowns: A story by an Inuk. *Peabody Journal of Education, 69*(2), 12–18.

Arnaquq, N. (2008). *Uqaujjuusiat—gifts of words of advice: Schooling, education and leadership in Baffin Island* (Unpublished master's thesis). University of Prince Edward Island, Charlottetown.

Assembly of First Nations. (2011, June 16). *Canadian Human Rights Act takes effect in First Nations communities—AFN calls on Canada to work with First Nations.* Assembly of First Nations. Retrieved from http://www.afn.ca/index.php/en/news-media/latest-news/canadian-human-rights-act-takes-effect-in-first-nation-communities-afn

Battiste, M. (2008). Research ethics for protecting Indigenous knowledge and heritage: Institutional and researcher responsibilities. In N. Denzin, Y. Lincoln, & L. Smith (Eds.), *Handbook of critical and Indigenous methodologies* (pp. 497–510). Thousand Oaks, CA: Sage.

Battiste, M. (2010, June). *Aboriginal resilience and renaissance in forging a transsystemic reform of knowledge and learning.* Paper presented as the Lansdowne Lecture, First People's House, University of Victoria, Victoria, BC.

Brody, H. (1975). *The people's land: Eskimos and whites in the eastern Arctic.* Harmondsworth, England: Penguin.

Brody, H. (1987). *The living Arctic: Hunters of the Canadian north.* Vancouver, BC: Douglas & McIntyre.

Brody, H. (2001). *The other side of Eden: Hunter-gatherers, farmers and the shaping of the world.* London, England: Faber & Faber.

Carr, M. (2001). *Assessment in early childhood settings: Learning stories.* London, England: Sage.

Carr, M. (2010, January). *Aotearoa! New Zealand and learning stories.* Paper presented at the Investigating Quality Sharing Circle, University of Victoria, Victoria, BC.

Davis, W. (2009). *The wayfinders: Why ancient wisdom matters in the modern world.* Toronto, ON: House of Anansi Press.

De Lissovoy, N. (2010). Decolonial pedagogy and the ethics of the global. *Discourse Studies in the Cultural Politics of Education, 31*(3), 279–293.
Department of Indian Affairs and Northern Development. (1990). *Inuit*. Ottawa, ON: Ministry of Supply and Services Canada.
Duhaime, G. (2008). *Socio-economic profile of Nunavik, 2008 edition*. Canadian Research Chair in Comparative Aboriginal Conditions. Université Laval, Québec, QC.
Egan, K. (2002). *Getting it wrong from the beginning: Our progressive inheritance from Herbert Spencer, John Dewey, and Jean Piaget*. New Haven, CT: Yale University Press.
George, J. (2009, September 22). KRPF aims for three officers in every community. *Nunatsiaq Online*. Retrieved from http://www.nunatsiaqonline.ca/
Gould, S. J. (1977). *Ontogeny and phylogeny*. Cambridge, MA: Belknap Press of Harvard University Press.
Greenwood, M. L. (2009). *Places for the good care of children: A discussion of Indigenous cultural consideration and early childhood in Canada and New Zealand* (Unpublished doctoral dissertation). University of British Columbia, Vancouver.
Igloliorte, H. (2009). *We were so far away: The Inuit experience of residential schools; Curatorial text/timeline*. Ottawa, ON: Legacy of Hope Foundation with Aboriginal Healing Foundation, and the Library of Canada Archives.
Lesko, N. (1996). Past, present and future conceptions of adolescence. *Educational Theory, 46*(4), 453–472.
Mac Naughton, G., & Hughes, P. (2009). *Doing action research in early childhood research in early childhood studies: A step-by-step guide*. Maidenhead, England: Open University Press.
Martin, K. L. (2008). *Please knock before you enter: Aboriginal regulation of outsiders and the implications for researchers*. Teneriffe, Australia: Post Pressed.
Mashon, D. N. (2010). *Realizing "quality" in Indigenous early childhood development* (Unpublished master's thesis). University of British Columbia, Vancouver.
National Committee on Inuit Education. (2011). *First Canadians, Canadians first: National strategy on Inuit education 2011*. Ottawa, ON: Inuit Tapiriit Kanatami.
Pauktuutit Inuit Women of Canada. (2006). *The Inuit way: A guide to Inuit culture*. Ottawa, ON: Author.
Rinaldi, C. (2006). The construction of the educational project: An interview with Carlina Rinaldi by Lella Gandini and Judith Kaminsky. In C. Rinaldi (Ed.), *In dialogue with Reggio Emilia: Listening, researching and learning* (pp. 121–136). New York, NY: Routledge.
Rogers, S. (2010, January 28). For Inuit dying begins at birth. *Nunatsiaq Online*. Retrieved from http://www.nunatsiaqnewsonline.ca/
Rowan, M. C. (2010). Disrupting colonial power through literacy: A story about creating Inuttitut-language children's books. In V. Pacini-Ketchabaw (Ed.), *Flows, rhythms, and intensities of early childhood education curriculum* (pp. 155–176). New York, NY: Peter Lang.
Rowan, M. C. (2011). *Exploring the possibilities of learning stories as a meaningful approach to early childhood education in Nunavik* (Unpublished master's thesis). University of Victoria, Victoria, BC.
Smith, L. T. (1999). *Decolonizing methodologies: Research and Indigenous peoples*. Dunedin, New Zealand: University of Otago Press.
Statistics Canada. (2006a). *Community profiles—Inukjuak, Québec*. Ottawa, ON: Author. Retrieved from http://www12.statscan.ca
Statistics Canada. (2006b). *High school completion rates. Census of population* (Statistics Canada Catalogue No. 97-560-XCB2006036). Ottawa, ON: Author.
Tait, H. (2006). Inuit health and social conditions. *Aboriginal Peoples Survey*. Ottawa, ON: Statistics Canada.
Tulloch, S. (2009). *Building a strong foundation—considerations to support thriving bilingualism in Nunavut*. Nunavut Literacy Report. Cambridge Bay, NU: Nunavut Literacy Council.
Weenie, A. (2008). Curricular theorizing from the periphery. *Curriculum Inquiry, 38*(5), 545–557.
Wilson, S. (2008). *Research is ceremony: Indigenous research methods*. Blackpoint, NS: Fernwood.

Chapter Eleven

Taking Children's Rights and Participation Seriously

Cross-national Perspectives and Possibilities

Beth Blue Swadener, Lacey Peters, & Sonya Gaches

Researchers, practitioners, and early childhood community members are increasingly incorporating children's voices into their work related to the establishment, strengthening, and understanding of sociological, political, and educational systems situated within the field of early childhood (Clark, 2005; Habashi, 2008; Lundy, 2007; Swadener & Polakow, 2011). Many positive outcomes have resulted from children's participation in research and from more authentically including children in the planning and enactment of various projects, as well as working with children as co-researchers and consultants (Berson, 2009; Blanchet-Cohen & Elliot, 2011; Clark, 2011; Gunn, 2008; Lundy, 2006, 2007; Mac Naughton, Hughes, & Smith, 2007; Soto & Swadener, 2005). Undertakings such as these bring needed attention to the inclusion of children in decision-making processes that are directly affecting aspects of their lives. Further, the need for strategies that encourage children's unmediated voices is increasingly evident—particularly for children who are members of marginalized groups in their societies.

This chapter foregrounds the voices and participation of children as a means of resituating early childhood theory and practice. Drawing from a range of literature and research experiences, we ask a basic question—What are our obligations to children, vis-à-vis a child's-rights framework, in the context of resituating early childhood education and research in Canada and beyond? As U.S.-based researchers, we acknowledge the possible irony of writing a chapter focused on children's rights-based research, as the United States is now the only nation (with a population of over 1 million) *not* to have ratified the United Nations Convention on the Rights of the Child (UNCRC) (Office of the United Nations High

Commissioner for Human Rights [OHCHR], 1989). All of the Canadian early childhood scholarship, programs, and policy initiatives presented in this volume exist within a larger context of having children's rights as an official part of national and local policy. An implicit question in this chapter is, How might this national framework be leveraged in the process of resituating early childhood in Canada?

As co-authors and collaborators, we share a commitment to children's rights and we bring both collaborative and complementary experiences that have helped shape our efforts to enhance children's rights and participation in our lives and work. Beth has long been a leader in reconceptualizing early childhood policy, theory, and methodologies, and is a cross-national researcher focused on sub-Saharan Africa and children's rights. Sonya is a long-term classroom teacher who recently transitioned to teacher education and research in a university context. Building on several years in the preschool classroom, Lacey has a strong commitment to working with children, families, and professionals to promote early childhood practices, programs, and policy inclusive of all people's perspectives. Following a brief review of literature focused on children's rights and participation and the UNCRC, we share our collective and individual experiences examining programs, planning, policy, and research in local and global contexts. We offer these as examples of resituating early childhood from a rights-based perspective.

Resituating Early Childhood and the UNCRC

Historically, children have been seen as "unfamiliar and different in research" (Lahman, 2008, p. 282). They are simultaneously portrayed as memories of adults; younger, less-capable adults; and those over whom adults have control. Given this view and other views of children (Clark, 2004; Corsaro, 2005; James & Prout, 1997; Qvortrup, 1994; Walkerdine, 1993) as distinctive kinds of world citizens, the United Nations Convention on the Rights of the Child (UNCRC) has recognized that "childhood is entitled to special care and assistance" (Preamble). The adult need to *protect* children is specifically addressed in the Article 19 of the UNCRC:

> States parties shall take all appropriate legislative, administrative, social and educational measures to protect the child from all forms of physical or mental violence, injury or abuse, neglect or negligent treatment, maltreatment or exploitation, including sexual abuse, while in the care of parent(s), legal guardian(s) or any other person who has the care of the child.

The need to *provide* for children can be found in Article 24, ensuring good-quality health care, safe drinking water, nutritious food, and a clean and safe environment, and in Article 27, which recognizes "the right of every child to a standard of living adequate for the child's physical, mental, and spiritual, moral, and social development." Within the context of the United States, this need to protect and provide for children can be illustrated by the numerous child welfare, advocacy, and legal agencies that have been developed to protect and provide for children.

Furthermore, Article 3 of the UNCRC requires that "in all actions concerning children, whether undertaken by public or private social welfare institutions, course of law, administrative authorities or legislative bodies, the best interest of the child shall be a primary consideration." At times, determining what is in the best interest of the child leads to conflicting agendas due to divergent cultural beliefs and values, including tensions between parents and children and cultural constructions of childhood that take a more communitarian perspective rather than an individual one. (For an in-depth discussion of these cultural tensions and complexities, see the Una Working Paper 8, 2011, *Children's Rights in Cultural Contexts*, (http://www.unaglobal.org/en/page/reports).

Rights to protection and provision are generally more widely recognized and embraced than the participatory rights of children and how those participatory rights are enacted within an international context. The UNCRC "assure(s) to the child who is capable of forming his or her own views the right to express those views freely in all matters affecting the child, the views of the child being given due weight in accordance with the age and maturity of the child" (Article 12). In addition, Article 13 provides children the right to freedom of expression as well as the right to relevant information. Concerns about these participatory rights are among the reasons that the United States has not ratified the UNCRC: these rights are often perceived as a threat to parental rights and authority. U.S. policies and practice have privileged adults over children, and parental rights over children's rights. Similarly, provision for children is considered a private responsibility of the family rather than a public or shared responsibility of the state. This view of children inhibits children's voices and views from being actively sought and given due weight.

Since the release in 2005 of the United Nations General Comment No. 7 (OHCHR, 2005) on "Implementing Child Rights in Early Childhood," there has been increased support for researchers, educators, and policy makers to provide opportunities for young children, specifically under the age of eight, not only to express their views and experiences but also for this information to be taken seriously. Comment No. 7 states that the "young child's right to express their views and feelings should be taken into account in the development of policies and services, including through research and consultations" (OHCHR, 2005, p. 7). Furthermore, it stresses that these are the rights of all children, regardless of their age.

A growing body of literature has affirmed that young children can tell adults about their lives and experiences and the concerns that they have for the people and environments with whom and with which they directly interact (e.g., Alderson, 2011; Alderson & Morrow, 2000; Lundy & McEvoy, 2009; Mac Naughton & Smith, 2008; Mac Naughton, Smith, & Davis, 2007; O'Kane, 2000, 2007; Polakow, 1993; Soto & Swadener, 2005). Findings from these studies contradict traditional neoliberal views of the child as passive participants, incapable of contributing valid information. We find that these undermining views are manifested in research or program planning that is conducted on or about children, with little or no involvement of the children's thoughts, experiences, or perspectives. Moving toward research, policy, and program planning that acknowledge children's rights and agency, we share the following assumptions with Mac Naughton, Hughes, and Smith (2007):

- Young children can construct valid meanings about the world and their place in it.

- Young children know the world in alternative (not "inferior") ways to adults.

- Young children's perspectives and insights can help adults to understand their experiences better. (p. 460)

With this being said, and while efforts to promote rights-based approaches increase, there are inherent risks related to motivations for reframing ways we think about integrating children's perspectives into adult agendas. Tokenizing children's participation is viewed as one of the most prevalent issues; however, the trend to include children as collaborators, co-researchers, and co-constructors can also be considered overused, or misappropriated (Blanchet-Cohen & Rainbow, 2006; Einarsdottir, 2011; Hart, 1992). More recently, critiques have been voiced among early childhood scholars cautioning that the movement toward children's inclusion in decision-making processes can become a fetishized practice, or a disingenuous obligation (Dockett, Einarsdottir, & Perry, 2009; Shier, 2001, 2011). The desire to entangle the perspectives of children with those of their adult counterparts stirs significant debate and begs the question, What does it take to position children within politics of care? In addition, considering the fact that adults do play such an important role in children's rights-based approaches to research and policy, it is imperative we critically reflect upon our roles as partners, facilitators, disseminators, and change agents. Researchers grounding their work in children's rights-based approaches consider reflexivity and the explication of power dynamics and ethical considerations an integral component of the implementation of research carried out with children (Blanchet-Cohen, 2006; Grover, 2004; Shier, 2001).

Lundy (2007) critiques the concept of "voice" as a means of capturing the full extent of the obligation under Article 12 when considered in the light of the other provisions of the UNCRC and suggests that a legally sound approach to Article 12 of the UNCRC would emphasize four factors: Space, Voice, Audience, and Influence, as follows:

- *Space:* children must be given a safe opportunity to express a view;

- *Voice:* children must be assisted to both form views and express them freely;

- *Audience:* children's views must be listened to; and

- *Influence:* children's views must be given due weight. (p. 933)

While much of the focus of participatory activity has been on Space and Voice, a rights-based approach will also focus on ensuring Audience and Influence by ensuring that children's views are taken seriously in all aspects of research and evaluation (Una Children's Rights Learning Group, 2010, p. 9). These categories frame adults as duty-bearers in support of children's right not only to be heard but also to have their ideas given due weight.

In a similar vein, Shier's Pathways to Participation model provides a helpful framework for pushing our work and our thinking toward opportunities and obligations for child participation. We have found it useful to draw parallels between Lundy's four factors and Shier's pathways model. Shier (2001, p. 111) delineates between levels of participation and openings, opportunities, and obligations (see Figure 1). The first two levels of Shier's model, listening to children and supporting them in expressing their views, are comparable to Lundy's description of space and voice. An audience is created as children's views are more actively sought by their peers and adults. A threshold for UNCRC compliance is achieved when children have influence, are involved, and "share power and responsibility in decision making"(Shier, 2001, p. 110).

Shier (2001) adds another dimension to levels of participation, namely, openings, opportunities, and obligations (see Figure 1). Openings are "a personal commitment or statement of intent to work in a certain way" with children (p. 110). Thus children are supported and given the space to express their views. Shier (2001) defines opportunities as a set of circumstances that enable those commitments to come to fruition through available resources, skills and knowledge, and development of new procedures or approaches. Obligation occurs at a policy level for an organization so that it becomes part of the built-in system (Shier, 2001). While openings, opportunities, and obligations can occur at all levels of participa-

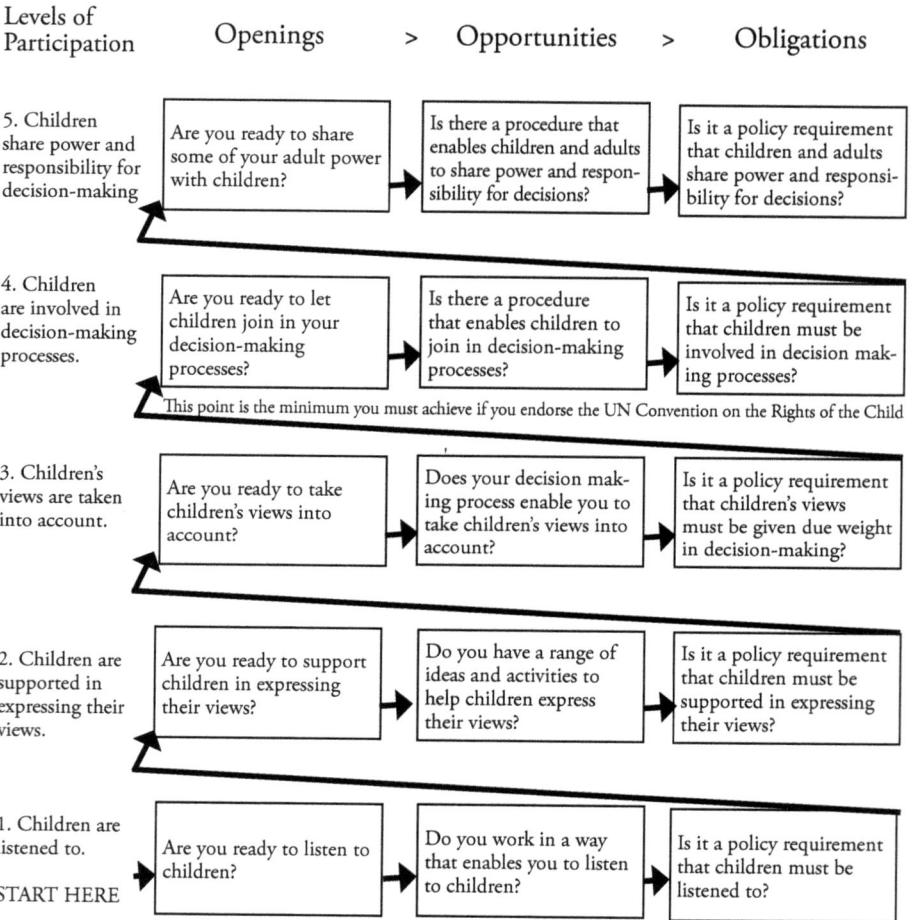

Figure 1. Shier's Pathway to Participation (2001, p. 111)

tion, for the *minimum* standard to be met to be in full compliance with the UN Convention on the Rights of the Child, children would *have* to be listened to, they would *have* to be free to express their views, and their "views must be given due weight in its decision-making" (Shier, 2001, p. 111). Shier (2001) contends that the highest level of participation is fully sharing power and responsibility for decision making with children. While recognizing the tremendous amount of work we have to accomplish in the United States in order to enact the highest level of participation, we look to examples from several national and local contexts.

Opening Spaces for Child Participation and Voice: Cross-national Examples

Continuing to draw from Shier (2001, p. 111) and the framework found in Figure 1, this section provides examples from three national contexts—Australia, Northern Ireland, and Canada—that were part of a seven-country study of children's rights and voices in research, policy, and practice, including program planning that Beth conducted between 2007 and 2010. These examples are not intended to generalize to all work with children in a particular setting, nor to essentialize the complex and rich array of projects in which children's voices are foregrounded and views given due weight. Rather, our intention is to draw from Beth's work with colleagues in these national contexts in relation to Shier's Pathways to Participation model. Further, the examples discussed are intended to open spaces for reconceptualizing power sharing with children in our collective work. We would also assert that each of these examples resituates the roles of adults and children in program planning, research, and advocacy for children.

Australia

Some of the most powerful work on reconceptualizing and resituating early childhood research and practice comes from colleagues in Australia (À Beckett & Proud, 2004; Giugni, 2006, 2011; Grieshaber & Cannella, 2001; Mac Naughton, Hughes, et al., 2007; Ryan & Grieshaber, 2005; Taylor & Richardson, 2005), a country that ratified the UNCRC early on and continues to strengthen its systems for protecting and enhancing children's rights. While this section focuses on one initiative in particular, it should be acknowledged that countless other examples can be drawn from the work of early years colleagues in Australia.

The Centre for Equity and Innovation in Early Childhood (CEIEC) at the University of Melbourne has long engaged in child rights-based research and community consulting related to issues of social justice, inclusion, and program planning. While a visiting scholar at the Centre, Beth had the opportunity to visit a number of Australian municipalities that have participated in the UNICEF Child Friendly Cities initiative, including several of the communities in the Melbourne metropolitan area. Another initiative, started in 2003, was the development of Municipal Early Years Plans (MEYPs) for each local government authority in Victoria. This was in response to a growing interest in the early years arising from national and international research that demonstrated the importance of early childhood experiences on health and development outcomes and a recognition that the diversity and fragmentation of the current early childhood sector was creating difficulties for families. Plans were intended to provide direction for the development and coordination of children's services.

When developing their MEYP, the City of Port Phillip challenged the ways in which council policies and services were traditionally developed and delivered so that children's rights, interests, and needs were afforded greater attention (Una Children's Rights Learning Group, 2010). The resulting plan presents a long-term, common vision for Port Phillip and clarity of purpose. The City of Port Phillip's MEYP vision states that

> Port Phillip is a city where childhood is honoured and all children are cherished and supported as active citizens with a voice of their own, secure in their identity and culture; where they are able to play, learn and contribute to their environments, surrounded by nurturing adults and supportive communities. (City of Port Phillip, 2005)

The plan identifies priority areas and specific actions to be achieved over a three-year time frame. Five principles were identified to underpin the council's actions: honoring childhood, valuing play, respecting children as active citizens, fostering a child's right to grow in healthy and supportive community environments, and understanding the importance of family. A three-year action plan was also developed and implemented that involved all council departments.

Port Phillip approached the Centre for Equity and Innovation in Early Childhood, which led to the Respecting Children as Citizens in Local Government Project (Mac Naughton & Smith, 2008; Smith, Alexander, & Mac Naughton, 2008; Smith & Smale, 2007). Kylie Smith and colleagues have worked closely with this city council in a child consultative process used in planning across sectors.[7] The process was led by a councilperson and later mayor, who shared the vision of taking children seriously, and facilitated by Smith and colleagues. Conversational interviews with preschool children, videotaping of story hours and other programs for infants and toddlers, focus groups consisting of parents and others working with children, and a public display of children's art related to making their community safer were major components of the consultative process. While many in the community felt that the children's views would be whimsical or self-centered, and a waste of time and funds, the project yielded child-generated ideas, several of which were acted upon by the Port Phillip City Council and its various government sectors. One powerful example of this was the children's experiences of crossing busy streets at crossing lights and feeling that they didn't have enough time to cross the many lanes of traffic or weren't able to find a crossing light close to where they needed one to cross streets safely. This resulted in a longer period of time for the walk lights to be on, resulting in benefits not only for children but for everyone, as well as in an additional stop light being installed.

---

7   The following City of Port Phillip examples were excerpted from a vignette in Una Children's Rights Learning Group, 2010.

Another issue addressed with the children related to their call for an increase in rubbish bins. In this case, the city's response was not to increase the bins but instead to share information with the children about the city's recycling policies and to educate the wider community to take rubbish home rather than leaving it on the beach. The councilperson leading this initiative acted to make changes where possible, but when she wasn't able to enact changes that the children recommended, she let the young consultants know why and ensured children that she would continue to monitor the issues. This demonstrated how this council recognized young children as active citizens whose ideas and concerns are as valid and important as those of adults. This can be viewed as an ethical encounter, not as a campaign for votes as these children are unable to vote. A critical aspect of the project was its emphasis on child consultation; after actions were taken, officials reported back to children and their interactions were grounded in respect for children.

We would argue that the Port Phillip example reflects Shier's (2001) fifth level of participation, in which children share power and responsibility for decision making (see Figure 1). The openings for sharing adult power with children included creating a process in which children's views were solicited and given due weight. The opportunities for children and adults to share power and responsibility for decisions included the use of a consultative process in which specific actions, whether taken or not taken, were shared with children for the sake of transparency and accountability by those in policy-making positions. Finally, the obligation to shared power that *requires* children and adults to take shared responsibility for decisions was reflected in the city's policies and practices with its youngest citizens. In the following sections, Beth discusses examples of child participation from her cross-national study.

In my visits to programs in other municipalities, I noted the impact of consulting with children in health contexts and early childhood programs. At one health center, children requested that more of the communication be made directly with them and not just to a parent. They wanted to be talked to and not talked about. In another instance, children wanted to have more pictures on public signs for those who couldn't read or speak English. Early childhood programs using a child rights-informed framework on a daily basis provided many opportunities for children's views to be discussed and given due weight. Some of these examples foreshadow strategies employed by Sonya and her colleagues, as discussed in a later section of this chapter.

While these examples have focused on consulting with children in community contexts, it should be noted that countless other child rights-based initiatives in research, early childhood teacher education, and professional development and Indigenous initiatives also provide frameworks for resituating early childhood research, policy, and practice in this national context.

Northern Ireland

Researchers at Queens University (including Laura Lundy, Lesley McEvoy, Bronagh Byrne, and Paul Connolly) and their community partners have been working with young children as co-researchers for several years (e.g., Lundy, 2006, 2007; Lundy & McEvoy, 2009; Lundy, McEvoy, & Byrne, 2011). Their research and consulting work with NGOs is anchored in the UNCRC and involves children in all phases of research. Other projects have dealt with postconflict and diversity issues in Belfast, Northern Ireland. I have had the opportunity to visit Belfast three times since 2009 and have collaborated with Laura Lundy and Bronagh Byrne on the Una Children's Rights Learning Group (http://www.jliced.org/) and other projects. This section highlights work that involved young children as consultants and co-researchers. Lessons learned from these studies contribute to methodological possibilities for the involvement of children in research by examining the implications of adopting an explicit UNCRC-informed approach to engaging children as co-researchers (Swadener & Polakow, 2011, p. 710). Lundy and colleagues (2011) were commissioned by Barnardo's Northern Ireland (a children's charity) to carry out research related to strategies for promoting educational attainment and positive engagement with school for children from socially disadvantaged areas—specifically, planning of after-school programs.

In this project, two Children's Research Advisory Groups (CRAGs) (Lundy & McEvoy, 2009) were established, composed of four Year One children (age 4–5 years) per school. Thus, strategies used with children were primarily visual and kinesthetic and involved capacity building with the children. (Lundy et al., 2011, p. 719). Consultations were held at the school, with measures taken to assure these were safe spaces, where children could freely express their views. Children contributed directly to the development of the research questions and choice of methods, as well as in the interpretation of the data and dissemination of the findings.

Consistent with Article 12 of the UNCRC, Lundy and colleagues argue that children must not only be given opportunities to *express* their views but also be assisted in *forming* their views (Lundy, 2007). They further argue that a child's capacity to form a view is not determined by age but is instead influenced by information provided, social-cultural expectations, and levels of support (UNA, 2009; Lundy et al., 2011). Thus, capacity-building exercises were built into the consultative process with young children—and these exercises focused on "capacity building on the substantive issues underpinning the research" (Lundy et al., 2011, p. 720). The child advisory groups discussed reasons that children go to school, what they learn, and why children have to go to school, in order to establish the broader aims the study. The team then focused on the research questions the funder (Bernardo's Northern Ireland) had posed. Children were shown photos of types of things that would help children "settle into Year One" (Lundy et al., 2011, p. 721) and what would be hard for children. In later stages of the project, children in the advisory groups helped develop research questions, made decisions about methods for the larger study, and were involved directly in data interpretation. Children interpreted results of a picture survey that included images in photos taken by other children. Finally, given that most of the four- to five-year-old children were not able to write and that some were not comfortable expressing their views through drawing, an artist worked with children in each school to make a large collage. "Children offered their ideas and the artist drew them, adapting the images as the children developed their suggestions" (Lundy et al., 2011, p. 729). Children were also welcome to draw their ideas.

This study and other work of Lundy and colleagues underscore what it might mean to truly give children's views due weight and also reflect the power sharing and decision making in the fifth level of Shier's (2001) participation model. As Lundy and colleagues (2011, p. 733) observe, "The key to involving children as co-researchers in a way that is respecting of their rights is ultimately dependent on how the children are perceived by the adult researchers." Treating children with respect and recognizing their agency and competence are critical. Lundy and colleagues (2011) conclude,

> As in all truly rights-based activity, not only are children's rights respected but the capacity of the duty bearers to fulfill their obligations to children is also enhanced. Working alongside children in order to research and gain understanding of the views and experiences of their peers is in itself a means of realizing children's rights. (p. 734)

Returning to the Shier (2001) participation model, Lundy and colleagues' work in this project can be seen as reflecting the fifth level, in which children share power and responsibility in decision making—in this case, contributing to decisions in all phases of the research. Openings and opportunities for child participation were clearly provided, and the research team set an explicit requirement that children/co-researchers on the advisory groups and adults would share power and responsibility for decisions related to the research. Where a governmental body set this policy standard in the Port Phillip example, a research team working with an NGO adopted a similarly rigorous interpretation of child participation in this Northern Ireland context.

Canada

Several of the chapters in this volume provide examples that can be read as reflecting and respecting children's voices, consistent with a children's rights-based approach. The growing use of learning stories, documentation with children, and culturally relevant practices in early childhood in Canada also speaks to ways in which childhood and children are understood. Work in Canada has long focused on First People or Indigenous communities, resettled refugees (see Kirova, this volume), and migrant groups. Judith K. Bernhard has long worked with linguistically and culturally diverse communities and young children, and Veronica Pacini-Ketchabaw and colleagues have worked with early years educators in reconceptualist work, emphasizing anti-colonial and feminist theories, including employing collective biography (as in this volume). Enid Elliot has focused on the lives of caregivers and used rights-based programming and consultation with children, particularly focusing on outdoor environments (Blanchet-Cohen & Elliot, 2011). The work of Rachel Heydon and Luigi Iannacci (2008) on de-pathologizing childhood respects children's right to be heard and understood beyond risk-laden labels, as does Luigi Iannacci and Bente Graham's chapter on binaries in early childhood (this volume).

As part of my international work on children's rights and voices I have collaborated with Natasha Blanchet-Cohen, who worked with the Institute for Child Rights and Development at the University of Victoria (BC) and is now working in Montreal, with focus on refugee and immigrant children and youth. This institute is part of the Child Watch International Research Network and its mission is to "enhance the capacity of individuals, organizations, and governments, to effectively use the UN Convention on the Rights of the Child to transform systems and create peace and dignity for children and our world" (http://www.childwatch.uio.no/key-institutions/north-america/centre-for-global-studies-uni-victoria.html). Some of the work of this group has focused on resettled refugees and migrant communities, as well as First People. Members of the institute have played critical roles in UNCRC comments, related research, and Canadian initiatives at the community and provincial levels.

Natasha collaborated with Enid Elliot on a study of four early childhood programs investigating young children's and educators' perspectives on engagement and learning possibilities outdoors, using a rights-based methodology. Children were engaged in interactive activities and focus groups (Blanchet-Cohen & Elliot, 2011). The combined perspectives of teachers and children and the value placed on natural spaces led to an increase in opportunities for outside play and "motivated educators to support children's interactions outdoors by mediating policy and societal fear of the risk of outdoor play" (p. 757). Their results underscored the value of a learning community supporting children's full use of outdoor space and the "important role of adult allies in advocating for rights-based programming" (p. 757).

I use the above examples to reference a few of the many possible ways that a child-rights perspective can contribute to a resituating of early childhood in Canada and beyond. Whether implicit or explicit, a focus on respecting and listening to children, giving their views and opinions due weight, and interrupting adultist patterns that limit children's full participation complements much of the work documented in this volume.

In 2011, Lacey, Sonya, and Beth shared a panel on children's rights and participation in research with Kimberly Bezaire at the annual meeting of the American Education Research Association. Kim's work foregrounds children's classroom experiences during free play, as well as children's perceptions of adult researchers. Children actively participated with Bezaire in an inquiry and exploration of the influence of play on early literacy development, with a focus on boys. One of the ways that she gave children's perspectives due weight was by collaborating with children to create a picture book documenting their responses to her research. The study culminated in the creation of a picture that was inspired, and co-authored by her child participants. The book is also used to inform adults on the topic of children's participation in research.

Applying These Ideas Closer to Home

After working with colleagues in several countries focused on child rights-based research, policy, and practice, Beth sought to apply some of these approaches in research projects closer to home, in Arizona. Lacey was part of a series of statewide studies that Beth was co-directing, and Sonya became our collaborator in a child consultation process inspired by the work of many of the colleagues whose work is briefly discussed in earlier sections in this chapter. This work motivated us to implement a child consultative approach to the qualitative component of a statewide mixed-method early childhood study in Arizona.

In 2009, Beth and Lacey began working on the Family and Community Case Study (FCCS) in Arizona, part of a larger project evaluating a voter-approved initiative aimed at improving the quality and accessibility of systems of children's services in Arizona. FCCS employed qualitative interview and focus group methods to document experiences of parents/primary caregivers raising young children, community providers supporting children and families, as well as preschool and kindergarten children. Participants represent the distinctive geographic, socioeconomic, cultural, and linguistic regions of the state (Arizona University Consortium, 2011, 2012; Joanou, Holiday, & Swadener, 2012).[8] Interviews with children were intended to provide adults with insight into their daily-lived experiences, with a particular focus on family, community, health, and their early care and education experiences.

For those of us invested in children's rights-based research there was a strong desire to find an opening and opportunity (see Figure 1, Shier, 2001) for the "un-

---

8   A consortium of the three state universities in Arizona carried out FCCS, each situated within respective urban, rural, and border communities. Beth, Lacey, and Sonya worked in the central region of the state, recognized as being predominately urban.

mediated" (Swadener & Polakow, 2011, p. 1039) voices of our youngest citizens to be included in this project. In the planning stages of the larger project, members of the research team realized the child interview protocol was awash with "adult ideological conceptions" (Mandell, 1988, p. 442). Therefore, we decided we needed our own child research consultants. We turned to Sonya, who was both a university colleague and an elementary multi-age (grades 1–3) classroom teacher.

Child Rights and Consultation in the Classroom

When Beth and Lacey approached me about having the first, second, and third graders in my classroom become research consultants I thought it would be a wonderful opportunity to expand upon the children's rights-based experiences I was already facilitating in my classroom. My team-teaching colleagues and I had made it a point to provide multiple opportunities for students' voices to be heard and taken into account. We also created opportunities for sharing power and responsibility through authentic participation in the classroom decision-making and curriculum choices (Shier, 2001).

One way in which we did this was through our weekly Town Hall Meetings and Neighborhood Meetings. Town Hall Meetings occurred each Monday with all three classes of multi-age students. Neighborhood Meetings were conducted once a week in each multi-age classroom. Town Hall Meetings were facilitated by teachers, but the Neighborhood Meetings were led by each "neighborhood's" mayor (a neighborhood was one class of twenty-five multi-age students). Mayors were selected by students who used a blind job application process conducted two or three times a year. All students completed, by themselves or by dictation, job applications that asked why they would be good candidates for these positions. Neighborhood councils, a group of randomly selected students facilitated by an adult, reviewed these blind applications (they were coded and the names removed) and decided together who would hold which classroom jobs, including that of mayor. Students were active participants in all of these meetings, focusing on how children help one another, our classroom communities, the multi-age program, and the school. They presented classroom problems to the group, sought answers together, and then implemented potential solutions. When students were concerned about the high number of students who kept losing pencils, students implemented masking tape name-flag pencil toppers and brought in additional pencils to be sold at the town's "Mercado." When students felt that some students went to the bathroom just to get out of work, they requested sign-out sheets and would remind one another during class to hurry back. Students also initiated cleanup crews to come in during school recess times to reorganize common areas and make signs providing their classmates with helpful hints on how to use those areas more neatly.

Even within the constraints of our school's curriculum and adopted resources, our multi-age program created openings and opportunities for students to move beyond these adult directives. At times this meant that we had to fight for our students' right to choose which books to read and which stories (or other genres) to write. We actively sought children's views in what they wanted to learn and how they would learn it. Our classroom had a binder entitled "Things Grown-Ups Expect You to Learn This Year." Students knew that these were the standards that "had" to be learned, but they were encouraged to go beyond or in another direction from these directives. At the beginning of a new unit of study, usually thematically created by the teachers based on required state and local standards, the class worked together to brainstorm a list of what students knew about the topic, a list of things they wanted to learn more about, and how they wanted to go about learning them. The challenge then became how to fit everything into our days given the amount of time and resources we had, as well as the policy requirements of how the administrative adults mandated and regulated this use of time and resources. While we had created the openings and opportunities for children's voices to be heard and for children to participate in the multi-age program, the administration did not see the value and felt no obligation to support this participation (Shier, 2001).

However, with the openings and opportunities that we had been able to create in the multi-age program, the students were well prepared for their work as research consultants on the FCCS child interview protocol. It was an easy fit to use techniques from our thematic unit brainstorming sessions and Town Hall and Neighborhood Meetings. Specifically we used procedures from "Think, Pair, Share" and other cooperative learning approaches (Kagan, 1989) and community-building practices (Kriete, 2002). Working in small groups, children met to brainstorm and discuss possibilities. Each small group chose one member to act as a scribe. This scribe was to record all of the children's ideas. Two questions were used as the guiding prompts to the groups: What should we talk to five-year-olds about? How can we make interviews with kids more fun? After each question was posed to the whole class, time was provided for children to think silently about their answers, followed by small group discussions.

Children took turns sharing their ideas in the small groups according to the procedures decided upon by each small group. The scribes recorded their group's ideas. Groups were then directed by the adult facilitators (Beth, Lacey, and Sonya) to decide upon their top three ideas. Each small group was called upon in turn to share these ideas. Beth then recorded these ideas on the class interactive whiteboard. In addition, the adult researchers kept notes so that other key thoughts and exchanges among the children could be captured for further analysis. Printouts from the interactive whiteboard, as well as the children's small group lists, provided final documentation of the children's ideas. This activity occurred at the end of the day in one of the final weeks of the school year. The students were so engaged in this activity that I had a great deal of difficulty getting everyone to pack up their backpacks and leave for the day. In fact, while I was taking most students to the school buses and parent pickup area, a couple of students who attended the after-school program lingered behind at the end of the day, giving Beth and Lacey even more ideas, reluctant to let their research consultation end.

Talking with Young Children about Their Experiences

Beth and Lacey used the information we gathered from our child consultants to make revisions to the original interview protocol developed for the child interview component of FCCS. We combined the perspectives of our consultants in Sonya's class with those who participated in similar meetings at the two other school sites across the state. The opportunity to interact with the child consultants not only provided opportunities to build a stronger awareness of young people's expertise on children and childhoods, but this experience also led adult researchers to challenge their assumptions about children's abilities to express themselves. During our conversations with the larger research team we discussed how we were all impressed by the depths of children's thoughts. Questions from our child research consultants included the following:

- How do you feel when your parents leave you?

- Do you feel like you are ready to go to kindergarten?

- Do you like physical or imaginary things?

- Do you have friends who like you but not each other?

Although the child consultation meetings were important in shifting our adult perspectives, we encountered issues related to integrating the consultants' suggestions into subsequent iterations of the interview protocol. Members of the research team were working under contract. The possibilities for us to build an interview protocol inclusive of children's perspectives were limited, considering that our primary aim was to gather information to address questions related to the larger external evaluation project. Many of the questions shared by the consultants related to topics other than family, community, health, and care and education; thus, an ethical tension emerged concerning whether it would be beneficial to add questions to the protocol. The following are examples of such questions:

- What is your favorite color?

- What do you concentrate on?

- What time do you go to bed?

In a different regard, several members of the larger research project were apprehensive about including children's questions (e.g., What are you afraid of? or How do you feel when your parents leave?) directly into the protocol, as they assumed children would discuss topics controversial or contentious in nature. This point illustrates the way in which adults based the inclusion or exclusion of children's perspectives upon their assumptions and biases of how other adults would respond to hearing children discuss more weighty or socially complex topics. This example also sheds light on an interesting contradiction in that the child consultants (older children) were afforded the opportunity to express their views freely, yet adults inhibited the opportunities for the younger child interview participants to engage in conversations that may have led to topics considered taboo or age inappropriate. It is important to note that the reluctance to give children's ideas due weight in this instance was caused by numerous factors situated outside of our research project, and within broader social contexts. Several of the members of the larger statewide FCCS research team argued that children's thoughts on the aforementioned topics would fall out of line with the central purpose of the evaluation project; as a result, children's ideas tended to be reappropriated to better fit the adult agenda, or were dismissed altogether.

In relation to Shier's (2001) model, we created openings and opportunities but there was no obligation by the outside contractor or others in the process to include children's recommendations. The child consultants' perspectives were given due weight and their ideas were incorporated into the interview protocol in any way possible. We were thus able to achieve higher levels of openings and opportunities with the consultative process, meeting the threshold of children's participation rights in accordance with the UNCRC. However, because we are operating in a context in the United States, a country that does not recognize the UNCRC, and there is no mechanism for children's opinions to be given due weight in a state system, we were unable to achieve the requirements connected to the obligations of children's participation.

Further, we were able to find openings and opportunities at various other points of the project. Throughout the phases of data collection, children's feedback was used to enhance the interview protocol. The information that children provided was used to ensure that adults remained sensitive and responsive to their needs and preferences. More pointedly, a total of forty-five children were interviewed in two separate waves of data collection and each interview was individualized to afford each participant the opportunity to express her or his views in any way that was most comfortable. As an example, several children were more inclined to use the drawing and writing activities, while others found playdough and other manipulatives to be more useful. A critical point to bring up is that our efforts to create a flexible interview protocol provide evidence that children were supported in expressing their views (the second level of Shier's model) and that we provided a range of activities to facilitate alternative, more "child-friendly" approaches to interviewing. This in turn helped to elicit children's perspectives in a more authentic, unmediated manner; as a result, adults were provided the opportunity to gain a better understanding of young people's perceptions of their daily-lived experiences. Generally speaking, we learned how children participate in family, community, and cultural practices; examined ways in which children make sense of social rules and expectations; gained insight into children's values and preferences for particular activities (as they relate to work and play); and became further aware of the influence of popular cultural on children's play and learning. This information was integrated into various reports disseminated by members of the FCCS team to illustrate how operations within the systems of early childhood care and education affect children and families.

It is clear that our efforts as a research team to involve children in the data collection phases of the study set an important precedent for creating "openings" that bring young people's perspectives into our work. Furthermore, the interviews with children brought us to the third level of Shier's model, but only to the point of providing opportunities for children to express their views. For instance, as a research team we involved children in our decision-making processes pertaining to our interviewing procedures. As mentioned, changes to our protocol were continuously made based on the feedback that the child participants provided. However, as we move into the dissemination phases of this project we are coming to realize that the capacity to include children's perspectives in other decision-making processes is constrained as a result of the lack of mechanisms in place to give children's thoughts due weight. Thus, we are working to build stronger awareness of the potential to learn from children, and use their ideas and opinions to guide the decisions made in relation to early childhood programming and policy.

Closing Reflections

In this multi-vocal chapter we have attempted to share both international and highly localized examples of what resituating early childhood in a child-rights framework might offer the field. We acknowledge the tensions in reconceptualist scholarship, including those between cultural relativism and universals, as well as between poststructural theories and structures intended to protect and to empower children. Several readings and critiques of the UNCRC, including some of our own writing, construct aspects of human/children's discourse and policy as individualistic, Western, and neoliberal (summarized in Una Children's Rights Learning Group, 2011). Yet, we contend that the UNCRC does offer a powerful set of principles and guidelines for deepening our commitment to act with children and not on or about them. In critical theory terms (e.g., Gramsci, 1971), there are moments of good sense and bad sense in anchoring policy and practice in children's rights (e.g., Ndimande & Swadener, 2011). Clearly, local and cultural context must be considered and national and local policies developed through an inclusive consultative process.

It is also important to remember the intensification of neoliberal early education policies and practices (see Curry & Cannella, this volume), which often serve to silence children (and their teachers) and have little regard for their agency, creativity, modes, or views. The pressures on early educators to implement increasingly narrow curricula also limit the rights of children to a full range of early experiences and opportunities. While utilizing a child rights-based framework in resituating early childhood may seem a modernist notion in some ways, it can actually serve as a radical interruption of the status quo.

Proponents of child rights-based work can do only so much without a more supportive policy climate. Even in the most "progressive" and child-affirming national contexts, there remain many barriers to the full enactment of the UNCRC. Jørgensen, Leth, and Montgomery discuss this in the context of Denmark, where they describe the "weak and relatively invisible" enactment of children's rights (Jørgensen et al., 2011, p. 839). Many would find this surprising, given the fact that Denmark enacted legislation to protect children's rights long before the UNCRC was written. Yet, Jørgensen and colleagues argue that many immigrant, refugee, and Indigenous children have not had the full benefit of Denmark's progressive policies. As we resituate early childhood research, practice, and policy for *all* children, particularly those at the margins, a rights-based framework is consistent with a strong equity agenda. The UNCRC can serve as a critical tool to be used against oppressive forces and forms of social and educational exclusion.

Examples in this chapter are largely contextualized by social and political mechanisms within the respective countries—countries that not only have ratified the UNCRC but also have scholars who are using participation rights in compelling ways with young children. We have sought to unpack fundamental elements of each project in order to explore possibilities for promoting children's participation and reframing adult understandings of children's roles in U.S. early childhood contexts. In doing so, we have found it helpful to utilize Shier's levels of participation. We do not do so to reify linear or developmental models, but rather to complicate and challenge assumptions about what collaborating fully with children might entail. In fact, Shier (2011) continues to shift and enhance his perspective, and has changed his representations to move beyond a linear pathway to a more metaphorical model. Moreover, we use these examples to engage in a critical analysis of children's roles and responsibilities within society, as they are afforded opportunities to participate, contribute to substantive decisions and policies, and express their views.

References

À Beckett, C., & Proud, D. (2004). Fall from grace? Reflecting on early childhood education while decolonizing intercultural friendships from kindergarten to university and prison. In K. Mutua & B. B. Swadener (Eds.), *Decolonizing research in cross-cultural contexts* (pp. 147–158). Albany, NY: SUNY Press.

Alderson, P. (2000). Children and researchers: Participation rights and research methods. In P. Christensen & A. James (Eds.), *Research with children: Perspectives and practices* (pp. 240–259). London, England: Falmer Press.

Alderson, P., & Morrow, V. (2011). *The ethics of research with children and young people* (2nd ed.). London, England: Sage.

Arizona University Consortium. (2011). *Initial report: Family and community case study*. Tempe, AZ: Technical Report of the First Things First External Evaluation, University Consortium.

Arizona University Consortium. (2012). *Final report: Family and community case study*. Tempe, AZ: Technical Report of the First Things First External Evaluation, University Consortium.

Berson, I. R. (2009). Here's what we have to say! Podcasting in the early childhood classroom. *Social Studies and the Young Learner, 21*(4), 8–11.

Blanchet-Cohen, N., & Elliot, E. (2011). Young children and educators engagement and learning outdoors: A basis of right-based programming. *Early Education & Development, 22*(5), 757–777.

Blanchet-Cohen, N., & Rainbow, B. (2006). Partnership between children and adults? The experience of the International Children's Conference on the environment. *Childhood, 13*(1), 113–126.

City of Port Phillip. (2005). *Creating a child-friendly Port Phillip: Implementation plan 2005–2009*. Port Phillip, Australia: Author. Retrieved from http://www.portphillip.vic.gov.au/default/Implementation_Plan.pdf

Clark, A. (2005). Listening to and involving young children: A review of research and practice. *Early Child Development and Care, 175*(6), 489–505.

Clark, C. D. (2011). *In a younger voice: Doing child-centered qualitative research*. New York, NY: Oxford University Press.

Corsaro, W. A. (2005). *The sociology of childhood* (2nd ed.). London, England: Sage.

Dockett, S., Einarsdottir, J., & Perry, B. (2009). Researching with children: Ethical tensions. *Journal of Early Childhood Research, 7*(3), 283–298.

Einarsdottir, J. (2011). Icelandic children's early education transition experiences. *Early Education & Development, 22*(5), 737–756.

Giugni, M. (2006). Conceptualising goodies and baddies through narratives of Jesus and Superman. *Contemporary Issues in Early Childhood, 7*(2), 97–108.

Giugni, M. (2011). "Becoming worldly with": An encounter with the early years learning framework. *Contemporary Issues in Early Childhood, 12*(1), 11–27.

Gramsci, A. (1971). *Selection from the prison notebooks of Antonio Gramsci*. New York, NY: International.

Grover, S. (2004). Why won't they listen to us? On giving power and voice to children participating in social research. *Childhood, 11*(1), 81–93.

Grieshaber, S., & Cannella, G. (2001). *Embracing identities in early childhood education: Diversity and possibilities*. New York, NY: Teachers College Press.

Gunn, R. (2008). The power to shape decisions? An exploration of young people's power in participation. *Health and Social Care in the Community, 16*(3), 253–261.

Habashi, J. (2008). Language of political socialization: Language of resistance. *Children's Geographies, 6*(3), 269–280.

Hart, R. A. (1992). Children's participation: From tokenism to citizenship. In *Innocenti Essays 4* (pp. 1–44). Florence, Italy: UNICEF International Child Development Centre.

Heydon, R., & Iannacci, L. (2008). *Early childhood curricula and the depathologizing of childhood.* Toronto, Canada: University of Toronto Press.

James, A., & Prout, A. (Eds.). (1997). *Constructing and reconstructing childhood.* London, England: RoutledgeFalmer.

Joanou, J. P., Holiday, D., & Swadener, B. B. (2012). Family and community perspectives: Voices from a qualitative statewide study in the southwest U.S. In J. Duncan & S. Ohe (Eds.), *Early childhood education services: The "heart" and the "hearth" of communities—international perspectives.* New York, NY: Palgrave Macmillan.

Jørgensen, P., Leth, I., & Montgomery, E. (2011). The Children's Rights convention in Denmark: A status report on implementation. *Early Education & Development, 22*(5), 839–862.

Kagan, S. (1989). The structural approach to cooperative learning. *Educational Leadership, 47*(4), 12–15.

Kriete, R. (2002). *The morning meeting book.* Greenfield, MA: Northeast Foundation for Children.

Lahman, M. (2008). Always othered: Ethical research with children. *Journal of Early Childhood Research, 6*(3), 281–300.

Lundy, L. (2006). Mainstreaming children's rights in, to and through education in a society emerging from conflict. *The International Journal of Children's Rights, 14*(4), 1–24.

Lundy, L. (2007). "Voice" is not enough: Conceptualising Article 12 of the United Nations Conventions on the Rights of the Child. *British Educational Research Journal, 33*(6), 927–942.

Lundy, L., & McEvoy, L. (2009). Developing outcomes for educational services: A children's rights based approach. *Effective Education, 1*(1), 43–60.

Lundy, L., McEvoy, L., & Byrne, B. (2011). Working with young children as co-researchers: An approach informed by the United Nations Convention on the Rights of the Child. *Early Education & Development, 22*(5), 714–736.

Mac Naughton, G., Hughes, P., & Smith, K. (2007). Young children's rights and public policy: Practices and possibilities for citizenship in the early years. *Children & Society, 21,* 458–469.

Mac Naughton, G., & Smith, K. (2005). Exploring ethics and difference: The choices and challenges of researching with children. In A. Farrell (Ed.), *Exploring ethical research with children* (pp. 112–123). Maidenhead, England: Open University Press.

Mac Naughton, G., & Smith, K. (2008). Engaging ethically with young children: Principles and practices for listening and responding with care. In G. Mac Naughton, P. Hughes, & K. Smith (Eds.), *Young children as active citizens: Principles, policies and pedagogies* (pp. 167–205). London, England: Cambridge Scholars.

Mac Naughton, G., Smith, K., & Davis, K. (2007). Researching with children: The challenges and possibilities for building "child friendly" research. In J. A. Hatch (Ed.), *Early childhood qualitative research* (pp. 167–205). New York, NY: Routledge.

Mandell, N. (1988). The least adult role in studying children. *Journal of Contemporary Ethnography, 16*(4), 433–467.

Ndimande, B. S., & Swadener, B. B. (2012). Children's rights and cultural tensions in South Africa. *International Journal of Equity & Innovation in Early Childhood, 10*(1).

Office of the United Nations High Commissioner for Human Rights. (1989). *Convention on the Rights of the Child.* New York, NY: United Nations.

Office of the United Nations High Commissioner for Human Rights. (2005). *United Nations Convention on the Rights of the Child, General Comment No. 7.* Geneva, Switzerland: Author.

O'Kane, C. (2000). The development of participatory techniques: Facilitating children's views about decisions which affect them. In P. Christensen & A. James (Eds.), *Research with children: Perspectives and practices* (pp. 136–159). London, England: Falmer Press.

O'Kane, M. (2007, February). *The transition to school in Ireland: What do the children say?* Paper presented at the International Centre for Early Childhood Development and Education conference, Vision Into Practice: Making Quality a Reality in the Lives of Children

Polakow, V. (1993). *Lives on the edge: Single mothers and their children in the other America.* Chicago, IL: University of Chicago Press.

Qvortrup, J. (1994). Childhood matters: An introduction. In J. Qvortrup, M. Bardy, G. Sgritta, & H. Wintersberger (Eds.), *Childhood matters. Social theory, practice and politics* (pp. 1–24). Aldershot England: Avebury.

Ryan, S., & Grieshaber, S. (2005). Shifting from developmental to postmodern practices in early childhood teacher education. *Journal of Teacher Education, 56*(1), 34–45.

Shier, H. (2001). Pathways to participation: Opening, opportunities, and obligations. *Children and Society, 15,* 107–117.

Shier, H. (2011). "Pathways to participation" revisited: Learning from Nicaragua's child coffee workers. In B. Percy-Smith & N. Thomas (Eds.), *A handbook of children and young people's participation perspectives from theory and practice* (pp. 215–229). New York, NY: Routledge.

Smith, K., Alexander, K., & Mac Naughton, G. (2008). *Respecting children as citizens in local government: Participation in policies and services project.* Port Phillip, Australia: City of Port Phillip.

Smith, K., & Smale, J. (2007, October). *Child participation in local government.* Paper presented at the workshop for MUTANT, Utrecht, the Netherlands.

Soto, L. D., & Swadener, B. B. (2005). *Power and voice in research with children.* New York, NY: Peter Lang.

Swadener, B., & Polakow, V. (2011). Introduction to the special issue on children's rights and voices in research: Cross-national perspectives. *Early Education & Development, 22*(5), 707–713.

Taylor, A., & Richardson, C. (2005). Queering home corner. *Contemporary Issues in Early Childhood, 6*(2), 163–173.

Una Children's Rights Learning Group. (2010). *Children's rights in Una and beyond: Transnational perspectives* (Una Working Paper 7). Belfast, Northern Ireland: Una. Retrieved from http://www.unaglobal.org/en/page/reports

Una Children's Rights Learning Group. (2011). *Children's rights in cultural contexts* (Una Working Paper 8). Belfast, Northern Ireland: Una. Retrieved from http://www.unaglobal.org/en/page/reports

Walkerdine, V. (1993). Beyond developmentalism? *Theory & Psychology, 3*(4), 451–469.

List of Contributors

Editors

Veronica Pacini-Ketchabaw is Professor and Coordinator of the Early Years Specialization in the School of Child and Youth Care at the University of Victoria. She has written extensively on the history of child care in Canada; the experiences of young children and early childhood educators in early childhood settings; and posthumanist, poststructural, postcolonial, and anti-racist feminist perspectives in early childhood education. She is editor of *Flows, Rhythms and Intensities in Early Childhood Curriculum* (Peter Lang), and co-editor of the journal *Canadian Children*.

Larry Prochner is Professor of Early Childhood Education and Chair of the Department of Elementary Education in the Faculty of Education at the University of Alberta. He is author of *A History of Early Childhood Education in Canada, Australia, and New Zealand*, and co-editor of *Recent Perspectives on Early Childhood Education and Care in Canada*.

Authors

Dr. Judith K. Bernhard is a professor in the School of Early Childhood Education, Faculty of Community Services at Ryerson University in Toronto. Her research program has focused on the impact of migration on family functioning.

Gaile S. Cannella, the series editor for Rethinking Childhoods, is the Velma E. Schmidt Endowed Chair in Early Childhood Studies at the University of North Texas. Her books included *Deconstructing Early Childhood Education: Social Justice and Revolution*; *Childhood and Postcolonization: Power, Education, and Contemporary Practice*; and *Childhoods: A Handbook*.

Daphney L. Curry is an instructor of Early Childhood Education and Reading in the College of Education at Midwestern State University. She is currently a doctoral candidate in reading and early childhood at the University of North Texas. Her research interests focus on new literacies and family literacy.

Katherine Davidson is Assistant Professor in the Faculty of Education at the University of Western Ontario, instructing in educational psychology/special education and in literacy. She practiced occupational therapy in the school system and taught for thirteen years in general and special education settings. Her research is in reading disabilities research utilization.

Sonya Gaches is Assistant Professor of Practice in Early Childhood Education at the University of Arizona, and a recent doctoral graduate of Arizona State University. With extensive classroom experience, particularly in mixed-age lower primary, she is currently working with future teachers and graduate students in a program emphasizing funds of knowledge and community-informed early education practices.

Bente Graham has taught mainstream and special education in a range of elementary grades in Ontario. She is a former elementary school principal and is currently an instructor at the Trent School of Education and Professional Learning, where she teaches and coordinates the Language and Literacy course and the Supporting Literacy and Learners with Special Needs course.

Luigi Iannacci has taught mainstream and special education in a range of elementary grades in Ontario. He is an associate professor at the Trent School of Education and Professional Learning, where he teaches and coordinates the Language and Literacy course and the Supporting Literacy and Learners with Special Needs course.

Anna Kirova is Professor of Early Childhood Education in the Department of Elementary Education at the University of Alberta. Her research focus is on the need for understanding the culturally and linguistically diverse children's experiences of schooling and the possibility such an understanding offers for culturally responsive pedagogy.

Kathleen Kummen is a faculty member in the Department of Early Childhood Care and Education at Capilano University. She is also a Ph.D. candidate at the School of Child and Youth Care at the University of Victoria. Her research interests focus on exploring theory and practice in the pre-service training and ongoing professional development of early childhood educators.

Rachel Langford is the director of the School of Early Childhood Studies at Ryerson University in Toronto. Her research and publications focus on early childhood teachers' work and history, professional preparation, and the Canadian childcare movement. She is the principal researcher on a three-year SSHRC (Social Sciences and Humanities Research Council) project that investigates professionalism as a Canadian childcare movement strategy in an era of neoliberalism.

Lacey Peters is a Ph.D. candidate in Early Childhood Education at Arizona State University and has worked with preschool children in various capacities, primarily as a classroom teacher. She has served as a research assistant in three mixed-method, early childhood projects; her dissertation research emphasizes children's voice and participation and focuses on the transition to kindergarten. She is also involved in early childhood teacher education.

Sherry Rose is a doctoral student in the Early Childhood Centre at the University of New Brunswick, working as a member of the Early Childhood Research and Development Team. At this point her research/teaching interests include curriculum, narrative documentation, and critical literacies.

Mary Caroline Rowan is a Vanier scholar, Ph.D. student at the University of New Brunswick, and an instructor of comparative education at Concordia University. She is interested in working with community stakeholders on crafting childcare programs grounded in Inuit ways of knowing and being.

Beth Blue Swadener is Professor of Justice and Social Inquiry in the School of Social Transformation at Arizona State University. Her research focuses on internationally comparative social policy, with a focus on sub-Saharan Africa and children's rights. She has published nine books, including *Reconceptualizing the Early Childhood Curriculum*; *Children and Families "At Promise"*; *Decolonizing Research in Cross-cultural Context*; and *Power and Voice in Research with Children*. She also serves as Associate Editor of the *American Educational Research Journal*.

Deborah Thompson works as a caregiver in a childcare centre and as an instructor of early childhood care and education at a community college. She is currently completing a doctoral dissertation at the University of Victoria. Her research considers the implications of multi-age childcare.

Pam Whitty is Professor of Early Childhood Literacies, Curriculum, and Critical Studies at the University of New Brunswick in Fredericton, and Director of the UNB Early Childhood Centre. She has been involved with community-based action research for the past twenty years, and continues to co-author curriculum documents in New Brunswick.

RETHINKING CHILDHOOD

GAILE S. CANNELLA, *General Editor*

Researchers in a range of fields have acknowledged that childhood is a construct emerging from modernist perspectives that have not always benefited those who are younger. The purpose of the Rethinking Childhood Series is to provide a critical location for scholarship that challenges the universalization of childhood and introduces new, reconceptualized, and critical spaces from which opportunities and possibilities are generated for children. Diverse histories and cultures are considered of major importance as well as issues of critical social justice.

We are particularly interested in manuscripts that provide insight into the contemporary neoliberal conditions experienced by those who are labeled "children" as well as authored and edited volumes that illustrate life and educational experiences that challenge present conditions. Rethinking childhood work related to critical education and care, childhood public policy, family and community voices, and critical social activism is encouraged.

For more information about this series or for submission of manuscripts, please contact:

>Gaile S. Cannella
>Gaile.Cannella@unt.edu

To order other books in this series, please contact our Customer Service Department at:

>(800) 770-LANG (within the U.S.)
>(212) 647-7706 (outside the U.S.)
>(212) 647-7707 FAX

Or browse online by series at:
>www.peterlang.com

www.ingramcontent.com/pod-product-compliance
Ingram Content Group UK Ltd.
Pitfield, Milton Keynes, MK11 3LW, UK
UKHW022238230426
12048UKWH00018BA/1341